D1475522

MANAGING THE SKIES

Managing the Skies
Public Policy, Organization and Financing of Air Traffic Management

CLINTON V. OSTER, JR
Indiana University, Bloomington, USA

JOHN S. STRONG
The College of William and Mary, USA

ASHGATE

Published by
Ashgate Publishing Limited
Gower House
Croft Road
Aldershot
Hampshire GU11 3HR
England

Ashgate Publishing Company
Suite 420
101 Cherry Street
Burlington, VT 05401-4405
USA

Ashgate website: http://www.ashgate.com

British Library Cataloguing in Publication Data
Oster, Clinton V.
  Managing the skies : public policy, organization and
  financing of air traffic management
  1. Air traffic control - Management 2. Airlines -
  Management 3. Aeronautics and state
  I. Title II. Strong, John S.
  387 .7'4'0426

Library of Congress Cataloging-in-Publication Data
Oster, Clinton V.
  Managing the skies : public policy, organization and financing of air traffic management
/ by Clinton V. Oster and John S. Strong.
    p. cm.
  Includes bibliographical references and index.
  ISBN 978-0-7546-7045-2
  1. Airlines--Management. 2. Air traffic control--Management. 3. Aeronautics and state.
I. Strong, John S. II. Title.
  HE9780.O85 2007
  387.7'40426--dc22

2007025294

ISBN 978 0 7546 7045 2

Printed and bound in Great Britain by MPG Books Ltd, Bodmin, Cornwall.

Contents

List of Figures

List of Tables

Acknowledgements

We would like to acknowledge financial support for this research from:

- Government of Canada, Canadian Studies Faculty Research Grant Program and the program administrator Dan Abele.
- IBM Center for the Business of Government and the former Executive Director Mark Abramson.

We would like to acknowledge research support from:

- Mason School of Business, College of William and Mary, for providing research leave for John Strong.
- School of Public and Environmental Affairs, Indiana University, for providing research support for Clinton V. Oster, Jr.

We were fortunate to have the opportunity to present our research and analysis in a series of seminars and meetings, including:

- Transportation Research Forum, March 2005.
- Transportation Research Board of the National Academy of Sciences, January 2006.
- ICAO/McGill Symposium on Air Navigation, September 2006.

We are grateful to the Government Accountability Office for inviting Clint Oster to participate in a daylong conference in October 2004 that assembled experts to exchange their views on how to improve the air traffic control system. The comments of each of the participants in that panel had an impact on this work.

We would link to thank the following people for extensive and candid discussions, reviews, comments, and questions. Their willingness to share their time and ideas and to discuss a full range of issues related to air navigation organizations is greatly appreciated.

Basil Barimo
Sharon Barkeloo
T. Martin Blaiklock
Ben Berman
John Crichton
Mark Dayton
Gerald Dillingham
Jack Fearnsides

Rod Fewings
Terry Fudakowski
Richard Golaszewski
Ian Hall
John Heimlich
John Hennigan
Terry Kelly
Sid Koslow
Glen MacDougall
Cliff Mackay
Robert McCulloch
Paul McGraw
Donna McLean
John Meenan
Doug Mein
Vahid Motevalli
Bob Poole
David Schaffer
Rob Thurgur
Jim Wilding

We also would like to thank Guy Loft of Ashgate Publishing for his diligence in working with us through the entire project.

We gratefully acknowledge the contributions made by all of the persons and organizations mentioned here. The book is much improved as a result of their ideas. Any errors, of course, are our own.

Clinton V. Oster, Jr.
John S. Strong
May 2007

SECTION ONE
Setting the Stage

With the forecast growth in air traffic, the air navigation series providers (ANSPs) throughout the world all face challenges of handling an increasing number of flights in a safe and efficient manner. Within the airspace they control, there also is an increasing number of international flights which will require them to interact more frequently with other ANSPs. The natural question that emerges is whether there are some approaches to organizing, funding, and operating ANSPs that are more effective and better suited to these challenges than others. That is the topic of this book.

This book is organized into five sections. Section One, which contains Chapters 1 to 3, sets the stage for the discussions that follow. There are few topics where the discussion is more laden with acronyms and specialized language than air traffic control. The result is that to the uninitiated, air traffic control seems like an incredibly complex topic well beyond their comprehension. Chapter 2 removes some of the mystery from the topic by explaining many of the more commonly used terms, by providing a description of the basics of how an air traffic control system works, and by explaining the basic differences in some of competing technologies. The goal is not to delve into the technical details, but to describe the basic functions and approaches that are common to air traffic control systems around the world so that the policy options about how to provide these services can be discussed and understood. In the last twenty years, as described in Chapter 3, many countries have moved away from traditional government agencies to a variety of organizational forms with a more commercial orientation as a means of providing these services.

Section Two of the book, Chapters 4 through 7, examines the international experiences with air traffic management in mature aviation markets. Air navigation and air traffic control services were once provided almost exclusively by government agencies. New Zealand and Australia were two of the first countries to change to a different form of provision and they are discussed in Chapter 4. Canada took a different approach which is examined in Chapter 5 and the United Kingdom took a still different approach, as discussed in Chapter 6. Europe presents a set of challenges with a large number of separate ANSPs operating in a relatively small geographic area that mirror many of the challenges faced in other parts of the world and is described in Chapter 7.

Section Three of the book examines international experiences in countries with emerging aviation markets. Chapter 8 sets the stage by looking at the challenges of establishing and operating air navigation systems in developing countries. Chapter 9 looks at Russia. Chapter 10 examines China. Chapter 11 looks at India and the challenges presented by rapid growth in air travel. Chapter 12 looks at the myriad of challenges in Africa and Latin America.

Section 4 of the book, Chapters 14 through 16, turn to the situation in the United States, the last major country in the world where air traffic services are still provided by a government agency and funded by excise taxes and general tax revenues. Chapter 14 reviews the history and evolution of the provision of air traffic control services in the United States. The problems facing the FAA today are not new problems and have their origins years, or even decades ago. Chapter 15 reviews the changes made to FAA's organizational structure in 2004 and examines the challenges that remain for the FAA, if it is to be able to accommodate the expected growth in air traffic. Chapter 16 examines the possible alternatives for reform of the FAA and how well these potential reforms might do in confronting FAA's major challenges.

The final section of the book, Section Five, Chapters 17 and 18, examines the cross-cutting issue of labor relations and the lessons learned. Chapter 17 looks at the challenges posed by labor issues and why labor relations are more contentious with some organizational structures and funding mechanisms than others. It also describes the major labor challenges ahead both in the United States and elsewhere in the world. Chapter 18 compares the strengths and weaknesses of the different organizational structures that are used in different countries throughout the world. This chapter then presents the major lessons that can be drawn from these comparisons and explores what the future might hold.

Chapter 1

The Global Air Traffic Control Challenge

The Worst of Times and the Best of Times

The 2000–2001 period illustrated both the worst of times and the best of times for the air traffic control system, at least in North America. These were the worst of times because of the growing problem of delays in the air transportation system. In the first nine months of 2000, fully one quarter of all passenger airline flights in the United States, affecting 119 million passengers were either delayed, canceled, or diverted. The average delay for these flights exceeded 50 minutes. The media reported at the time that airline service had become so unpredictable that some business travelers were flying to their destinations the night before important meetings rather than in the morning so as to be sure not to miss them. Complaints about air travel were up 16 percent in 2000 over the previous year.

To be sure, there were many reasons for the delays including strong growth in air travel, weather, inadequate runway capacity at airports, and unrealistic scheduling by some airlines. But in late 2000 and 2001, the inability of the air traffic control system to keep up with the growth in air travel was getting more and more of the blame. The airlines were quick to point the finger at the air traffic management system operated by the Federal Aviation Administration (FAA) for the delays claiming that there weren't enough controllers or that there wasn't enough room in the sky under FAA rules. There were also growing public concerns about safety as the number of runway incursions, or near misses on the runways as the media was referring to them, were increasing throughout the late 1990s.[1]

At the same time, more and more people were beginning to question whether FAA was capable of addressing these problems. In 1995, US Government Accountability Office (GAO) had designated the air traffic control modernization program as a high-risk information technology initiative because of its size, complexity, cost, and problem-plagued past. Adding to the concern was that in 1999, FAA's financial management had also been designated as high risk by GAO. Throughout the 1990s, a series of studies by independent commissions had called for major reforms in how air traffic control was provided in the United States. These problems were not confined to the United States. Much the same thing was also happening in Europe as delays attributed to air traffic control problems were growing sharply throughout the late 1990s.

As beleaguered as the air traffic control systems seemed to be in 2001, the tragic events of September 11, 2001 set the stage for what might be considered the best of

---

1 "Near Misses on Runways Spark Debate at Hearings," *Pittsburgh Post-Gazette*, July 1, 2002, Page A-12.

times, at least in terms of air traffic control performance. The first hijacked aircraft hit the New York World Trade Center at 8:46 am on September 11. By 9:26 am, the FAA had banned all takeoffs by civilian aircraft and at 9:45 am, FAA ordered the first unplanned shutdown of US airspace in history. At the time, there were more than 4,500 aircraft – about 3,300 commercial and about 1,200 private – in the air using the air traffic control system under instrument flight rules (IFR).

Nothing like this had ever happened before. There were no procedures, there were no plans to follow, there had been no drills, and both Canadian and US air traffic control had to work together very closely to do things neither had done before. On a normal day in the US air traffic control system, about 20 aircraft are rerouted each hour. On September 11, controllers rerouted 1,100 aircraft in the first 15 minutes of the shutdown. Of the planes in the air at the time the order was given, nearly two thirds were landed within the first hour and the skies over the contiguous 48 states were clear of all commercial and private flights by about 12:15, only two and a half hours after the order was given.

Domestic flights weren't the only challenge. With US airspace closed, the flights already en route to the United States from abroad had to be rerouted somewhere and Canada took up the challenge. More than 250 international flights carrying 44,000 passengers were diverted to Canadian airports. Atlantic Canada bore the brunt of the diverted trans-Atlantic traffic and the small community of Halifax, Nova Scotia alone took over 40 aircraft. The airport converted one of its two runways into a massive parking lot and packed the jets together as closely as possible. The community turned high schools, arenas, and churches into temporary shelters for more than 7,000 passengers. A similar story unfolded at the small community of Gander, Newfoundland where 39 aircraft were diverted. Vancouver handled many of the trans-Pacific flights.

The US and Canadian air traffic control systems did an astonishing job on September 11. They managed to clear the airspace by landing 4,500 commercial and private aircraft under highly stressful circumstances in less than three hours without a single accident or even a single report of a loss of separation. It was a remarkable performance and a testimony to the skill and dedication of the air traffic controllers in both countries. But the dedication and skill of the air traffic controllers won't be enough to accommodate the expected future growth in air traffic unless some important changes are made to the air traffic control system, not only in the United States, but throughout the world.

Growth in Worldwide Aviation

In 2006, according to the International Air Transport Association (IATA), airlines around the world carried an estimated 2.1 billion passengers, of whom 743 million were in international service.[2] Between 2006 and 2010, passenger traffic was expected to grow at an average annual rate of 4.8 percent, so that by 2010, well over 2.5 billion passengers would be carried. Air cargo was forecast to grow at an even

---

2   Fact Sheet: IATA www.iata.org/pressroom/facts_figures/fact_sheets/iata.htm.

faster rate. The region with the fastest expected growth is the Middle East, with the Asia-Pacific region the second fastest. The slowest growth is expected in North America and Europe, but even in these more mature markets, the growth is expected to be between 4.3 and 4.4 percent per year. By 2010, Asia is expected to be the largest market, surpassing the US domestic market which has historically been the world's largest. Even the United States, with slower forecast growth is expected to reach one billion passengers per year by 2015. By 2020, worldwide airline passenger traffic is expected to be at least double what it was in 2006.

This forecast growth is good news for the world economy. Aviation's global impact is estimated at $2.96 trillion, equivalent to 8 percent of world gross domestic product (GDP).[3] The industry is responsible for 29 million jobs and 25 percent of all companies' sales are dependent on air transport. Air transport and particularly air cargo are especially import to economic growth in developing countries where surface transportation infrastructure is often lacking. But the benefits of air transport will come only if the growth can be accommodated.

Strains on the Air Traffic Management System

The forecast growth is troubling news for the world's 160 Air Navigation Service Providers (ANSPs) who provide the navigation and air traffic control services that allow these aircraft to fly safely and efficiently to and from their destinations.[4] No air traffic management system currently in place can handle the volumes of traffic forecast for 2010 or beyond. For the worldwide aviation system to run smoothly, for the forecast growth rates to be achieved, and for the economic benefits of aviation to be realized, ANSPs throughout the world are going to have to expand their capacity to manage aircraft.

Expanding capacity or switching to more modern technologies pose far greater challenges in air traffic management than in perhaps any other sector of the world economy. Changing from one technology to another in air traffic control is difficult because the system must operate continuously with extreme accuracy and reliability 24 hours a day, 365 days a year. An interruption of service even for a matter of seconds can put aircraft at risk – modern jet aircraft typically cruise at about 570 miles per hour or a little over 250 meters per second. No matter when a transition from one technology to another is made, there will almost certainly be planes in flight during the transition. To the extent that a new system requires aircraft to have different equipment than the system it replaces, then either all aircraft will have to have capability of using both the old and the new system or the two systems will have to be operated together until all the aircraft have been reequipped. In air traffic control, it's not enough to develop an improved technology; a smooth transition from the old technology to the new technology must also be developed.

---

3   Fact Sheet: Economic and Social Benefits of Air Transport, www.iata.org/pressroom/facts_figures/fact_sheets/economic_social_benefits.htm.

4   Air Navigation Service Provider is the term most typically used to describe the organizations that provide air traffic control services and also air navigation services. These two activities together are also often referred to as air traffic management.

While domestic travel will usually be entirely within the air traffic management system of a single country, international flights will have to operate within the air traffic management systems of two or more countries. If an airplane is making the transition from the air traffic control system of one country to that of another, the systems of the two countries must be able to communicate with one another so that the aircraft can be smoothly "handed off" from one system to another. The aircraft must also be able to operate with the system of each country through which it passes. If one country upgrades the technology in its system, that new technology must also be able to communicate with the technology of the second country.

The air traffic management systems operated by the 160 ANSPs in the world comprise the network that will have to accommodate the forecast growth in air travel. Because traffic must flow over the network, the full benefits of upgrading one part of the network won't be realized if the other parts of the network aren't upgraded as well. It does little good for one country to increase the capacity of their air traffic management system if an adjacent country through whom traffic must also flow doesn't upgrade their system as well. Air traffic management systems within the network that have outdated equipment or low capacity can become as bottlenecks in the system that can have ripple effects on systems thousands of miles away.

Chapter 2

How Air Traffic Control Works

Introduction

There are few topics where the discussion is more laden with acronyms and specialized language than air traffic control. For most people, listening to experts talk about air traffic control is much like listening to people converse in a foreign language they've never studied. Acronyms like ANSP, VFR, IFR, TCAS, CRCO, ARTCC, TRACON, ADS-B, WAAS, and GNSS are only the beginning of mysterious terms. The result is that to the uninitiated, air traffic control seems like an incredibly complex topic well beyond their comprehension. Such perceptions are unfortunate because the apparent complexity limits the ability of otherwise intelligent people to participate in, or even understand, discussions of the important air traffic control policy issues faced around the world.

This chapter will try to remove some of the mystery from the topic by explaining many of the more commonly used terms and by providing a description of the basics of how an air traffic control system works. The explanation will be based on how systems currently work in the United States, but where there are important differences between the US practice and practices elsewhere, these differences will be noted. Similarly, how some alternative technologies might be used will also be discussed. To be sure, air traffic control can be complex in its details, procedures, and equipment. The goal here is not to delve into the technical details, but to describe the basic functions and approaches that are common to air traffic control systems around the world so that the policy options about how to provide these services can be discussed and understood by a broader range of people.

Two Distinctions

An air traffic control organization's main functions are to keep aircraft separated, that is prevent airplanes from colliding with one another either in the air or on the ground, and to move aircraft along efficient flight paths from their origin airport to their destination airport. Air traffic control also may provide weather and navigation information to pilots. To understand how these tasks are accomplished, there are two distinctions that are useful to make at the beginning. The first is between "visual flight rules" and "instrument flight rules" and the second is between "controlled" and "uncontrolled" airspace.

If an aircraft is operating under visual flight rules, or "VFR," then it is the responsibility of the pilot of the aircraft to maintain separation from other aircraft so as to avoid collisions. The basic method of maintaining separation under these conditions is through the concept of "see and avoid" where pilots look out the cockpit window and make sure they don't get too close to other aircraft. When the visibility is good, when there aren't too many other aircraft in the vicinity, and when aircraft are traveling at relatively low speeds, this method can work well. As discussed in Chapter 14, from the beginning of flight until the end of the 1920s, this was the only method of air traffic control that was needed. As aircraft and navigational aids improved, it became possible for flights with properly equipped aircraft and properly trained pilots to be conducted at night or in weather conditions where visibility is poor, such as flights in fog or through clouds. In these flights, control of the aircraft and navigation is accomplished solely by reference to cockpit instrumentation. These flights are governed by what are called instrument flight rules or "IFR". Under instrument flight rules with reduced visibility, the traditional see and avoid approach isn't sufficient to maintain aircraft separation and avoid collisions, so aircraft operating under these conditions must be separated by the air traffic control system or by other technologies.[1]

Airspace is divided into "controlled" airspace and "uncontrolled" airspace. In controlled airspace, air traffic control separation is provided to all aircraft operating under instrument flight rules.[2] In controlled airspace, if flights operating under visual flight rules are present, the IFR flights have the responsibility of separating themselves from VFR flights and VFR flights have the responsibility of separating themselves from both IFR flights and from other VFR flights. In the United States, airspace above 18,000 feet is essentially reserved for IFR flights only. Most of the rest of the airspace in the US is also controlled, but allows both IFR and VFR flights. Some airspace in the US is uncontrolled. Typically uncontrolled airspace is below 1,200 feet and away from busy airports. In uncontrolled airspace, both VFR and IFR flights have responsibility for separating themselves from all other aircraft.

Of course, these distinctions are not always as sharp as the above discussion would imply. While air traffic controllers have no responsibility for VFR aircraft, they will provide traffic advisories for VFR aircraft on a "workload permitting" basis. The practice of see and avoid can also be made more effective by technologies such as traffic collision avoidance system (TCAS) and the automatic dependent surveillance system (ADS-B) which enhance the pilot's ability to detect and avoid nearby aircraft.

A Typical Flight

Perhaps the easiest way to describe how the air traffic control system works is to follow a typical passenger airline flight from beginning to end. A commercial airline flight, whether passenger or cargo, will have a flight profile that includes the following steps:

---

1   There are technologies available that can enable aircraft flying under instrument flight conditions to avoid collisions with one another. Such technologies will be discussed later in this chapter.

2   In many countries, there are several categories of controlled airspace, each with different restrictions about what aircraft can operate under what conditions.

- Preflight: This portion of the flight starts on the ground and includes fueling and loading passengers, baggage, or cargo onto the aircraft and pre-flight checks.[3]
- Pushback and Taxi: The aircraft is pushed back from the gate and taxis to the runway for takeoff.
- Takeoff: The pilot powers up the aircraft and proceeds down the runway.
- Departure: The plane lifts off the ground and climbs to a cruising altitude.
- En route: The aircraft travels across the country at cruising altitude and nears the destination airport.
- Descent: The pilot descends and maneuvers the aircraft toward the destination airport.
- Approach: The pilot aligns the aircraft with the designated landing runway.
- Landing: The aircraft lands on the designated runway, taxis to the destination gate, parks at the terminal, and the aircraft is unloaded.

Preflight

Prior to the flight, while passengers, baggage, and any cargo are being loaded on the aircraft, the pilot does the final walk-around inspection of the aircraft. The aircraft used for passenger airline flights are equipped to fly in a wide variety of weather conditions and typically follow instrument flight rules. The pilot, or more typically for a commercial passenger flight the airline's dispatch office, files a flight plan with the air traffic control tower. The flight plan contains the airline name and flight number, the type of aircraft, the intended airspeed and desired cruising altitude, and the route of flight including the departure and destination airports. The flight plan will accompany the flight through the air traffic control system and provide the necessary information to controllers about the flight's destination and route. In the United States, flight plan information is entered into the Federal Aviation Administration (FAA) host computer. Once the flight plan has been checked and approved, the pilot is given clearance and the computer generates a flight progress strip, which contains all the necessary information for the flight and which will be transmitted from controller to controller until the plane reaches its final destination. Flight progress strips originated as small strips of paper used to track a flight. In some systems, these strips were manually passed from controller to controller as the flight progressed through the system. In some countries, including much of the United States, these paper strips have been replaced by computer systems which pass the information along and display it on computer screens.

In air traffic control systems that handle a large amount of traffic, one of the challenges is when the number of flights destined for an airport in a given period of time exceed the capacity of that airport to handle the flights. When that happens, one alternative is simply to have the aircraft fly in circles near the airport until they have an opportunity to land. For years, this was the standard practice throughout the world and in some places it still happens. This practice, however, was expensive for the airlines because of the fuel burned while circling. More importantly, it posed a

---

3   Some passenger flights also carry cargo.

safety risk if a plane deviated from a holding pattern into the path of another plane. In the past, some midair collisions have resulted from such deviations.

A better approach is to monitor when such a situation is likely to arise and hold the plane on the ground at the origin airport until it can fly directly to its destination and land right away. In the United States, all air traffic control is overseen by the Air Traffic Control System Command Center, which monitors the entire system, including weather conditions. When a delay at the destination airport is anticipated, perhaps due to weather or other reasons, the flight may be held on the ground and delayed from taking off. These ground holds are used to make sure that no part of the air traffic control system is overloaded beyond its capacity. Holding an aircraft on the ground prior to takeoff is preferred for both safety and economic reasons to having that aircraft circle in the air at the destination airport, waiting for the congestion to ease so that the plane may land. In Europe, EUROCONTROL's Central Flow Management Unit serves a similar function.

Pushback and taxi

The ground controller is responsible for all ground traffic, including aircraft taxiing from the gate to the takeoff runway and, for arriving aircraft, from the landing runway to the gate. When the aircraft is ready to depart and the ground controller has determined that it is safe, the pilot is directed to push back from the gate. If a tug is used to push the airplane back from the gate, that tug is usually operated by airline personnel. The aircraft then taxis to the runway under the direction of the ground controller. When the plane reaches the designated takeoff runway, the plane is "handed off," which means that the flight progress strip is passed, to the local tower controller who takes over responsibility for directing the flight. When a flight is passed from one air traffic controller to another, the pilot of the aircraft is instructed to change the radio frequency from the frequency of the controller which is handing the aircraft off to the frequency used by the controller which is receiving the handoff of the aircraft. For international flights throughout the world, these conversations between pilots and controllers are conducted in English. For local flights, controllers most commonly use the local language. To insure that the controller's instructions are clearly understood, the general practice is for the pilot to repeat the instruction back to the controller.

The portion of the flight when the aircraft is on the taxiway can be surprisingly dangerous, particularly at very busy airports and especially under conditions where weather, darkness, or airport configuration may limit visibility. At airports with multiple runways, taxiing aircraft must often cross one or more runways to get to the runway where they will takeoff. If an aircraft mistakenly taxis onto an active runway where another plane is taking off or landing, the result can be a catastrophic loss of life. Indeed, the worse aviation accident in history was in 1977 when two B-747s collided on a runway in Tenerife, Canary Islands killing 583 people. Runway incursions, collision hazards on the ground between an aircraft and another aircraft or other vehicle, remain a safety concern.

Takeoff

The local controller is responsible for making sure that aircraft taking off maintain a safe distance from one another during takeoff and initial climb. An airplane taking off or in flight leaves very turbulent air behind it, including a particular form of turbulence knows as wake vortex turbulence. If an aircraft flies too closely behind another aircraft, it can result in a very bumpy ride and in some cases a very dangerous condition. Complicating the controller's job is the fact that different aircraft leave behind them different amounts of wake vortex turbulence, so in spacing the aircraft during takeoff, the controller must be aware of the types of planes. When the local controller determines that there will be sufficient distance between aircraft and the one that preceded it, and that it's safe to take off, clearance is given to the pilot and the pilot may begin the takeoff run.

A critical safety aspect is making sure that the active runway is clear of other aircraft. The local controller provides the pilot with the radio frequency on which the pilot can talk to the next controller, and hands the plane off to the next controller, in this case the departure controller. The local controller will typically continue to monitor the plane until it is up to five miles from the airport. At some point within that five-mile radius, the plane is handed off to the departure controller.

Departure

Depending on the specific airport, the departure controller will handle the aircraft within about a 30 to 50 mile radius of the airport. Once the aircraft is airborne and out of visual sight, the question arises of how the controllers know where the aircraft is. In most cases throughout the world, the aircraft is tracked by radar. Originally air traffic control used what is known as primary surveillance radar (PSR). With primary surveillance radar a signal is transmitted which then bounces off the aircraft (or "paints" the aircraft as it is sometimes known) and is received back by the radar installation. What the controller viewing the radar screen would see from primary surveillance radar is basically a smudge for each aircraft within range of the radar. Keeping track of which smudge corresponded to which aircraft was often a difficult task and was often done by the controller observing which smudge moved in response to a command to a particular aircraft to turn.

The military use of radar faced a similar problem in distinguishing which smudge was a friendly aircraft and which was an enemy aircraft. They developed what was known as an Identification Friend or Foe (IFF) system. With this system, friendly aircraft were equipped with a radio transceiver called a transponder, receiving on the same frequency as the radar signal. When the radar signal would hit the transponder, it would send back a coded reply that identified the aircraft as a friend. This approach evolved into a civilian system called Secondary Surveillance Radar (SSR). Before the aircraft takes off, the pilot turns on the plane's transponder. The transponder detects incoming radar signals and broadcasts back a four-digit code that, when linked to information about the flight plan contained in the computer provides the air traffic control system with the aircraft's identification, destination, altitude, and airspeed. This information is displayed on the radar screen of the air traffic controller and makes it much easier for controllers to keep track of multiple flights.

At busy airports in the United States, the departure controller, who has control of the aircraft now, is located in a Terminal Radar Approach Control Facility, known as a TRACON. The TRACON airspace may contain more than one airport and will have well established air corridors for arriving and departing aircraft, and the departure controller will direct the plane to one of these corridors by giving the pilot the heading, speed, and rate of climb. The departure controller will use radar, in conjunction with transponders, to monitor the aircraft and maintain a safe distance between it and other aircraft. When the aircraft leaves the TRACON airspace, the departure controller hands off the aircraft to an Air Route Traffic Control Center (ARTCC) controller.

En route

The controllers responsible for the aircraft during the en route portion of flight are located in what are called in the United States, Air Route Traffic Control Centers, (ARTCC), more often just known as Centers. The upper airspace of the United States is divided into 21 different zones, each one controlled by a different Center. Within each of these zones, the airspace is divided into sectors, and each sector is managed by at least two controllers. The radar associate controller received the flight plan information prior to the flight entering the sector and works with the radar controller to maintain safe separation between aircraft. This involves communicating via radio with the pilot and providing instructions as to altitude, heading, and speed. There are both high altitude sectors (above 24,000 feet) and low-altitude sectors (below 24,000 feet). The controller will also provide the pilot with updated weather information. In some cases, pilots may request a deviation around bad weather and in other cases, the controller may direct the aircraft to alternative routings to avoid bad weather. These controllers will monitor the aircraft until it leaves their sector, at which point they will hand it off to the next sector's controller. Depending on the length and destination of the flight, it will likely pass through several sectors and several different Centers.

Descent

As the plane nears its destination, the controllers will move it from the high-altitude sectors to low-altitude sectors and merge the aircraft approaching a particular airport from various directions into one or more lines, with sufficient spacing between the planes so that they can proceed to land under the guidance of controllers at the TRACON. As the plane descends, it will get to within 50 miles of its destination airport and will enter airspace controlled by the destination TRACON.

Approach

At the TRACON, the approach controllers will merge the aircraft into a single line and align them in approach corridors for each of the runways used for landings. In order to merge planes into a single line, some may have to slow down, others may have to speed up, and still others may have to enter a holding pattern briefly. One of the challenges facing air traffic controllers in both the descent and approach phases is merging aircraft coming from several different directions into a single line of aircraft with proper spacing between them. When the plane is within 10 miles of the runway, the approach controller in the TRACON hands off the aircraft to the local controller in the tower.

Landing

The local controller uses both visual information and surface radar to make sure that it is safe to land and then clears the aircraft to land. As with takeoffs, making sure that the runway is clear of other aircraft is a critical controller responsibility. The local controller also provides the pilot with weather and runway condition information. Once the aircraft has landed, the local controller directs it to the appropriate taxiway and hands the plane off to the ground controller to direct the plane to the gate.

When described in simple terms, it all sounds easy; in fact, almost all flights are uneventful from an air traffic control standpoint. However, many things must function properly for the air traffic control system to work. Not only must the radars and transponders work well to allow the controllers to monitor the location of each aircraft, but the radios must also work well on the different frequencies to allow the controllers and the pilots to communicate and the pilots much switch to the right radio frequencies at the right time. Then the various computers must work well and communicate with one another to allow the handoffs from controller to controller. And, all of this must function without interruption 24 hours a day, 365 days a year.

Limitations of Ground-Based Radar Systems

The description of the flight presented above describes a ground-based radar system as is used in most of the world. Ground based radar systems are a proven and well understood technology. Such systems work together with ground-based navigational aids that can be used to determine an aircraft's position. However, radar is slow compared to how quickly the aircraft are moving. Radar antennas take about four and a half seconds to rotate through a cycle. For a controller to get an accurate picture of the aircraft's heading, requires three radar readings, which takes about 14 seconds if the aircraft is close but the lag in knowing the position and heading can stretch to 36 seconds for an aircraft in midflight.[4]

Ground-based systems have a second fundamental drawback that coverage is not available in all parts of the world and isn't even possible for flights over oceans. In areas where radar coverage isn't available, such as over the Atlantic and Pacific Oceans, controllers have had to rely on aircraft reporting their positions based on onboard equipment such as inertial navigation systems. Relying on reported positions doesn't provide as close control as radar based systems, and as a result aircraft have to be spaced further apart. A third drawback is that ground-based navigational aids require a maintenance infrastructure to keep them operational. In some developing countries, an adequate maintenance infrastructure may not be in place, which could compromise the reliability of the system.

---

4   Tim Doyle and Andrew T. Gillies, "Smart Skies," *Forbes*, February 26, 2007.

Global Navigation Satellite Systems

These coverage limitations of ground-based systems have lead to increasing interest in satellite-based systems, more generally called Global Navigation Satellite Systems or GNSS. GNSS are worldwide positioning systems based on a series of satellites in medium earth orbit, about 12,000 miles above the surface of the earth. The International Civil Aviation Organization (ICAO) endorsed the use of satellite navigation in its Future Air Navigation System (FANS) design. In 1996, ICAO endorsed the development and use of GNSS as a primary source of future navigation for civil aviation and began developing and publishing Standards and Recommended Practices (SARPS) in 2001. Satellite-based systems could provide both navigational information and, by providing air traffic controllers with the location, speed, and direction of aircraft, could provide the information needed to maintain separation as well.

The United States developed and operates the Global Positioning System (GPS) and Russia is developing a similar system called GLONASS which is not yet operational. The European Commission plans to develop its own system, called Galileo. GPS systems are widely used in ground and water transportation and are increasingly found in automobiles. The GPS system was originally based on 24 satellites in six different orbits, although some additional satellites have been added to increase availability. The GPS satellites were placed in orbit by the US Department of Defense, beginning in 1978 and made available for civilian use in the 1980s.[5] In 1994, the United States informed ICAO that it would offer the GPS standard positioning service to support civil aviation at no charge to users. The GLONASS system is planned to have 24 satellites while the Galileo system is planned to have 27 operational satellites with three spares.

GPS works according to the geometric principle of triangulation. A GPS receiver measures the time it takes for the signal to reach it from a specific satellite to calculate the distance to that satellite. In principle, if you know the distance to three satellites and the specific location of those satellites, you can calculate your precise position in three dimensions (longitude, latitude, and altitude). Each satellite has an extremely accurate atomic clock so that it can broadcast the precise time the signal is sent. If a GPS receiver also has an atomic clock, it can then determine the time it takes each signal to arrive and thus the distance to that satellite. If a measurement is taken from a fourth satellite, then the time can be determined without the GPS receiver having its own atomic clock. Thus, in practice, a GPS receiver must be able to receive signals from four satellites to determine its location. If the receiver can determine it's location at different points in time, it can also determine the direction of travel and speed as well as whether it's climbing or descending. The information the satellite sends tells the receiver which specific satellite it is, where it is located at that specific time, as well as the day and time the signal is sent. The more satellites a GPS receiver can receive signals from at any given time, the more accurately the

---

5   Initially, the signal available for civilians was intentionally degraded by a process called Selective Availability to prevent military adversaries from using the highly accurate system. Selective Availability was turned off in May 2000 which improved the accuracy of the civilian system.

receiver can determine its position. The GPS system also has a system of worldwide monitor and control stations that maintain the satellites in their proper orbits and adjust their clocks.

Enhancing GPS accuracy

Unfortunately, there are some factors that can reduce GPS accuracy. The satellite signal can slow slightly as it passes through the atmosphere. GPS receivers have a built in model that calculates the average amount of delay, which partially corrects for this effect, but not fully. A second source of inaccuracy can be orbital errors which are errors in the satellite's reported position. There can also be clock errors when the receiver's clock is not quite as accurate as the satellite's clock. GPS signals will pass through clouds, glass, and plastic, but are blocked or reflected by objects such as buildings and mountains. This issue is less of a factor for aircraft than for ground applications, but can still affect aircraft operating at relatively low altitudes in mountainous terrain. The greater the number of satellites visible to the receiver, the greater the accuracy, but the relative position of the satellites matters as well. GPS works best when the satellites are located at wide angles relative to each other and is less accurate when the satellites are closely grouped. It is also possible under some circumstances for satellites to transmit incorrect signals without warning users.

To overcome these potential problems, augmentation systems are used to improve the accuracy and reliability of satellite-based systems. Such augmentation systems can be aircraft based, satellite based, or ground based. Aircraft-based systems work by providing integrity checks on the satellite based navigation. One such system requires the aircraft to receive signals from five satellites instead of the minimum of four satellites. That system then compares the navigation information of various subsets of four satellites out of the available five to make sure that they are all consistent with one another. If they are not, then the pilot is alerted. A variant of this system uses six satellites to detect a faulty satellite and then to exclude it from navigation calculations.[6] Another approach is to use information available to the aircraft from other sources as a check on the information from the satellite systems. For example, the altitude reading from the aircraft's barometric altimeter can be used as a cross check as can information from the aircraft's inertial navigation system or information from ground-based navigational aids.[7]

Another approach is satellite-based augmentation systems. With such systems, a network of reference stations on the ground collect the satellite signals. These reference stations are, of course, at fixed locations so it's possible for them to determine how accurate the satellite information is and to calculate a series of differential corrections, including information about whether a specific satellite should or should not be used. That information is then sent to users via geostationary satellites. The FAA operates a satellite-based augmentation system known as WAAS,

---

6   These kinds of systems are known as Receiver Autonomous Integrity Monitoring Systems or RAIMS.
7   These kinds of systems are known as Aircraft Autonomous Integrity Monitoring Systems or AIMS.

the Wide Area Augmentation System to provide aircraft navigation for all phases of flight. WAAS consists of 25 ground reference stations across the United States that monitor satellite data and compare it with their surveyed locations. WAAS uses two master stations, one on each coast of the US to collect the data and create GPS correction information and two geostationary satellites to send the information to users. WAAS was commissioned for use in 2003. WAAS only provides coverage for the United States, but Europe and Asia are developing similar approaches with the European Geostationary Navigation System (EGNOS) and the Japanese Multi-Function Satellite Augmentation System (MSAS).

A third approach is ground-based augmentation systems. Ground-based augmentation systems are similar to satellite based systems in that they too have a system of ground reference stations that collect information from satellites and calculate differential corrections. With a ground-based system, these corrections are broadcast to the aircraft using a Very High Frequency Data Broadcast (VBD). Ground based augmentation systems are well suited to provide the navigation information necessary to conduct precision approaches within a terminal area. One example of such a system is the Local Area Augmentation System (LAAS) being developed by FAA.

A basic question with satellite based navigation systems is whether they provide navigational information of sufficient accuracy to allow landing in poor weather conditions with reduced visibility. With such landing, the defining criteria is the decision height (or decision altitude), which is the minimum altitude above the runway when the pilot must be able to see the runway or the runway's approach lights in order to continue with the landing. Category I operations are where the decision height is no lower than 60 meters (about 197 feet) with a runway visual range of not less than 550 meters (about 600 yards). Category II has a decision height between 30 meters (about 98 feet) and 60 meters and a runway visual range of not less than 350 meters (about 380 yards). Category III has several subsets and has even lower decision heights and even lower runway visual ranges. WAAS is expected to eventually provide Category I service. Ground based augmentation systems support Category I operations and are believed to have the potential to support Category II and Category III operations.

Collision avoidance and free flight

A satellite based navigation can also support safety enhancements such as Automatic Dependent Surveillance – Broadcast, known as ADS-B. An ADS-B system would use the information from satellites coupled with ground-based stations to determine the aircraft's position as described above. Then that information would be automatically broadcast to other aircraft in the area that were equipped to receive these signals and to air traffic controllers on the ground. The displays in ADS-B equipped aircraft would show pilots the location of other aircraft in their vicinity, with a lag in information of only about a second. Ground stations using an approach called multilateration could provide similar information to aircraft not equipped with ADS-B but detected by radar to these displays so that pilots and air traffic controllers would see the same information on their displays. Weather information and information about temporary flight restrictions could also be added. ADS-B could reduce the risk both of midair collisions and runway incursions by giving pilots better situational awareness. It could also reduce controller workload by allowing pilots to take a greater role in maintaining separation from other aircraft. And, because satellite-based systems can determine the location of aircraft with greater precision than radar, ADS-B could help increase the capacity of the airspace system by allowing aircraft to fly more closely together without compromising safety.

ADS-B is already being used successfully on a limited basis in the United States. Alaska presents a particularly challenging flight environment because of the combination of weather and mountainous terrain. Since 2000, FAA has installed five ground based stations and equipped 200 aircraft with ADS-B instrumentation. Accident rates have dropped sharply as a result. Embry Riddle Aeronautical University has equipped all of its training planes with ADS-B and experienced a dramatic drop in loss of separation incidents.

Satellite-based navigation systems could also lower the cost and speed the implementation of a concept known as "free flight." With the current air traffic control system, aircraft in the en route portion of flight are typically guided by air traffic control along predetermined paths in the sky. These paths are similar to single lane highways where planes line up to traverse the skies. Following these paths makes it easier for air traffic controllers to maintain separation between aircraft. However, for many flights, following these predetermined paths results in longer flights than simply flying in a straight line between the origin and the destination. Similarly, following these predetermined paths may prevent aircraft from operating at their optimal altitudes. The result is an increase in the time of travel and in fuel consumed compared to a system where flights could proceed directly from origin to destination.

Free flight would allow aircraft to proceed directly from origin to destination using the most direct and efficient flight path. It would put the responsibility for maintaining separation on the pilots of the aircraft, aided by systems that detected potential conflicts, rather than on air traffic controllers. One way of providing the necessary information to pilots to maintain separation would be a satellite-based navigation system with ADS-B. Another way would be to use TCAS, which stands for Traffic alert and Collision Avoidance System. TCAS is conceptually similar to ADS-B, but does not require a satellite-based system. Recall from the description of a flight earlier in this chapter than the radar system works in concert with the transponders in each aircraft. Radar interrogates the transponder and the transponder responds with information about the identity of the flight, it's altitude, speed, and direction. A TCAS system interrogates the transponders of the aircraft in surrounding air space and uses the responses to build the equivalent of a map of the surrounding airspace that shows the position, bearing, and speed of the other aircraft. A TCAS system can also use that information to detect the threat of possible collision and issue instructions to the pilots to allow them take actions to avoid that collision. However, TCAS is not as accurate as ADS-B, so its use in this role may be limited.

While free flight offers some potential benefits to aviation, it also has some limitations. One concern is the extent to which it would be workable in highly congested airspace. A second is that while it offers advantages for the en route portion of flight, the potential advantages are less obvious in congested terminal airspace where aircraft must be aligned and spaced properly to land on specific runways. A third concern is that all aircraft operating in the airspace would have to be properly equipped for either a satellite based system or a ground radar based system to work.

Controllers in the future

Systems such as ADS-B and concepts such as free flight raise the issue of how the role of the air traffic controller might change with the possibilities opened up by new technology. Traditionally, air traffic controllers have directed every move of each of the aircraft that were their responsibility. They instructed the pilots the altitude, speed, and direction to fly and when to change any of those parameters of flight. In part because of the early limitations of ground based navigational aids and in part to ease the task of keeping separation between aircraft traveling at high speeds, controllers directed aircraft along pre-determined pathways in the sky. These pathways, by being at different altitudes for travel in different directions, made the task of keeping airplanes separated largely one of maintaining the proper distance between an aircraft and the plane traveling the same pathway in front of it. As jet aircraft were introduced and cruising speeds became much faster, even in daylight in clear weather the process of see and avoid by looking out the cockpit window simply wasn't adequate. Quickly moving aircraft left too little time to react when planes were on a collision course and the pilots had only their eyesight to detect the potential danger. Air traffic controllers were in much better position to see potential collisions on their radar screens much further in advance and give pilots the instructions needed to avoid the collision. As computer capability increased, programs were able to detect potential collisions even sooner and alert controllers of the danger.

Technology such as ADS-B can give pilots much better situational awareness than simply looking out the cockpit window and, with computer assistance to identify potential conflicts with other aircraft, have the potential to transfer much of the responsibility for separation back to the pilots. The job of the controller at en route control centers would become less one of directing the aircraft's every move and more one of monitoring the aircraft in a sector to ensure that potential loss of separation situations were resolved without any compromise to safety. In congested airspace surrounding busy airports, however, controllers would still likely retain their traditional role of directing aircraft. Notwithstanding the improved situational awareness systems like ADS-B can give pilots, it might still be easier and safer to have a controller directing aircraft how to line up with proper separation for a landing runway than have the pilots try to make the arrangements among themselves. Any motorists who have ever found themselves uncertain about whose turn it was to go next at a four-way stop sign can appreciate that similar uncertainty among aircraft aligning themselves to land could have far more serious consequences. Thus new technologies would have the capacity to change the role of air traffic controllers, but those changes would vary greatly between en route centers and TRACONS and even vary across airports and time of day depending on how busy the airports were and how complex their runway configurations were.

The challenge of changing technologies

It's one thing to develop a new technology that can improve air traffic control and it's another thing to introduce it safely. The challenge is that the air traffic control system must operate continuously without any interruption. Moreover, no matter when a transition is made from one system to another, there will inevitably be some flights in progress at the time of the transition.

The need for uninterrupted service has several implications. One is that the new system is likely to have to be installed in parallel with the existing systems since both will have to operate either simultaneously or nearly simultaneously. Similarly, to the extent that the new system requires aircraft to have different equipment, then either all aircraft will have to have capability of using both the old and the new system or the two systems will have to be operated together until all the aircraft have been reequipped.

A second implication is that it may be easier to implement a series of incremental changes rather than wait for a single large technological leap. Incremental changes are likely easier to adapt to from the perspective of training personnel, both in air traffic control facilities and equally importantly in the pilot workforce. Incremental changes may also be easier to test prior to implementation to ensure that there are no unanticipated problems. It may also be easier to implement incremental changes within a shorter time horizon and thus to match incremental changes more closely to the most pressing needs of the system. A large technological leap must be designed for the forecast needs of the system and the larger the technological leap, the further the forecast needs to look into the future. Finally, it may be easier to maintain interoperability across systems in different regions of the world with smaller incremental changes than with large technological leaps.

Look how far we've come

While the challenge of developing and implementing new technologies to meet the needs of the world's aviation system can seem daunting, it's worth reflecting on how far we've come. Many of the past changes in air traffic control were precipitated by accidents both in the air and on the ground at airports. Those kinds of accidents, while still occurring occasionally, have been dramatically reduced to the point where near misses are now considered newsworthy. This improvement has come as the amount of airline traffic has increased dramatically. In 1929, for example, passenger and cargo airlines operating worldwide flew 90,000,000 revenue aircraft kilometers. By 2005, that figure had grown to 30,845,000,000 revenue aircraft kilometers which represents an average annual growth rate of over 8 percent sustained over 76 years.[8]

---

8   Based on ICAO data provided by the Air Transport Association at http://www.airlines. org/economics/traffic/World+Airline+Traffic.htm.

Chapter 3

The Evolution of Air Navigation Services

In the second half of the twentieth century and the early years of the twenty-first century, the aviation industry grew to become a major contributor to the world's economy, making about 55 million flights a year worldwide (over 150,000 flights per day) by 2005 and carrying about 1.6 billion passengers. World War II had stimulated rapid development in aviation technology. It became apparent in the early 1940s that the civilian air transport industry was poised for rapid growth whenever the war was over. But for air transport to prosper there were both technical and political obstacles to overcome.

The Chicago Convention and the Responsibilities of the States

The successful growth of both military and civil aviation led to recognition of a need for global "rules of the sky". In looking to develop a basic structure, public and business leaders in aviation looked to the maritime law in developing "Rules of the Air" from "Rules of the Sea," in particular the importance of transit rights and international waters.

At the same time, designing a overall structure for aviation operations required a set of principles as to how, where, and when planes could fly. The original aviation policies drew from the experience of railways, by establishing principles for fixed air routes that resembled a three-dimensional railroad in which separation was a key concern. This hybrid system is still largely in place today, although technology is creating new opportunities to move from the relatively rigid air route system to a more flexible system.

In 1944, the United States and its allies conducted discussions that eventually led to the Convention on International Aviation held in Chicago in November. The Chicago Convention, as it became known, lasted for five weeks as delegates from 52 nations considered the many issues critical to the growth of international civil aviation.

The 96 articles adopted at the Chicago Convention establish the privileges and restrictions of all Contracting States and provide for the adoption of Standards and Recommended Practices (SARPs) regulating international air transport. The Convention accepted the basic principle that every State has complete and exclusive sovereignty over the airspace above its territory and provides that no scheduled international air service may operate over or into the territory of a Contracting State without its previous consent. The Chicago Convention also established the International Civil Aviation Organization (ICAO), as a specialized agency of the United Nations and charged with coordinating and regulating international air travel.

Of particular importance to air navigation and air traffic control is Article 28 of the Chicago Convention which states:[1]

Each contracting State undertakes, so far as it may find practicable, to:

(a) Provide, in its territory, airports, radio services, meteorological services and other air navigation facilities to facilitate international air navigation, in accordance with the standards and practices recommended or established from time to time, pursuant to this Convention;

(b) Adopt and put into operation the appropriate standard systems of communications procedure, codes, markings, signals, lighting and other operational practices and rules which may be recommended or established from time to time, pursuant to this Convention;

(c) Collaborate in international measures to secure the publication of aeronautical maps and charts in accordance with standards which may be recommended or established from time to time, pursuant to this Convention.

Virtually every country in the world involved in air transportation is a signatory to the Chicago Convention. Thus, providing air navigation services is ultimately the responsibility of a State or consortium of States and every Air Navigation Service Provider (ANSP) has the same basic responsibilities and provides the same basic set of services.

The Move to Commercialized ANSPs

While during the first few decades following the Chicago Convention air navigation and air traffic control services were provided by government agencies, there is no requirement in the Chicago Convention that the services be provided directly by the State itself. Indeed, ICAO states in Annex 11, para. 2.1.3 that, "When it has been determined that air traffic services will be provided, the States concerned shall designate the authority responsible for providing such services." Clearly, under ICAO guidelines a State can designate another organization to provide the services, but prior to 1987, air navigation services in all countries were provided directly by civil servants working in government owned and operated facilities. In 1987, Airways Corporation of New Zealand was formed as a state-owned enterprise and took over air navigation responsibilities from the Ministry of Transport. Since then, over forty other States have established commercialized ANSPs.

The terminology used in describing the growth in commercialized ANSPs can be confusing or even misleading as various people talk about "commercialization" or "corporatization" or "privatization." ICAO uses the term "autonomous authorities" as synonymous with commercialized air navigation service providers.[2] ICAO defined commercialization quite generally as, "An approach to management of facilities

---

1   Convention on International Civil Aviation done at Chicago on the 7th Day of December 1944, http://www.icao.int/icaonet/arch/doc/7300/7300_orig.pdf.

2   The Civil Air Navigation Services Organisation, *Corporatisation of Air Navigation Services*, August 1999, page 3.

and services in which business principles are applied or emphasis is placed on development of commercial activities" while they define privatization as, "Transfer of full or majority ownership of facilities and services to the private sector."[3] The Civil Air Navigation Services Organisation (CANSO) uses the term corporatization of air navigation services.[4]

Perhaps the most useful discussion of how to define commercialization is found in a January 2006 study by MBS Ottawa, "Commercialization is the range of organizational options and regulatory frameworks that introduce business practices into what is, or traditionally was, the province of a government department."[5] The MBS report additionally notes that a prerequisite for commercialization is the introduction of some form of financial autonomy into the ANSP.

The motivation for the move to commercialized ANSPs have varied from country to country, but there have been some common themes. The first is the need to supplement limited government resources to fund capital investments and modernization. This need has been translated into efforts to establish greater financial autonomy and through dedicated revenue sources, which did not have to compete with other government priorities. A second theme has been a desire to improve the ANSP's ability to respond to the needs of the users. A third, somewhat less common theme was the desire to sell off air navigation as a means to provide an injection of cash into the government treasury. Finally, while not a primary motivation for moving to a commercialized ANSP, virtually all of these organizational restructurings have resulted separating the regulation of air traffic control from its operation. Indeed, most commercializations have clarified the government's role as that of providing safety regulation and oversight.

A notable exception in the trend toward commercialized ANSPs has been the Federal Aviation Administration (FAA) in the United States, although recent efforts to establish a more independent Air Traffic Organization within FAA represent small steps in this direction. Air traffic control in the United States remains provided by this government agency funded by taxes rather than user fees. Indeed, the United States is the sole remaining developed country not charging users directly for air traffic control services.[6] Worldwide, only 21 out of the 180 countries providing ATC services do not charge user fees. Besides the United States, the others all tend to be small and/or poor countries with only a single airport receiving commercial air service (and that airport generally does charge landing fees). But there is no separate charge for the terminal, en route, or over-flight functions of ATC in these countries.[7] Moreover, in the United States, the FAA both regulates the air traffic control system

---

3   International Civil Aviation Organization, I*cao's Policies on Charges for Airports and Air Navigation Services*, Doc 9082/7, 2004, Appendix 3.

4   The Civil Air Navigation Services Organisation, *Corporatisation of Air Navigation Services*, August 1999.

5   MBS Ottawa, Inc., *Air Traffic Control Commercialization Policy: Has It Been Effective?*, January 2006, page 16.

6   *Resolving the Crisis in Air Traffic Control Funding* by Robert W. Poole, Jr. and Vaughn Cordle, Policy Study 332, Reason Foundation, May 2005, page 15.

7   *Tariffs for Airports and Air Navigation Services*, International Civil Aviation Organization, Doc 7100 (2002) as reported in *Resolving the Crisis in Air Traffic Control*

and also operates that same system. To be sure, there are separate branches within FAA that operate and regulate the system, but the FAA still retains and is accountable for both operation and regulatory activity.

Comparisons of ANSP Performance

The MBS Ottawa study mentioned above represents the most extensive and consistent study of comparative ANSP performance across a range of countries, operating environments, and organizational structures. The study examined commercialized ANSPs in ten countries: Australia, Canada, France, Germany, Ireland, Netherlands, New Zealand, South Africa, Switzerland, and the United Kingdom. All of these ANSPs except the UK were commercialized prior to 1997. The FAA was also examined as an example of a non-commercialized government department approach.

In addition to a compendium of legal descriptions of the ANSPs and extensive interviews with ANSP managers, employees, regulators, and customers, the study conducted a trend analysis of several performance indicators for the period 1997 through 2004. A trend analysis is limited because it only indicates the direction and rate of change for each indicator for each ANSP and doesn't account for differences in the sizes or absolute performance measures of ANSPs. Keeping these limitations in mind, the findings of the study are significant. The MBS study concluded that commercialization did not have an adverse impact on safety, while it improved customer service and modernization. The commercialized ANSPs made the transition from regarding government as their client to responding quickly to the needs of the aviation community. The study concluded that "Costs were generally reduced, significantly in some models, while financial stability was maintained, and most areas of public interest remained neutral or positive when commercialized elements were introduced."[8]

Some of the specific findings that supported these general conclusions are worth highlighting:

- With respect to safety, all nine commercialized ANSPs in the study for whom safety data were available had a downward trend in ATM-related safety incidents per IFR movement. It wasn't possible to compare that experience with FAA because FAA doesn't have reliable comparable data.[9]
- Total ANSP costs per IFR movement were down for Australia, New Zealand, the United Kingdom, and Canada while they were up 23 percent for FAA. As a result, en route unit rates had a downward trend for Australia, New Zealand, Canada, with the United Kingdom rates moving slightly higher. More generally, charges to users have been reduced whenever revenues have exceeded costs.[10]

Funding by Robert W. Poole, Jr. and Vaughn Cordle, Policy Study 332, Reason Foundation, May 2005, page 15.

8   MBS Ottawa, Inc., *Air Traffic Control Commercialization Policy: Has It Been Effective?*, January 2006, page 9.

9   Ibid, Figure 5.2, page 35.

10 Ibid, page 48.

- The cost reductions did not appear to come at the expense of air traffic controller salaries in the commercialized services. Air Traffic Control Operator pay was up about 20 percent for NAV CANADA and NATS (in the United Kingdom). Data were not available for Australia and New Zealand. While air traffic control operator pay did increase at these commercialized units, there appeared to be more emphasis on cost control. For FAA, air traffic control operator costs were up over 40 percent. Moreover, while the ratio of all staff to controllers was down 5 percent for FAA, it was down more for Australia, New Zealand, NATS, and NAV CANADA. All of the commercialized ANSPs except Airservices Australia experienced a growth in traffic over the period, as did FAA, but it's difficult to compare the change in the number of controllers because it's not clear if the staffing starting points were comparable. Nevertheless, the number of air traffic controllers was up about 2 percent for FAA, up about 10 percent for NAV CANADA, unchanged for NATS, down 5 percent for New Zealand, and down 15 percent for Australia.
- Air traffic control induced delays have been a major concern at FAA and NATS. Such delays were up 150 percent for FAA but down almost 50 percent for NATS. Delays were not an issue with the other commercialized ANSPs in the MBS Ottawa study.

The results of the MBS study are more insightful when viewed in the context of the findings of a comparison of US and European en route centers that was done by EUROCONTROL.[11] That study found that the operating costs per flight hour were about 60 percent higher in the selected European Centers than in the selected US Centers. Two main reasons for the higher European costs relative to the United States were that US controllers both work more hours than their European counterparts and also handle more aircraft per hour worked.[12] In addition, the support costs in the European centers, defined as the operating costs other than those for the air traffic control operators were substantially higher than in the United States primarily because of the greater relative number of support staff in the European centers. Interestingly, the study did not find any systemic differences in the complexity of the traffic in the US and in Europe.[13]

When these two studies are viewed together, it appears that the FAA has some productivity advantages inherent in the geographic scope and traffic density of its responsibilities, coupled with different traditions of what constitutes a normal work week. However, it also appears that recently, the commercialized ANSPs have made much more progress in reducing costs and improving productivity than has the FAA.

---

11 Performance Review Commission, *A comparison of performance in selected US and European En-route Centres*, Eurocontrol, May 2003.

12 Ibid, page 93.

13 Ibid, page 94.

Dimensions of Performance for ANSPs

Each ANSP faces a different operating environment and no two operate or are organized exactly alike. In examining and comparing the performance of ANSPs, there are ten important dimensions to consider.

1. Safety.   The most critical element of air traffic control is the ability of the system to maintain separation between aircraft both in the air and on the ground. All ANSPs maintain that safety is their highest priority and it is embedded in the culture of air traffic controllers. However, not all ANSPs are equally effective in providing safe service.

2. Separation of Operation from Regulation.   The value of arms length regulation, where the organization that regulates how a system should be operated is not the same organization that operates the system is well recognized in virtually all sectors of the economy and in most segments of the aviation industry. For many years in many countries, however, the same government agency that operated the air traffic control system also regulated it. As more and more countries have moved to a more commercial approach to providing air traffic control services, they have also moved to separate regulation from operation. Some countries have put more separation between regulation and operation than others and some have yet to separate the functions at all.

3. Matching Cost Drivers to Revenue Drivers.   A critical issue for every ANSP is how it is funded, and how this funding mechanism is linked to the costs of operating the system. If the factors that drive the costs of an air traffic control system aren't closely matched to the factors that drive the revenues, the share of the revenue contributed by each segment of the industry may not reflect the share of the costs that segment imposes on the air traffic control system. A second potential problem is that changes in how the industry operated, for example the mix of aircraft or the pattern of flights, could have much different impacts on revenue than it did on costs.

4. Effective Capital Investment.   A modern air traffic control system is a capital intensive operation. It's critical that the capital investments that are made deliver the expected performance, are completed on time, and are completed within budget.

5. Financial Structure and Capacity.   Aviation activity, both commercial and private, has historically varied with the business cycle. An important element of ANSP financial structure is the ability to weather the financial implications of variations in traffic brought about by the normal business cycle or other external events. In addition, there is a need to be able to undertake long-term financing to match long-term capital investment programs.

6. Need for Economic Regulation.   While there are many ANSPs around the world, the provision of air traffic control services in a given geographic area is not suitable for competition and is more safely provided as a monopoly. However, granting a monopoly to a service provider immediately raises the question of whether the service provider will exploit that monopoly power and charge user fees or taxes that are above that necessary to cover costs.

One way to guard against this possibility is to make sure that the incentives or the governance structure is designed to prevent monopoly abuses. Another approach is to regulate the prices charged and the services rendered.

7. Organizational Independence.   One recurrent problem that ANSPs have encountered when they were government agencies is that other parts of the government may impose decisions or actions that affect air navigation, even if the reasons are unrelated to the efficient operation of the air traffic control system. In some cases, the decisions might prevent consolidation so as to preserve jobs in a particular location; in other cases, a decision might involve budget or personnel reductions in response to overall government deficit concerns.

8. Clear Lines of Accountability.   For an organization to operate effectively, it must have a clear set of objectives and a well defined system of accountability to judge its performance in achieving those objectives.

9. Ease of Interoperability.   With the past and anticipated growth in international traffic, the ability of an air traffic control system to interact smoothly with adjacent air traffic control systems – interoperability – is increasingly important. To the extent that ANSPs are restricted in their choice of equipment suppliers, perhaps to ones from the same country, or operate with different incentives, then interoperability will be more difficult to achieve.

10. Pursuit of Social and Political Goals.   In most countries, there are aviation activities that are deemed to be valuable to society but may not be able to pay for the costs they impose on the air traffic control system without undue financial hardship. Maintaining airport services in small or remote communities or supporting small private aircraft in the air traffic control and air navigation system are two examples frequently cited as being in this category. One possibility would be to support these activities out of a country's general fund. A more common approach is to cross subsidize losses in providing these services with surpluses generated by charging more than the cost for other services. Such cross subsidies are easier to do under some organizational structures than under others.

SECTION TWO
International Experiences in Mature Aviation Markets

There are approximately 160 air navigation service providers (ANSPs) worldwide. The transformations and restructurings undertaken by some of these organizations illustrate many of the challenges and lessons in improving air navigation performance. In this section, a selected group of ANSPs in developed aviation markets are examined. Chapter 4 looks at Airservices Australia and Airways New Zealand, two of the first ANSPs to move to a more commercial structure, albeit while retaining different forms of government ownership. Chapter 5 examines the experience of NAV CANADA, a private, non-share capital corporation that provides air navigation for the second largest airspace service in the world. Chapter 6 looks at the United Kingdom's National Air Traffic Services (NATS), which is yet another different organizational form. NATS is responsible for the planning and provision of air traffic services in United Kingdom (UK) airspace and (by international agreement) over part of the north Atlantic. NATS is structured as a Public-Private Partnership (PPP) with the government owning 49 percent of the shares, a group of British airlines owing 42 percent, the employees owing 5 percent and BAA, plc, the operator of most British airports owning 4 percent. Chapter 7 examines European air navigation, which faces the particular challenge of managing congested and constrained airspace through a system of national and multinational air navigation providers.

Chapter 4

Australia and New Zealand[1]

Introduction

New Zealand and Australia undertook fundamental changes in the organization, financing, and operation of air navigation services over the past two decades. Both Airways New Zealand and Airservices Australia have become much more commercially oriented, developed sound and sustainable financial structures, and have become much more effective in their capital program design and implementation. Airservices Australia has been at the forefront on a variety of technology innovations, while Airways New Zealand has provided a model for working closely with aviation customers.

Australia

Airservices Australia is a wholly government-owned corporation providing air navigation services. The Australian Flight Information Region covers 11 percent of the earth's surface, including both Australian airspace and also international airspace over the Pacific and Indian Oceans. Airservices also manages upper-level airspace (above 30,000 ft) under contract to the neighboring Pacific Island Flight Information Regions of the Solomon Islands and Nauru and lower–level airspace in the Pacific Ocean region at five airports for the United States Federal Aviation Administration.

Airservices manages air traffic operations for more than three million domestic and international flights carrying some 47 million passengers. The corporation has a fixed asset base of about AUD $500 million, has about 3000 employees, including 1000 air traffic controllers working from two major centers in Melbourne and Brisbane, and 26 towers at international and regional airports. Airservices also provides aviation rescue and fire services at 19 smaller Australian airports. Airservices revenues were AUD 681 million in 2005–2006, with profit after tax of AUD 94 million. Capital spending has been approximately AUD 100 million annually.

Background

In 1938, the Australian Department of Civil Aviation was established, along with a comprehensive set of State Air Navigation Acts. Civil aviation grew rapidly, especially immediately after the Second World War, leading to the government's

---

1 Much of the information in this chapter is drawn from the annual reports and corporate plans of Airservices Australia, available at www.airservicesaustralia.com, and from Airways New Zealand at www.airways.co.nz.

purchase of all shares in Qantas and significant public development of airports. The continuing role of government in airlines, airports, and air navigation was reinforced by the evolution of a domestic "Two Airline Policy" into one in which Qantas provided international services and Ansett provided domestic services.

In the 1980s, the government undertook a consolidation of its transport activities, creating a new Department of Transport and Communications, followed by the establishment of the Civil Aviation Authority in 1988, with responsibility for the provision, operation, financing, and regulation of air navigation services. Also significant was the establishment of the Federal Airports Corporation in 1986, with this state enterprise assuming responsibility (initially) for seventeen major airports by 1988. The 1980s also marked a significant change in the air navigation operations; in 1985 the government contracted with the Australian national communications satellite system (AUSSAT), to become the first country in the world to use satellite technology for air navigation on a national scale. Overall, these government restructurings were intended to make the public sector transport activity more efficient with a more commercial orientation. It should be noted that even prior to these changes, financing of air navigation services had charges had been based on aircraft charges, rather than passenger taxes or general fund revenues.

A series of government commissions, studies, and academic analyses increasingly challenged the continuation of this aviation policy, leading to the end of the two airline policy and de facto deregulation in 1990. The resultant growth in new airlines, services, and passenger demand led to new demands on aviation infrastructure, spurring another restructuring of government aviation operations. Beginning in 1994, the government's airport privatization program was launched. (Twenty-two airports, including the four major airports representing three-fourths of all traffic, were privatized by 2002.)[2]

Growing concerns about the ability of the government to finance needed modernization and concerns about safety performance in a booming aviation market led to another round of organizational changes. Under the 1995 Air Services Act, the Civil Aviation Authority was split into two parts, with Airservices Australia created to provide air navigation services, while regulatory authority was transferred to the Civil Aviation Safety Authority. This structure gave Airservices greater operational, investment, and financial autonomy, while separating safety oversight and regulation responsibility.

Transition to the new organization

While Australian air navigation had been one of the first to corporatize in 1988, the 1995 reforms were extremely important in establishing that air navigation was to be operated on commercial principles. This 1995 restructuring established Airservices as a Government Business Enterprise; this organizational status was amended in 1997 to that of a Commercial Authority, owned by the Australian Government.

---

2   See "Airport Privatization in Australia," Case HKU150, Centre for Asian Business Cases, School of Business, University of Hong Kong, August 2001.

Airservices is governed by a Board appointed by the Minister of Transport, who in turn designate a chief executive.

The new Airservices corporate plan was built around six areas:

1. Safety: improve and maintain highest levels of safety performance;
2. Environment: implement practices that help reduce the impact of aviation on the environment, especially reduced fuel consumption and carbon emissions;
3. Operational performance: seek greater efficiency and innovation in technology;
4. Customers and markets: improve customer involvement and satisfaction; extend market reach to provide services to other countries;
5. Employees: to develop a more skilled and flexible workforce;
6. Owners: to meet the Government's requirements for financial returns and increasing shareholder value.

A number of issues faced Airservices at its inception. First was the need to modernize Australia's air navigation technology, moving from a system that still has many features from the 1940s to an advanced system that had been studied since 1990, and was ready for implementation. A year before the establishment of Airservices, the government had signed a major contract with Thomson-CSF to develop and implement the Australian Advanced Air Traffic System (TAAATS), which introduced greater automation including electronic flights strips rather than paper, and enabled the consolidation of flight information regions and a significant reduction in the number of air traffic control centers as well. TAAATS represented a system that would place Australia near the forefront of air traffic management. While there were a number of implementation challenges and delays, the transition to TAAATS was completed by early 2001.

A second issue was the need to review the revenue and costs structures that had been in place for some time. Improvements were made to cost accounting systems, and a major cost reduction effort was undertaken. On the revenue side, some aircraft charges were not particularly well-aligned with costs, so a three-year pricing reform program was implemented, including location-specific charges for fire, rescue, and terminal area charges. A key change was the shift in charging aircraft on the basis of the services they used, rather than on the basis of the type of fuel they consumed.

Airservices also faced requirements to plan for the increase in air traffic expected for the 2000 Olympic Games, as well as the critical need to establish a longer-term operating and development plan for Sydney airport. Sydney also was critical as it had been faced with persistent safety issues related to airport and airspace operations.

The transition to the new organizational model proved challenging. The period was marked by the 1997–98 economic downturns across Asia, with significant effects on international air traffic to and from Australia. This created additional strains on Airservices' finances, resulting in a decline in operating profits and an overall net loss (including restructuring charges of AUD 80.7 million) of AUD 33 million. Significant losses also occurred in 1998–1999 fiscal year. However, as traffic began to recover, and greater productivity was achieved, Airservices financial performance began to recover. Airservices had been able to achieve significant cost savings, with real price reductions in charges of 20 percent in the 1997–2001 period.

The challenges of 2001

The collapse of Ansett Airlines (the second largest airline, representing one-fourth of Airservices revenues) in August 2001 caused major effects on Airservices' operations, including financial aspects of being a significant creditor because of the air navigation charges due. This situation was then made even more challenging a month later with the worldwide downturn in air traffic in the wake of the September 11 terrorist aircraft attacks in New York and Washington, and by the outbreak of SARS in 2002. Overall, revenues fell from AUD 583 million to AUD 511 million, which was only partly offset by a AUD $21 million reduction in expenses. However, Airservices' cost containment programs and adjustments to capital programs to take into account the downturn in the operating environment and the financial difficulties of the airlines enabled Airservices to still post a profit for 2001–2002 and to maintain its AAA debt ratings.

Operationally, Airservices' completion of the TAAATS system enabled new ways of improving performance and efficiency and, working with airline and aviation customers, to identify new initiatives in upgrading the system. In addition, 2001–2002 saw important technological innovations in the introduction of Reduced Vertical Separation Minima (RVSM), allowing more direct and fuel-savings routings. This made Australia one of the first countries to implement RVSM over continental and oceanic airspace. In Sydney, the commissioning of the Precision Runway Monitoring radar system enabled better management of aircraft arrival on parallel runways, increasing safety and reducing delays (especially in poor weather conditions). Initial work also was undertaken on datalink technology, leading to operational trials of Automatic Dependent Surveillance-Broadcast technology in 2003. Innovation also was evident in financing, as Airservices undertook the structuring and execution of the largest cross-border lease transaction for air navigation, enabling the company to access over AUD 900 million for capital funding on very attractive terms.

Airservices outlook

By 2006, Airservices had continued its strong track record of technological innovation. The company also was embarking on major changes with respect to air navigation operations, to safety concerns, and to organizational restructuring.[3]

Air navigation operations

Airservices Australia has been a leader in adapting technology to its service environment, with particular advances in using communications technologies to improve flight efficiencies and capacity.

---

3   See Airservices Australia, *Annual Report 2005–2006*, and Airservices Australia, *Corporate Plan July 2005–June 2010*.

Following the major technology upgrade of TAAATS and a new National Airspace redesign in 2003, Airservices launched its "tailored arrivals" program at Sydney and Melbourne, in conjunction with Boeing and European air navigation and aeronautics supplies. The tailored arrivals system transmits approach and landing clearance instructions electronically to aircraft, so that pilots and controllers don't have to engage in multiple voice communications. The system is linked directly to an aircraft's Flight Management System, so that the electronic data guide the aircraft on a steady descent profile along the most efficient path to the runway. The program has demonstrated substantial reductions in delays, noise, fuel burn, and emissions.

In 2005, Airservices endorsed its Service Delivery Environment (SDE) program, a major initiative in airspace management to be phased in over three years. Under SDE, air traffic control would be organized along three functional streams of service – upper airspace, the high density East Coast operations, and Regional operations. This structure should facilitate the more rapid implementation of ADS-B datalink technology in upper airspace, and more specific attention to solving congestion and capacity issues in the East Coast region.

In 2006, Airservices began working closely with the Australian Defense Force with a goal of more integrated air traffic management across the country's airspace, through joint use facilities and terminal control operations in the Perth region.

Overall, Airservices Australia has delivered significant technology benefits to airlines. The adoption of flex-tracks has enabled airlines to work with Airservices to develop routes on a daily basis that take into account winds and weather patterns, saving significant flight times on transpacific routes. A second innovation has been in the area of dynamic re-route planning, in which real-time meteorological and aeronautical information is used to recalculate optimal routes even after an aircraft is in flight. This has helped reduce delays and provide more efficient routings. A third innovation is in "user preferred routes" in which airlines and Airservices cooperate to plan a unique three dimensional flight path for an aircraft on a particular flight. This ability to plan has helped airlines manage operations much more efficiently.

Airservices is trialing the use of flex-tracks in the other Flight Information Regions it covers, in addition to the transpacific routes. Of particular interest is the application to flights from the east coast of Australia through the Indonesian Flight Information Regions, where weather conditions can change rapidly. In the longer term, this approach to air navigation could be extended to the Indian Ocean and the Arabian Sea, both which are busy airspaces where flex-tracks hold promise for improved efficiency in operations.

Airservices also has begun to spread its wings beyond Australia. In 2004, the company signed an agreement to license its aeronautical information products worldwide. The most significant of these activities was launched in 2005, when Airservices began a contract to provide air navigation services at six US Federal Aviation Administration towers in the Pacific Region.

Safety

The second stage of National Airspace Plan rollout that was begun in 2003 came under sharp criticism for reducing the degree of air traffic control supervision in some sectors.[4] In the wake of these criticisms, Airservices began to develop and implement safety enhancements by expanding ATC activity in specific airspace regions. In other areas, the failure to achieve targeted reductions in air navigation incidents led to a review of key indicators and targets, with emphasis on improving the ability of Airservices to identify and recover from operational errors. Lastly, the separation of air navigation regulatory functions (undertaken by the Civil Aviation Safety Authority) from air navigation operations has provided better oversight of safety matters.

Organizational reform

Airservices and the Australian government have a shared objective to maintain a leadership role in international air navigation services. By 2005, there was growing concern that Airservices' organizational structure might not be efficient or flexible enough to manage expected growth, introduce new technology, or to take advantage of growing opportunities in the global air navigation market.

In 2005, Airservices launched a comprehensive restructuring, centralizing many support functions. The changes in organizational structure complemented changes to Airservices' status as a Government Business Enterprise, resulting in greater capacity to operate on a commercial basis and to seek more international opportunities to provide air navigation services.

New Zealand

Airways New Zealand has played a major global role in air navigation, in large part because it was the first government air traffic control organization to be transformed in to a commercial government corporation in 1987. This unprecedented step spurred many other countries (who also were struggling to deal with growing aviation requirements and difficult fiscal environments) to re-think long-held ideas about the best ways to organize and manage air navigation services.

Airways manages a sizeable portion of airspace (37 million square kilometers) in the Southern hemisphere, and handles about 1 million aircraft movements annually. The company has two flight information regions, two area control centers, sixteen control towers, and six international airports. Airways has just under 700 employees. Chartered to operate on a commercial basis, Airways received no government funding and pays dividends to the government as its shareholder. Revenues were approximately NZD 131 million in fiscal 2006, with profit after tax of NZD 13 million. Airways paid a dividend of NZD 8 million in fiscal 2006, in addition to providing a return on equity capital for the government. Airways has about NZD 111 million in assets, with very low leverage compared to other commercialized air navigation providers (debt was 24 percent of total capital in 2006).

---

4   See Australian Civil Aviation Safety Authority, "Airspace Management Reform in Australia," September 2006, available at www.casa.gov.au/media/2006/DOTARS06_155WT.htm.

Background

The Airways Corporation of New Zealand (Airways) was established in April 1987 as a State-Owned Enterprise, as part of a major set of economic reforms implemented by the government in 1985. Previously, air traffic control operations had been under the direction of the Ministry of Transport, which had responsibility for both the service delivery and regulatory functions of air navigation and airports. The costs of providing these services were paid for from the Government Treasury, as part of general fiscal policy. While there was a tax on aviation fuel, this revenue was not specifically allocated to civil aviation infrastructure.

In the mid-1980s, the New Zealand Government was facing ongoing macroeconomic and fiscal difficulties. After decades of extensive public intervention in the economy, a new government launched a series of radical economic reforms aimed at reducing the role of the public sector in the economy. In order to reduce the burden on the government budget, Airways was established as one of nine State Enterprises, to be run on commercial principles. Policy and regulatory functions and oversight were expressly reserved to respective government ministries or specifically designated agencies.

Beyond a commercial objective and company governance structure, the transformation contained two additional dimensions that proved critical to Airways' sustainability. The first was the shift to user charges directly applied to aircraft activity. This created a well-defined revenue source that could be used to address both operating and capital needs. A second factor was Airways' new ability to raise capital on its own account in private financial markets. Given the legacy of limited government funds, Airways faced substantial recapitalization requirements, that could now be addressed by required sizeable capital investments that being able to tap capital markets.

Within its first seven years, Airways was able to achieve improved efficiency and reduced costs through consolidation of facilities and adoption of commercial practices. Also, the switch to user fees gave a greater voice to commercial and private aviation in setting objectives for performance and for costs. In its initial decade, Airways was able to achieve real (inflation-adjusted) reductions in air navigation revenues of thirty percent, while managing improved operating performance and while launching a major capital modernization program.

Outlook

By 2006, Airways' strategy continued to be centered on three main planks – more efficient air navigation operations, improving safety performance, and sustaining its financial performance.

Air navigation operations and safety

The financial pressures faced by the airline industry have had multiple sources, from major event-driven crises (September 11 air terrorism, SARS) to challenges from industry drivers such as lower yields and high and volatile fuel costs. In recent years, Airways has renewed its efforts to ensure that its air navigation operations and programs are in line with the challenging context of civil aviation. Strategically, Airways states its goal as "to provide the air navigation service that our customers want and can afford."[5]

Through 2006, Airways had not increased its air navigation service charges for eleven years, and committed to maintaining them for an additional three years. Capital projects have been oriented to modernizing its radar network, enabling more efficient flow management and thus reducing the fuel burn of airlines. Another major effort was the rehabilitation of the main runway at Auckland, which necessitated major modifications to the operating practices of Airways' busiest facility. A third major capital project involved fundamental changes to controller training, developing innovative air navigation simulation technologies in partnership with leading animation and IT companies. The "Total Control" software project has enabled Airways to train controllers in a much more realistic simulation environment than previously had been possible.

Looking further ahead, Airways has adopted a long-term strategy for air navigation known as "Required Navigation Performance" (RNP). RNP recognizes that flight management systems no longer restrict aircraft to "highways" controlled by ground-based navigational aids. In response, Airways has developed a concept of "pipelines" in which aircraft flight profiles will be monitored and managed from departure to arrival, with explicit goals of safety performance and accuracy in location and time profiles. The emphasis is on making sure that transitions to satellite-based technology meet performance targets as they are implemented. This technological approach would provide the aircraft operator greater flexibility to reduce route mileage and to optimize climb and descent profiles. In terminal airspace, Airways has increased its efforts at collaborative decision-making which enables airlines to jointly work with Airways to manage priority flights and services in the event of disruptions or delays.

Safety

Traditional safety benchmarks of airspace incidents involving loss of separation indicate that Airways continued to improve and remained one of the world's leading air navigation organizations in terms of incident rates. One aspect of Airways Safety Management System has been its "Just Culture" philosophy, in which a goal is open reporting, analysis, and lessons to be learned from incidents. Airways' management believes that this philosophy has raised incident reporting levels and has enhanced safety as a result. However, incident reporting policies and practices were sharply criticized in the wake of issuance of the official Coroner's report on the 2003 fatal crash of an Air Adventures private aviation aircraft. The Air Adventures accident has challenged the underlying philosophy of voluntary reporting and has prompted the Government and Airways to re-think approaches to safety oversight and regulation, which were ongoing in early 2007.

---

5   Airways New Zealand Annual Report 2006, p. 6.

Financial and organizational performance

Twenty years after its commercialization, Airways remains one of the world's most respected air navigation organizations. Airways has retained its full financial self-sufficiency, largely independent from government control. In the five years prior to 1987, air navigation activities ran a deficit of NZD 120 million, while in the twenty year period since commercialization, Airways has provided the New Zealand government with over NZD 180 in dividends and taxes paid. Airways' record of operational and commercial performance began a trend that has culminated in widespread adoption of similar organizational structures for air navigation around the globe.

Chapter 5

Canada

NAV CANADA is a private, non-share capital corporation that owns and operates Canada's civil air navigation system (ANS), which is the second largest ANS operation in the world. NAV CANADA provides air traffic control, flight information, weather briefings, aeronautical information services, airport advisory services and electronic aids to navigation. NAV CANADA operates seven area control centers, over 100 airport control towers and flight service stations, and seven flight information centres. These facilities manage over 12 million aircraft movements annually, including takeoffs, landing, and overflights. The corporation has 5,300 employees and annual revenues of over C\$1.1 billion.

History and Background[1]

Canada's air traffic services had historically been provided by Transport Canada as a governmental function. Canada's airline deregulation in the mid-1980s spurred rapid growth in air traffic, especially in major cities such as Toronto. At the same time, federal government fiscal constraints led to major budget cuts, including the air navigation system. Of particular concern was a growing shortage of air traffic controllers at key locations. This resulted in major delays to airlines and to business aviation. The air traffic controllers' union began to raise concerns that the rising workload, required overtime, and reduced budgets were affecting safety.

Concerns about the performance of the air traffic system began to be shared by all stakeholders. Together, the airlines, unions, and business aviation recommended that the government explore commercialization options to improve the performance of air traffic services. Following a series of studies, the Transport minister, Doug Young, made such a recommendation. A team was established within Transport Canada to analyze the potential benefits and costs of commercialization. This small team undertook a comprehensive review of organizational alternatives, international experiences, revenue and user fees, capital investment, financing, and regulatory issues. The team recommended further public consultations, which were launched in early 1994.

The consultation process was extraordinarily thorough, built around an advisory committee that included virtually all stakeholders in the air traffic system: airlines, airports, unions, pilots, general and business aviation, safety organizations,

---

1 For a comprehensive review of Canadian air traffic management and the establishment of NAV Canada, see G. McDougall, "The Privatisation of the Canadian Air Navigation System," in *Defining Aerospace Policy*, edited by K. Button, J. Lammersen-Baum, and R. Stough, (Aldershot, England: Ashgate, 2004), pp. 13–50.

and equipment suppliers. The resulting consultation reports concluded that a commercialized ANS structure would be better able to provide improvements to services, while maintaining system safety.

The consultation process also concluded that a variety of organizational options could be effectively undertaken, and that these options were likely to provide many benefits compared to continued government provision:

- better procurement decisions and management,
- access to capital markets for funding,
- a more stable user-funded system more responsive to customers.

The study team evaluated five key areas covering:

1. Organizational options for commercialization.
2. Safety regulation.
3. Economic regulation.
4. International experience and lessons.
5. User charging systems and fees.

As the review process unfolded, it became clear there was strong support for shifting the underlying funding structure from the Air Transportation Tax (based on a percentage of ticket prices paid by travelers) to a user fee structure. Studies indicated that user fees based on internationally-agreed guidelines and practices would produce revenues that would not only enable full cost recovery, but also provide enough money to fund debt service for capital market finance.

Another result of the study was recognition that Canada was missing a significant source of revenue in the form of overflight charges, especially for flights between Europe, Asia and the United States that transited Canadian airspace. Previously, these services had been provided at no charge to commercial airlines and other aircraft operators. Recognizing this opportunity, the government instituted a fee system that generates about C$ 200 million annually. These incremental charges enabled revenues for the Canadian ATS to about equal costs for the first time. This changed the perception of the financial viability and attractiveness of the Canadian ANS, and gave increased importance to the value of the assets and activities being considered – especially if they were to be transferred from governmental to private control.

The adoption of overflight fees and the general commitment to shift from a ticket tax to user fees also shifted the nature of discussion about organizational alternatives. While the air carriers were supportive of a shift to user charges, they also felt strongly that they should play a significant role in ANS governance (this became known as "user pay, user say"). This spurred additional interest by other stakeholders in governance.

In this context, the government chose to establish a special-purpose, private, non-share capital corporation that would purchase and operate the ANS. Because of the corporation's non-share capital status, there were no shareholders to receive profits. This structure meant that any surpluses of revenue over costs could be used for capital investment, to pay down debt, or to go towards reducing future air navigation charges. The associated financial reporting structure required that any surpluses in a given period would be directed into a reserve fund account.

Since there would be no shareholders, the Canadian Corporations Act provided for member organizations that could nominate Board directors. The agreed Board structure has fifteen members:

- 4 directors nominated by air carriers,
- 1 directors nominated by business aviation,
- 2 directors nominated by unions,
- 3 directors nominated by government,
- 4 directors appointed by the above 10 members,[2]
- the CEO of NAV CANADA.

This board structure is designed to provide major stakeholders a significant role in governance. The Board is supported in these efforts by an Advisory Committee comprised of representatives from various aviation groups across Canada.

Once the board structure was in place, the new corporation was empowered to negotiate the purchase of the ANS from the government. The detailed negotiations were complex, but led to an Agreement in Principle in December 1995 establishing sale price and terms and conditions to be resolved before transfer. The process was shaped by the commitment to a new user fee structure, so that value was determined on a net present value basis rather than on asset values (which presented significant valuation problems in themselves). Negotiations over valuation focused on growth and risk scenarios, as well as forecast of expected capital investments required (and the associated debt service costs).

Another issue involved the regulatory environment under a new structure. It was widely accepted that safety regulation would be retained by Transport Canada. With regard to economic regulation, concern that NAV CANADA would be a monopoly provider was tempered by three factors: the non-share capital status, legal requirements that limited charges to full cost recovery, and recognition that the presence of user groups on the Board would create incentives for efficiency and avoidance of "gold-plating" the system. As a result, economic regulation was minimal, based on legal requirement to adhere to certain principles, along with an appeal process to a government tribunal.[3]

The negotiation resulted in an agreed valuation of C$1.5 billion, to take the form of a cash payment to the government. Because there was no shareholder equity in the structure, the sale price and the initial working capital would have to be raised in debt markets, with future revenues pledged as collateral (a revenue bond structure). A high credit rating was received, based on the designated monopoly status, a stable and growing demand, a flexible user charge system with fees comparable to other

---

2   Once the initial board was established, the appointment of the four designated additional directors has now become the responsibility of the full board, rather than only the ten stakeholder directors.

3   To date, only two appeals have been filed, and were resolved in favor of NAV CANADA. One was denied by the tribunal in 2003, and the other in 2006.

countries, guaranteed government revenue support for the first two years, and the broad stakeholder support for the process and the organizational structure.

NAV CANADA was able to secure a C$3 billion credit facility. The company drew C$2 billion in actual borrowing, three-fourths of which was used to purchase the system from the government, and the remainder to provide working capital and to establish reserves. Legislation was enacted in June 1996, and NAV CANADA purchased the ANS from the government on November 1, 1996. Following the transfer, a bond offering was arranged to replace the majority of the bank loan with long term, lower cost permanent finance.

Labor provisions in the transition

Unions had supported a transfer of ANS from government to a new entity, in part because of growing workload and safety concerns, but also because under governmental operation they had been subject to a six year long wage freeze and because the right to strike was prohibited. The new organization extended existing job security provisions, as well as the provisions in existing collective agreements. Nevertheless, there was a dramatic reduction in staff. Of the 6,300 employees transferred from Transport Canada, over 1,000 staff were reduced in the first three years after 1996.

NAV CANADA Performance 1996–2001

The first five years of operation saw significant improvement in operational and financial performance, with improvement in a number of safety indicators. The implementation of the user fee system resulted in 11 percent lower charges to air carriers than would have resulted from prior tax-based system. Robust traffic growth of 20 percent led to building up a balance of C$ 75 million in NAV CANADA's rate stabilization reserve fund. NAV CANADA undertook an extensive capital investment program totaling about C$600 million over the 1996–2001 period.

NAV CANADA Performance After September 11

Other than the United States Federal Aviation Administration, no ANS provider was more dramatically affected by the events of September 11 than NAV CANADA. Immediately following the attacks and the closure of both US and Canadian airspace to civil aviation, the employees of NAV CANADA were able to guide 1500 aircraft to safe landing, including 239 US-bound international flights diverted from the North Atlantic to Canada. By the end of the day, all flights had been handled safely, without one single incident or loss of separation.

Once the operational situation had settled, NAV CANADA was faced with an immediate traffic and revenue decline of more than 10 percent, which would result in a C$100 million shortfall versus budget for fiscal 2002. Longer term, NAV CANADA anticipated a cumulative 2002–2005 revenue shortfall of more than C$ 360 million. If this shortfall came to pass, it would likely have made debt service more difficult, while making it much harder to sustain even a modest capital program. In this context, NAV CANADA adopted what it termed a "Balanced Approach" in which all stakeholders were asked to work together and each make a contribution to sustain the financial stability of the system.

Revenues

The rate stabilization reserve fund was depleted, running its positive C$75 million balance to a negative position of C$116 million. In effect, NAV CANADA was able to run an operating deficit, albeit with the intention of recouping these cumulative losses over the next five years. Rates, which were reduced 15 percent in 1999 and were to have been frozen until 2002, were raised 6 percent in 2002, an additional 3 percent in January 2003, and an additional 7 percent in August 2003. While these increases may seem significant at first, NAV CANADA's rate increases since 1999 have remained slightly below the overall inflation rates, and remain approximately 20 percent below the Air Transportation Tax it replaced. Air carriers were offered a temporary deferral of fee payments and an extension of payment terms to help manage their cash flow.

Cost savings and financial restructuring

Cost reductions were implemented in the form of cuts to management and board salaries and other compensation. A wage freeze was proposed, but not implemented, for unions. Suppliers were also required to provide concessions. Capital spending was reduced or deferred. Overall, annual cost savings of C$ 100 million were achieved. In addition, a review of capital assets led to two sale and leaseback transactions, which helped generate cash flow of C$ 56 million to support operations.

Overall, the successful initial period of operations from 1996–2001, along with its unique governance structure, strongly influenced NAV CANADA's capability to respond to this dramatic change in its operating and financial setting and outlook.

NAV CANADA's Current Performance and Outlook

The effects of the downturn continued to be felt by NAV CANADA through 2004. The severity and duration were worsened by the advent of the Iraq war, traffic declines in Asian markets resulting from SARS, and by the bankruptcy filing of Air Canada in October 2003. (Air Canada was NAV CANADA's largest single customer, and at the time of bankruptcy owed NAV CANADA C$45 million. NAV CANADA recognized this full amount as bed debt expense in its 2003 accounts.)

Through this time, the company sought to maintain operational and safety performance while managing its financial situation as best as possible. The rate stabilization fund (which had a positive C$75 million reserve as of September 11, 2001) was drawn down into deficit, reaching negative C$116 million by 2003. By the end of 2004, traffic volumes were close to 2001 levels, and NAV CANADA had made significant progress in paying down the deficit in its rate stabilization account.

By August 2005, the company had further recovered, with revenue increasing 13 percent over 2004. This increase was in part due to traffic growth, but more so from a further increase in charges of 7 percent, effective September 2004. The increased revenue enabled NAV CANADA to reduce the deficit in the rate stabilization account, ending with a surplus of C$63 million by August 2006.

Safety

While air navigation safety regulation remains a government ministerial responsibility under Transport Canada, NAV CANADA is responsible for operational safety and efficiency. Safety indicators have been maintained or improved since transition to private status. For example, one key metric, the rate of losses of separation between controlled aircraft has steadily declined from 1.36 per 100,000 movements in the last year of government operation, to 1.0 per 100,000 aircraft movements by 1999, to 0.77 per 100,000 movements in 2006. The company has met and sustained its goals of being in the top decile of ANS providers in terms of safety performance. Organizationally, NAV CANADA has moved toward implementation of an integrated Safety Management System and has adopted reporting and investigation procedures to identify and study incidents and problems.

Labor and operational initiatives

Of NAV CANADA's approximately 5,300 employees, there were just under 2,000 operational controllers by September 2005, representing a 14 percent increase from 1999. The company has achieved staffing level targets, although there is some discussion with unions about whether these targets reflect underlying needs in an environment of rapid traffic growth. There also have been staffing shortages at the Winnipeg and Edmonton Control Centres.

In 2005, the company concluded new collective bargaining agreements with most of their associated unions, including the Canadian Air Traffic Controllers Association (CATCA). These new contracts run for four years and were achieved with less rancor than had occurred in many prior negotiations. Improving labor relations remains a major issue, especially in the areas of staffing levels, training and employee involvement in project planning and implementation. This will become more important in the medium term, as NAV CANADA faces a large cohort of controllers eligible for retirement.

Given that labor represents more than 70 percent of total costs, continued productivity gains are required to keep cost growth below the level of traffic growth. NAV CANADA has sought to introduce operational initiatives to support productivity through technological improvements. These projects include national rollout of the Canadian Automated Air Traffic System (CAATS), one of the world's most advanced flight data processing systems. Other projects include enhanced computer displays, upgraded radars, and Instrument Landing System (ILS) replacements.

Rates and charges

In January 2005, NAV CANADA initiated a review of its customer charges, including the charging and cost allocation methodologies, the rate stabilization account, and the provision of aeronautical publications. The major proposed change was to reduce the aircraft weight factor in the formula for the Terminal Charge in two phases. The international convention of "charging units" defined by weight and distance has been an attempt to include cost drivers and some measure of ability to pay or value of service. Inclusion of a weight factor also recognizes that the majority of the infrastructure and operating costs of the Canadian ANS system is driven by commercial airlines operating large aircraft.

Studies undertaken for NAV CANADA indicate that a weight factor of 0.60 is consistent with costs, while the current 0.90 factor is a proxy for ability to pay by air carriers operating larger planes. However, given the recent performance of the industry, the type of aircraft flown by an airline is not a clear indicator of the carrier's financial health. Recognizing the need for transition, NAV CANADA proposed a change from the previous 0.90 to 0.85 for two years, and a further reduction to 0.80 beginning in September 2008.

The proposed NAV CANADA change represented a limited move away from this historical "ability to pay" system. In effect, the proposed charging system is moving to align charges closer to cost drivers. It also is consistent with proposals in Europe to apply a weight factor of 0.7 across its charging systems. In practice, the change would decrease charges for widebody aircraft, be roughly neutral for most jets, and raise charges for smaller regional jets and for propeller and turboprop aircraft. On a per passenger basis, NAV CANADA estimated that the new structure represented an increase of about C$0.54 for small aircraft and a reduction of about C$1.00 per passenger flying in larger aircraft.

Another aspect of the proposed changes is differential (lower) pricing for International Communication Services using data link technology rather than sole reliance on voice communication. This reflects the more extensive interaction and costs incurred by voice-only communication.

Overall, the changes in the system of charges were revenue-neutral in the aggregate, albeit with some higher (lower) changes for some users. Overall, the changes in the rates and charges system were designed to better align costs and charges; to better balance charges and costs for large and small aircraft; and to reflect the impact of lower cost ANS technologies.

The revised system of charges was implemented in September 2006. The additional surcharges that previously had been in place were removed, while base charges remained at prior levels. Taken together, this represented an average decrease in charges of 1.8 percent.

Among the other changes, the company has also announced an increase in the target balance of its Rate Stabilization Account (RSA) from $50 million to $75 million. Once the target balance has been reached, it will then be set at 7.5 percent of total annual expenses, excluding one-time non-recurring items, on an ongoing basis. While this is not of the magnitude of the shortfalls following September 11 and subsequent events, it represents a slightly higher reserve target than the actual reserve fund at that time. NAV CANADA intends to achieve the increase of $25 million through positive variances in operating results rather than through any increase in charges. This policy sets in place a mechanism where surpluses above a minimum reserve can be used to reduce (or lower an increase) in future charges.

Investment program

NAV CANADA's capital program follows an incremental approach with an emphasis on investing and upgrading with existing, proven technology. The company believes this approach minimizes technical, cost, and delay risks while maintaining connectivity to a currently functioning system. NAV CANADA has adopted a 3–5 year horizon as best matching ANS technology and system developments.

Since 1996, NAV CANADA has invested over C$600 million, with another C$400 million in commitments. Initially, investments were aimed at making the Canadian ANS infrastructure "catch up" with years of deferred investments. As this goal was achieved, there has been more attention on modernizing and enhancing the system.

For example, NAV CANADA's 2005–2008 Business Plan focuses on implementation of the CAATS system for automated exchange of operational data, more controller and ATC decision support tools, and enhancing area and satellite navigation coverage. There is an emphasis on making sure that investments match customer equipage, and that planning is focused on the issues that create the most value for system users, such as improving air traffic flow management and increasing airspace capacity and flexibility. NAV CANADA estimates that these technology and service initiatives will save users more than C$100 million annually in more efficient flight operations.

NAV CANADA capital planning has made a concerted effort to use "off the shelf technology" but adapt it in-house (if required) to meet needs. Alternatively, NAV CANADA develops ATM software itself in situations where it believes that suppliers are non-responsive or too costly. This approach has enabled NAV CANADA to develop commercial opportunities for systems and products that it has developed in-house. The best example of this is the sale to National Air Traffic Services (NATS) in the United Kingdom of touch screen based flight display systems for London airports and NAV CANADA's oceanic software for NATS' Shanwick Automated ATS.

Financial restructuring

As the economic and operational environment stabilized by 2005, NAV CANADA began looking ahead to future financing needs. The company considered proposing changes to its Master Trust Indenture (MTI) which governed one component of its debt financing. However, after discussions with bondholders, NAV CANADA has decided to leave the terms of the existing bonds unchanged and proceed with a new financing platform that will enable the issuance of additional debt as unsecured general obligations, subordinate to the MTI bonds. This should provide additional financial flexibility and capacity for the new capital program. By fiscal 2006, NAV CANADA had reaffirmed its AA rating and had refinanced C$700 million of debt, keeping its balance at C$2.175 billion. The company also had arranged an undrawn credit facility of C$683 million, providing additional financial flexibility.

At the end of fiscal year 2006, NAV CANADA had achieved total revenues of almost $1.2 billion, reflecting continued traffic growth. Operating expenses increased as well, in large part due to higher pension expense. Overall, there was a small surplus, allowing the rate stabilization account to grow to C$63 million. The rate stabilization account (RSA) has been reaffirmed as a valuable tool to manage industry downturns and to stabilize rates over longer periods, and the 7.5 percent of revenues target for the RSA establishes a benchmark for risk management.

Looking ahead

The stabilization of the company's financial position has enabled NAV CANADA to look further ahead. The company is entering a new stage, which is characterized by an ongoing review of operations, proposed revisions to the system of rates and charges, further modernization of the ANS system, an enhanced investment program, and restructuring the balance sheet to provide additional flexibility and lower cost financing.

Lessons from NAV CANADA

NAV CANADA has been successful in transitioning from government to a special non-share capital private corporation. Compared to the prior government operation, NAV CANADA has improved safety, reduced charges, and increased efficiency and productivity.

The extensive review and consultation process with system stakeholders made the transition from government to private provision more transparent acceptable to all parties. The process was focused on how to improve performance by examining options, rather than attempting to prescribe a particular model at the outset.

The replacement of the passenger ticket tax and general revenue funding by a system of user charges was facilitated by careful studies which identified new sources of revenue (overflight fees) and which indicated that charges would be in line with international levels and less than the tax being replaced. The adoption of a user charge system increased the desire for users to play a role in governance. The non-share capital organizational structure with board representation by stakeholders creates good incentives for cost control, improves capital program management, and reduces the need for economic regulation. There has been significant reductions in operating costs relative to past trends, and most of these savings have been passed on to users in the form of lower charges.

The non-share capital structure caused NAV CANADA to be heavily leveraged in its purchase of the air navigation system from the Canadian government in 1996. However, the company was able to retain some degree of financial flexibility with its credit facilities and has sustained a AA investment grade rating throughout the downturn. NAV CANADA's organizational structure turned out to be an asset in the wake of the severe downturn since 2001. The stakeholder model in effect required all parties to make contributions and sacrifices. The mandated requirement to cover the cost of service established a clear financial objective during the period, while the rate stabilization fund allowed the company to manage the consequences of the downturn over a longer period. In effect, the NAV CANADA stakeholder model served an equity-like risk bearing role during the period. Experience mattered in managing financial distress. The operating and performance record of NAV CANADA from 1996–2001 provided the company with credibility and support for its efforts to cope with the industry's crisis.

The customer orientation appears to extend to a capital program and planning approach that has been much better at both modernization and the development of new technology with respect to cost, delay, and performance. Much of Canada's ANS infrastructure is now among the best in the world.

Chapter 6

United Kingdom

National Air Traffic Services (NATS) is responsible for the planning and provision of air traffic services in United Kingdom (UK) airspace and (by international agreement) over part of the north Atlantic. NATS manages the UK's two flight information regions (FIRs), operates five air traffic control centers, and provides air traffic services at fifteen major UK airports. The Scottish FIR is the largest in Europe, and the London center is one of the busiest in the world. NATS handles 2.3 million flights annually; this traffic carries more than 220 million passengers.

History of Reform Efforts

At the end of World War II, air traffic services were placed in the Ministry of Civil Aviation, and subsequently were reorganized to achieve greater segregation of civil and military air traffic. Following a major study in 1961, National Air Traffic Control Services was established in 1962 as a unified civil/military organization to operate Britain's air traffic control. The shorter title and acronym NATS was adopted in the early 1970s. In 1972, NATS was absorbed into the newly-established Civil Aviation Authority (CAA). Service and regulatory aspects were linked as an act of policy. The Controller of NATS rotated between military and civilian staff on a three-year cycle.

The growth of aviation in the 1970s and 1980s put significant pressure on NATS to cope with more flights. Since inception, NATS had used a charges-based system, linked to internationally agreed formulas based on weight and distance flown.[1] However, the revenue produced by these charges did not always cover the full cost of providing NATS services, nor was it required to do so. In the 1970s, NATS lost money many years, and ran a deficit of £100 million in one year alone. Beginning in the early 1980s, the Thatcher Government imposed a requirement for charges that provided for full cost recovery.

Even with this operational change, NATS continued to struggle on the capital investment and planning. NATS' normal operating surpluses of about £50 million could only cover about half of investment needs. However, as part of the government, NATS was subject to an external financing limit known as the Public Sector Borrowing Requirement. As such, NATS became highly dependent on government grants for investment funds. These grants peaked at £130 million in 1993, but it was widely recognized that NATS was unable to fund the investment required to

---

1 While the precise weightings of the model varied across countries, the basic structure of a weight and distance component was generally accepted.

replace outdated equipment in the London center, let alone finance capital needed to keep pace with growth and changes in technology. Attempts to utilize private finance were also unsuccessful. In the early 1990s, projects for a new Scottish centre and for a new Flight Data Processing System failed almost completely, yet NATS paid contractors £95 million for these two projects.

NATS' operational and safety performance was widely respected. However, there was growing criticism of NATS' level of charges to airlines and its recurring difficulties in managing its investment program. Of particular visibility was NATS' largest project, the en route center at Swanwick, which opened more than five years late and £150 million over the £475 million budget. In addition, delays had begun to plague the system; in the late 1980s, the average flight was delayed 22 minutes, an extremely high figure. While efforts were made to increase capacity and efficiency, average flight delays were a still high 11 minutes in 1993.

Moreover, by the late 1980s there was growing concern about safety and the dual function of NATS as regulator and provider of air traffic services. By 1989, following a House of Commons Transport Select Committee inquiry, responsibility for ATS safety regulation was transferred to the CAA's Safety Regulation Group. A 1990 review of NATS by the Monopolies and Mergers Commission recommended the separation of regulation and safety activities, with a management structure led by a civilian chief executive appointed from the outside. The MMC report also added that the logical conclusion of these initial steps would be creation of a NATS organization independent of the CAA.

In 1993, the Conservative government announced that it was reviewing options for the privatization of NATS. Another Transport Committee review in 1994–1995 recommended that NATS be converted into a for-profit public sector company that would be able to borrow in capital markets. While this proposal was deferred, the Conservative government did act on a CAA proposal that NATS be restructured to achieve maximum possible separation within the existing legislative framework. In 1996, NATS was established as a separate company structure, wholly-owned by the CAA. This was generally viewed as a step in preparation for privatization.

The mixed experiences with privatization in the UK led to a re-thinking about how to restructure activities that had a substantial public interest component. Labour, who had previously declared "our air is not for sale," had come to recognize the need for a change in NATS. at In 1998, the incoming Labour government announced plans for NATS to be restructured as a Public-Private Partnership (PPP), to help NATS have more control over its operating budget and to be able to access additional capital for its deferred investment program. The restructuring also was intended to separate regulation of air traffic services from their provision, and to be more responsive to users.

The change to a Labour government in 1998 led to a review of organizational options, including:

- privatization as a regulated utility (similar to electricity and water companies),
- a non-profit trust (similar to NAV CANADA),

- a chartered independent publicly-owned company (similar to the BBC),
- a public corporation (similar to Airways New Zealand),
- a modified version of the Private Finance Initiative (similar to schools and hospitals). This model was rejected because it was limited only to individual projects or new investments. This would make systems modernization programs much more difficult.

The NAV CANADA model was rejected by the Labor government, ostensibly because it was believed that the structure might still be subject to the Public Sector Borrowing Constraint. While this may have been true if the exact NAV CANADA model had been adopted, Britain had a history of non-profit public trusts – particularly in the ports sector. It also was believed that NAV CANADA's structure gave fewer incentives for efficiency and might not be able to handle major capital programs.[2]

Following a consultation period, a regulated PPP structure was chosen. The Labor government concluded that this structure would provide a solution to the financial and operational problems of NATS, by untying NATS from the government budgetary constraints and capital restraints due to NATS falling under the Public Sector Borrowing Requirement. It was also believed that the PPP provided greater incentives for efficiency than either a public corporation or a non-profit structure. While NATS was not required to make a profit, it was expected to generate a return on capital employed of between 6 percent and 8 percent on average.

Perhaps most importantly, the government fiscal situation put increasing emphasis on the budgetary impact of the NATS PPP. There was much discussion about the need for other government transport programs to benefit from the proceeds of NATS' share sale.

The necessary legislation was introduced to Parliament in December 1999, and the Transport Act was approved in late 2000. The legislation provided for:

- a system of safety and economic regulation by the now-separate CAA,
- operating license conditions concerning public service obligations,
- government to retain a 49 percent shareholding and a "golden share," intended to preclude takeovers, and also to retain control over major corporate actions,
- government nomination of two directors with veto power on key,
- strategic issues.

Moving toward corporatization

The designation of NATS as a regulated PPP required a new structure focused on civil air navigation services. Military air traffic services were transferred to the Ministry of Defence. Given the pending regulatory structure, it was necessary to

---

2   NAV Canada had emphasized that its user-nominated governance structure provided strong efficiency incentives and a more applied focus to capital investment. They also noted that the non-profit structure was not subject to economic regulation, thereby reducing regulatory risk and allowing them to borrow at lower cost than regulated utilities.

transfer NATS from the CAA to direct government control, pending the sale of to private sector participants.

Following the sale, NATS was to be structured as a holding company with several subsidiaries. NATS En Route Ltd (NERL) is responsible for en route and oceanic air traffic services (ATS), while NATS Services Ltd would be responsible for airport ATS and business development. NERL is a regulated business which holds the monopoly of civilian en route air traffic control over the UK, while NSL competes for contracts to provide air traffic control at airports in the UK and overseas, as well as providing other services.

Financial structure and regulation

NATS' main source of income is regulated charges to airlines and airports. En route charges, which comprise about 75 percent of revenues, are based on an internationally-agreed, cost-based formula taking into account aircraft weight and distance flown.[3] NATS is particularly dependent on charges from transatlantic flights (including overflights from Europe), which represent about 15 percent of flights but 40 percent of revenues.

Under the PPP, en route charges are subject to price-cap regulation by the CAA using the RPI-X method. This approach sets prices at the level of the inflation less a factor to account for productivity. The larger the X factor, the greater the productivity improvements expected and the more the real price decline. For the first five years, X was set for 2001 at 2.2 percent, for 2002 at 4 percent, and for 2003 and 2004 at 5 percent.[4] Thus, after an initial adjustment, NATS was expected to meet progressive efficiency gains. NATS' management recognized the efficiency gains that would be required and felt that they could be achieved without detriment to operations or to the initially proposed £1 billion 10 year investment plan, especially given forecasts for strong traffic growth.

Regulations also provided an RPI-X structure for oceanic services, with an initial X setting of 2 percent for the initial five year period. Thus, the regulatory structure placed more pressure on NATS to achieve efficiency gains in en route services. These hoped-for improvements were supplemented by a delay incentive provision, which would reduce (increase) NATS revenues if en route delays were worse (better) than in 1999, subject to an overall cap of between £2 million and £5.7 million per year over the first five year period. No delay provision was established for oceanic services. In addition, a cap for terminal services was deemed unnecessary, because the British Airports Authority has responsibility for terminal services at London's airports which are provided under contract by NATS.

---

3   These are established by EUROCONTROL and collected on NATS' behalf by the EUROCONTROL Central Route Charges Office.

4   This profile of efficiency gains was expected to bring NATS level of charges to the European average by the end of the five year period.

Sale and initial ownership/management structure

The Transport Act included requirements for both the 49 percent government share and for a 5 percent stake to be held by NATS employees. The remaining 46 percent was put out for bids. Three consortia qualified for the next round of bidding: Nimbus (which included facilities and airport services group Serco), Novares, and the Airline Group (comprised of British Airways, bmi British Midland, Virgin Atlantic, Britannia, Monarch, easyJet, and Airtours). The Government had stated its intention to pick a single partner consortium.

After continuing discussions, on March 27, 2001, the Government announced it had selected the Airline Group as NATS "strategic partner". Both Nimbus and the Airline Group bids were viewed as very similar in terms of safety, security, and operations considerations. However, there were other differences on which the decision turned. The Nimbus proposal was seen as having a stronger financial structure, but with lower sale proceeds to the government. There also was more support for the Airline Group's bid from other airlines (who believed there would be more customer focus to their benefit) and from the employees (who believed that jobs and conditions would be more secure).

Initially, the Airline Group's bid of £845 offered £95 million more in sale proceeds than Nimbus' offer. The main reason for the difference was that the Airline Group had assumed a higher rate of growth in NATS' traffic and revenue. After their selection, however, the Airline Group told the government that traffic declines in 2000 and early 2001 meant that they could not afford the price they had bid. The deal signed in July 2001 reduced initial proceeds by £87 million to £758 million. (This was still slightly more than the original Nimbus offer.) There also was a provision for deferred proceeds at later dates, worth (at most) an additional £21 million. The partnership became effective in July 2001 after getting merger clearance by the European Commission. Day-to-day operation was to be handled by a senior executive team, reporting to a non-executive board from the Airline Group, the director of the International Air Transport Association (IATA), and three partnership directors appointed by the Government.

The net £765 million sale was completed in July 2001. The sale proceeds were financed overwhelmingly through borrowing by the Airline Group on behalf of NATS. Equity investment from the Airline Group was only £50 million, or only about 6 percent of the total acquisition funding.

NATS' initial financial structure saw NATS' debt rise to £733 million to cover the agreed sale proceeds. NATS pre-existing debt capital of £355 million was re-financed with a new £733 million loan. This loan was secured by NATS future revenues, not against the Airline Group as shareholders – as would have been expected if this was a conventional financial structure. In effect, the transaction was very similar to a project finance structure in which the equity participants paid in only minimal equity, and where the overwhelming share of funding was from borrowing by NATS itself. The structure was quite similar to a leveraged buyout of NATS.

Despite warnings from NATS and the CAA about this level of debt financing, the Government concluded that these fears were misplaced. The Government's financial advisors noted that any reduction in the amount of debt was likely to reduce sale proceeds pound for pound.

After the transfer, in addition to the acquisition borrowing, the Airline Group negotiated additional credit facilities of £690 million for capital programs, and an additional £30 million facility for working capital. Prior to the events of September 11, NATS was expected to borrow almost £1.5 billion. The Government's financial advisers concluded that this structure was adequate, and that it would be better for the shareholders to respond to additional needs if required.

NATS' Financial Difficulties after September 11, 2001

The UK government's desire to maximize sale proceeds and the resulting highly geared financial position made NATS vulnerable even to modest industry declines, which began occurring in 2000. The severe downturn in traffic after the September 11 terrorist attacks made NATS' financial structure non-sustainable and in need of immediate and dramatic restructuring. This restructuring took the better part of two years and it was not until 2004 that NATS' position was strong enough to again look to managing for the future.

The collapse of traffic left NATS facing an estimated £230 million revenue shortfall over four years. NATS' en route revenues were about 14 percent below forecast in the six months following September 11. In addition, because en route services had much higher margin than terminal area services, NATS' profits were reduced by approximately one-third as compared to forecast. These declines were severe enough to put NATS at risk of violating the terms of its credit facilities. NATS was forced to limit its borrowings under the credit line to only £24 million of the £690 million line. In effect, this put the entire £1 billion capital program on hold. Operating cash surpluses also were reduced, with some concerns that NATS would be unable to pay debt service on existing debt by early 2002.

While equity investors are commonly expected to bear business risks, the downturn after September 11 left the members of the Airline Group exposed to the same financial stress as NATS. They were unwilling and unable to infuse additional equity funds. The Government also was unwilling to supply additional equity capital without extended review. The Government's position was made more difficult in the context of the October 2001 decision to place Railtrack (the country's rail infrastructure company) into receivership. Between Railtrack and NATS, the result was tense relations between the government and financial institutions, as well as much public criticism of various privatization initiatives. In short, existing equity investors were unwilling or unable to serve a risk-bearing role.

Given the fragility of NATS' structure and the severity of the industry downturn, the need for a comprehensive solution was soon apparent. In such a setting, this type of financial distress can only be resolved through a mix of raising revenues, cutting costs, restructuring debt, and raising additional capital. Reflecting contributions from all stakeholders, the NATS restructuring has been described as NATS' "Composite Solution".

Revenues

NATS' regulated pricing structure could not be changed without CAA regulatory approval. This proved to be a major challenge, because NATS charges had already been among the highest in Europe, and because the airline users were themselves in financial difficulty. However, as the severity of the downturn became apparent, the CAA agreed to revise NATS' RPI – X structure to a constant RPI -2 percent, which is 2 percent – 3 percent more than originally agreed. With the RPI running about 3 percent, this was still much less than the 12 percent average nominal increase put in place by European ATS providers in 2002. This pricing change was expected to cost airlines £100 million more over the 2003–2010 period.

In addition, the regulator put in place a traffic volume risk sharing mechanism that allows NATS to raise its charges automatically to recover half or more of lost revenue, should traffic fall below the level forecast by NATS in its regulatory submissions.

Cost reductions

While it is generally felt that ATS costs are largely fixed (at least in the short run), the magnitude of traffic declines forced NATS to re-think its cost structure. NATS reduced support costs, deferred pension contributions and capital expenditures. Overall, NATS reduced costs by approximately £170 million over 4 years, representing about 10 percent of total costs.

Additional capital funding

After internal cost reductions and the relaxation of regulatory price caps by the CAA, NATS proposed an additional £130 million of equity investment, comprised of £65 million on equal terms from the Government and a new investment from BAA plc, the operator of London's main airports. The Government had required that any additional investment on its part be matched by private sector shareholder capital.

The introduction of a new shareholder resulted in a new ownership structure, with the government retaining its 49 percent share, the employees their 5 percent share, BAA plc with a 4 percent share, and the Airline Group's stake reduced to 42 percent. This new shareholding structure is quite remarkable, given that both the government and BAA's equity contribution exceeded that of the original $50 million from the Airline Group, yet BAA's shareholding is very small. This appears to be the result of BAA's stronger financial position but a reluctance to allow the major UK airports to have a major governance role in ATS. The contribution by BAA looks somewhat similar to customer financing.

The proceeds were used to reduce the debt financing from the original £733 million (plus subsequent borrowings of £24 million) to approximately £600 million. Once these additional funds were secured, NATS' credit ratings were strengthened, and the Company was able to replace the $600 million of bank debt with a bond issue that provided a much cheaper source of long term finance with fewer restrictions on company operations and investments.

The result was a balance sheet that was still highly leveraged but much less so than before. Leverage decreased from 117 percent of assets at the time of the PPP to 70 percent by 2006. The restructuring and financial turnaround enabled NATS to improved its credit rating to an A rating by 2006. In addition, the infusion of shareholder funds moved the basic financial structure of NATS away from project finance precepts to a more conventional corporate finance structure, in terms of the relationship of equity investment in relation to debt.

NATS' Subsequent Performance and Outlook

NATS financial structure was much improved by late 2003, but the volume and mix of traffic remained a challenge. The company lost £109 million in 2002–2003, and barely broke even in 2004. The advent and growth of low-fare carriers caused more discussion of the level of NATS charges compared to those in other European states. In addition, a major outage in summer 2004 caused significant traffic disruptions and delay, although without safety performance being affected.

By the end of 2004, traffic had recovered to pre-September 11 levels, with 2005 traffic growth of almost 5 percent. This revenue growth enabled NATS to report its first significant pre-tax profit of £69 million for the year ended March 2005, and enabled it to declare its first ever dividend. Operationally, NATS handled record traffic of over 2.2 million flights, with fewer delays and consistent safety performance. The stabilized industry and company environment has enabled NATS to finally move forward on its £1 billion investment program and to undertake significant partnerships with the Irish Aviation Authority, joint projects with Spain for next generation air traffic systems, and to work with and utilize NAV CANADA technologies for electronic flight data systems.

NATS announced a small profit of £1.8 million for the year ended March 2004, a major reversal from the losses of £29.1 million for the year end March 2003, and a loss of £79.9 million in the year ended March 2002 (which included the immediate effects of September 11). The strengthening financial performance continued through 2006. Recovering traffic growth led to record revenues of £586.7 million in the year ended March 2006, while net income of £57.4 million enabled NATS to pay its first dividend of £5 million to shareholders.

Laying a Strategy

By the end of 2003, it was clear that NATS needed to think more strategically toward the future. A £1 billion investment plan was launched, with the first phase focusing on replacing secondary radars at twenty sites. The program is aimed at reducing the numbers of control centers from four to two, and to upgrade flight data processing and communications in collaboration with European partners and with NAV CANADA. The investment program has a goal of handling three million operations annually by 2010.

NATS brought in a new senior management team in mid-2004, with private sector backgrounds involving large scale capital programs. This group moved quickly to bring a more commercial orientation, including greater operational accountability, more extensive efforts at capital project management, and emphasis on financial results as well as improving operational and safety performance. By November 2004 a new strategy (known as "21 Destinations") was laid out in 2005, providing explicit performance targets for safety, service, value and people. The strategy also made explicit NATS's goals to expand its organizational linkages with other ANS providers, and to play a leading role in any consolidation among ANS providers, especially in Europe.

Recent Performance

Safety

NATS has continued its high service standards, while improving its safety record. The number of cases of loss of separation (termed "airproxes" in NATS reporting) fell from 71 to 57 between 2005 and 2006, while the number of airproxes attributable to NATS fell from 27 to 18. In addition, the rolling three year average of airproxes has fallen from approximately 80 per year in the 1998–2003 period, to 65 per year in 2004–2006. The decline is even higher in term of rates of airproxes, given the record traffic of the past three years.

NATS also has launched new initiatives working with the Civil Aviation Authority (CAA) and general aviation to reduce the number of unauthorized infringements of controlled airspace. Another program involves working with airlines to mitigate growing numbers of "level busts," in which aircraft deviate from their assigned altitudes. Finally, there is a renewed effort to develop a better reporting culture that is focused on understanding and addressing air navigational errors form all parties.

Service, costs and efficiency

NATS handled record volumes of traffic in 2004–2006. Average delay per flight was 22 seconds in 2006, about the same as 2005, and much improved over the average delay per flight of between 71 and 130 seconds between 2000 and 2003. The average delay (attributable to NATS) per delayed flight also continued to decline.

Adjustments to controlled airspace are now undertaken in the context of an Operational Partnership Agreement (OPA), in which NATS' Service and Investment Plans are shared with customers (principally the airlines and airports), and in which the airlines share their planning data. This helps NATS to manage the rapid growth of low-fare carriers serving previously underutilized airports; previously, the launch and growth of this part of the market placed significant strains and management challenges on NATS services. NATS' long-term investment plan emphasizes upgrading of infrastructure and decreasing the reliance on legacy systems, aimed at reducing the system failures that occurred in the past and which trigger financial penalties as part of NATS' operating license from the government.

Since the PPP, costs have risen, but at a slower rate of growth that before the PPP and at a slower rate than traffic. The number of staff has been reduced by approximately 10 percent since 2002.

Regulatory review

NATS was subject to its second full regulatory review in 2005. This process was particularly important given the adjustments in the original RPI – X formula in the wake of 2001 events.

Airlines, especially low-fare carriers, complained to the CAA as economic regulator that NATS charges were too high. While NATS' charges had declined by 0.3 percent annually between 2001–2005 while other European charges rose by an average of 2 percent per year during the same period, NATS remained among the most expensive ANS providers in the region. NATS countered that their organizational and operating environment was fundamentally different than that of other European ANS providers, and that the high charges reflected these higher real costs.

The CAA proposed much more demanding financial controls for NATS' second five-year Charge Period from 2006 to 2010. The new regulatory framework calls for real reductions in NATS en route unit revenues averaging 3.4 percent per year, for a cumulative reduction over the five years of around 15 percent. CAA proposes to leave the price cap for the oceanic business broadly unchanged at 4 percent below the retail price index. The CAA stated that it believed that this regulatory framework would generate significant real price reductions for users. The CAA also increased financial incentives, including increasing the maximum delay penalty from £10 million to £24 million. The regulator accepted NATS investment program and plans and continued the risk-sharing arrangement by which charges may be adjusted if traffic falls substantially below base forecasts.

After an initial appeal, NATS accepted the regulatory framework. NATS views the regulatory changes as a significant management challenge, especially to requirement to reduce costs by an additional £50 million. NATS believes that while the changes will lower charges to users, it also will reduce profitability for both en route services unit (NERL) as well as the group as a whole. The regulated private structure of NATS institutionalizes the ongoing tensions between different stakeholders, including members of the Airline Group which are both customers and owners.

Looking Beyond Britain

Having emerged from its restructuring and its regulatory review, NATS has increased its attention to increased partnerships and linkages with other ANS providers. Joint ventures and investment programs have partnered with the Spanish ANS organization AENA, with NAV CANADA, and especially with the Irish Aviation Authority, where there are major efforts to integrate airspace management and charging mechanisms. NATS believes that European ANS providers will undergo a dramatic consolidation in the next decade, and it is preparing to expand its role as a strategic partner or potential owner or operator of air navigation services outside the UK.

This potential expansion of NATS activities will present challenges to the current regulatory structure and might encourage the current shareholders to reconsider their desire to hold equity positions in a broader, transnational ANS company. Given the increasing interest of cross-border private equity finance in airports, this could result in a quite different ownership composition for NATS.

Lessons from NATS

After a difficult early period and a lengthy restructuring, NATS has established a strong operating and safety record, an improved investment program, and has established a sound commercial and strategic footing. The level of charges remains high, and meeting tough regulatory standards will be a continuing challenge. Having to manage the PPP in the wake of industry upheaval meant that it took a prolonged period for management and the organization to become more focused on customers and users.

The transition from government to commercial status was strongly conditioned by government's preference to use a particular model for commercialization (Public-Private Partnership, or PPP). This preference led to a series of choices and compromises in implementation that placed NATS in a weak position at the outset. The government's desire to maximize sale proceeds overrode the objective of an improved ANS operation. This encouraged optimistic growth forecasts, inadequate risk assessment, and extreme gearing.

The role of the Airline Group as strategic partner was compromised by the project finance structure put in place. NATS was too highly leveraged, and the security structures for the financing looked only to NATS' cash flows rather than equity holders as risk-bearing entities. The initial unwillingness and subsequent inability of the Airline Group to make larger equity investments meant that equity holders bore only minimal risk in the initial structure.

The regulatory environment proved to be challenging and contentious, given the financial problems faced by both NATS and users. The process struggled to respond to the financial crisis, in part because of concerns about the viability of the entire enterprise and the conflicting incentives of shareholders. The subsequent regulatory review highlighted the challenges of balancing stakeholder interests at a time of industry change.

NATS remains a bit of a hybrid organization, especially given its shareholding structure. Industry change and consolidation present potential challenges to an ownership group that may have quite different interests and incentives.

Chapter 7

Europe

A Microcosm for Much of the World

Throughout the world, the two principal barriers to having seamless air traffic control are the fragmentation caused by so many different countries providing their own air navigation services and the frequent interoperability between these systems so that aircraft can move smoothly from one system to another. These are the same two barriers that Europe faces, but in a highly confined airspace. In this sense, European air traffic control presents a microcosm of the challenges much of the world faces.

The dominant characteristic of the air traffic control system in Europe is that it is highly fragmented. As Loyola de Palacio, the former European Union Commissioner stated, "The present system, dating back to the 1960s, is patched together from even older national systems. It segments European airspace into small, inefficient blocks which use a variety of different air traffic control technologies."[1] Consider for example that Europe's airspace covers 6,120 square kilometers but has 57 separate ANSPs with 75 area control centers employing 42,000 people. European airspace encompasses 114 large airports,[2] and handles about 8.1 million air traffic movements a year.[3] By contrast, the air traffic control systems of the US and Canada together cover nearly 20,000 square kilometers an area over three times as large, but control that space with two ANSPs who together operate 29 area control centers, slightly more than one third the number in Europe, together employing 35,450 staff. This airspace encompasses 104 large airports and handles 20 million air traffic movements a year.

Efforts to Reduce Fragmentation

At the beginning of the commercial jet transport era in the late 1950s, it became apparent that European fragmentation would become an increasing problem with the expected growth in air traffic and the higher speeds of the aircraft. In December 1960, representatives of Belgium, France, the Federal Republic of Germany, Luxembourg, the Netherlands and the United Kingdom took the first step toward the formation of EUROCONTROL by signing the EUROCONTROL International Convention

---

1   Business and Management Practices, Air Traffic Management, December 2006, SECTION: Pg. 21 Vol. 15 No. 4 ISSN: 0969–6725.

2   In this context a large airport is one that handles more than one million passengers per year.

3   "Single minded: The dawn of the Single European Sky will be a long time coming, and the route toward it remains a political minefield," *Flight International*, July 13, 2004.

relating to Cooperation for the Safety of Air Navigation. The original goal of EUROCONTROL was to have a single organization responsible for managing the upper airspace throughout Europe. Upper airspace is where airplanes are cruising in flight as opposed to lower levels where they are climbing or descending near airports. EUROCONTROL's plan was that three international Air Traffic Control centers were to be established to operate the upper airspace. However, despite these early intentions, reservations began to emerge quite soon after the signing of the Convention. In the 1960s and 1970s, the majority of the European States were not prepared to give up as much sovereignty over their own airspace as EUROCONTROL would have needed to fulfill the original vision. In the end, EUROCONTROL was able to establish only a single center, the Maastricht Upper Area Control Center in 1972, to control the upper airspace of Belgium, Luxembourg, the Netherlands and northern Germany. While this center represented the first time in history that air traffic in one country had been controlled from a center located in another, EUROCONTROL still fell far short of the original goal and European airspace remained fragmented.

A Basic Tension

The failure to establish a unified air traffic control system in Europe's upper airspace is the result of a long-standing basic tension in Europe between national sovereignty, a political consideration, and operationally efficient airspace design, an economic consideration. Recall that in 1944, the Chicago Convention accepted the basic principle that every State has complete and exclusive sovereignty over the airspace above its territory. While the Chicago Convention didn't require that the State itself provide air traffic control services in its airspace, countries have control of their airspace as a matter of national sovereignty and have the right to determine how air traffic control services will be provided.

Where countries are geographically large, such as Australia, Canada, or the United States, it's possible to have efficient airspace design while still having the country, or its designated organization, provide air traffic control services. In Europe, however, the countries are geographically smaller, so that having each country provide its own air traffic control services means that the airspace is inherently divided into units that are simply too small for the most efficient use. The result is that in Europe it takes an inordinate amount of coordination with a great many transactions between separate facilities for aircraft to move relatively small distances. To reconfigure the airspace so that it could be managed more efficiently would require that some countries would have to allow other countries or international organizations to manage traffic in their airspace. Reaching agreement on such arrangements proved almost impossible in the 1960s and 1970s, except for the single agreement involving Belgium, Luxembourg, the Netherlands, and part of northern Germany, and it remains difficult today.

Some Signs of Progress

While EUROCONTROL wasn't able to consolidate all control of Europe's upper airspace, it has found opportunities for international collaboration. In 1971, the

Central Route Charges Office (CRCO) was established to provide a centralized system for collecting a single charge per flight on behalf of the EUROCONTROL Member States and reimbursing the Member States with the charges collected. The system has evolved into one of the most efficient in the world and charges aircraft operators for each aircraft that used a given airspace; the exact cost being dependent on the distance flown, the weight of the aircraft, and the specific airspace through which the plane flies. The CRCO also offers its services to non-Member States by means of bilateral agreements. The main benefit to States of using the CRCO's central route charges system is that it is cheaper than employing traditional collection procedures. The CRCO combines a high recovery rate (average 99.48 percent for 1996–1999) with administrative costs which usually amount to little more than 0.5 percent of the charges collected.[4] Perhaps the most important feature of the CRCO was that it represented a willingness of the Member States to give up a very small amount of autonomy as part of a collaborative process.

In January 1986, the original EUROCONTROL Convention was amended and the original goal of unified air traffic control in the upper airspace was abandoned. Instead, the emphasis became on cooperation among the various ANSPs. In 1990, the European Air Traffic Control Harmonisation and Integration Programme (EATCHIP) was launched. This new approach to European air traffic management cooperation represented a movement away from an emphasis on more efficient consolidated airspace and instead, a movement toward making the best of a fragmented system by getting the various systems of the different countries to work together more smoothly. The initial challenge was to achieve harmonization of European air traffic services in all European Civil Aviation Conference (ECAC) States by 1998, by working towards the compatibility and interoperability of European ATM systems and procedures.[5] The program also developed EUROCONTROL's role as an air traffic management planning organization for Europe and provided the institutional framework to introduce common ATM facilities.

Growing Delays

By the late 1980s, air traffic had doubled from its early 1970s level and congestion and delays in the fragmented system were becoming a more serious problem. In 1988, the ECAC took another step toward collaboration and created a Central Flow Management Unit as a part of EUROCONTROL to make the best use of the available air traffic control capacity. At the time, there were only national flow management units operated by their own national administrations, but they typically were

---

4   EUROCONTROL History: 1963–2003, "40 Years of Service to European Aviation," http://www.eurocontrol.int/corporate/public/standard_page/history.html.

5   European Civil Aviation Conference members currently include: Albania, Armenia, Austria, Azerbaijan, Belgium, Bosnia and Herzegovina, Bulgaria, Croatia, Cyprus, Czech Republic, Denmark, Estonia, Finland, France, Georgia, Germany, Greece, Hungary, Iceland, Ireland, Italy, Latvia, Lithuania, Luxembourg, Malta, Moldova, Monaco, Netherlands, Norway, Poland, Portugal, Romania, Serbia, Slovakia, Slovenia, Spain, Sweden, Switzerland, The former Yugoslav Republic of Macedonia, Turkey, Ukraine, United Kingdom.

limited to geographic areas that were too small to be effective. The agreement to participate in a central flow management process was a second important indication of a willingness to give up some autonomy to join in a collaborative process. The Central Flow Management Unit did not become fully responsible for air traffic flow management, however, until March 1996.

Figure 7.1 shows the European traffic volumes and delays from 1997 through 2005. While part of the delays in Europe were due to airport capacity, most of the delays were because of air traffic control, and those delays were increasing sharply when the Central Flow Management Unit became operational. The average delay per flight figures shown in the figure may seem modest, but these are annual averages across all of Europe. Traffic in Europe is much heavier in June, July, August, and September, and there was considerable variation in delay across the various parts of Europe. As the figure indicates, after the peak year of delays in 1999, ATC delays have been brought down significantly to the point where, while still a problem, they are now not much larger than airport delays. The Central Flow Management Unit has played a major role in reducing these delays.

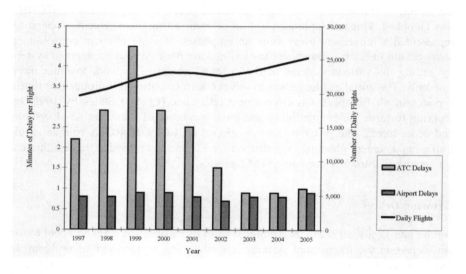

Figure 7.1   European flights and delays

Single European Sky

By 1999, average delays in some parts of the system of nearly 30 minutes per flight continued to plague European aviation.[6] In December, European Commissioner Loyola de Palacio launched the Single European Sky initiative. The legislation

---

6   "Air Travel in Crisis," *Aviation Week and Space Technology*, Vol. 151, No. 17; Pg. 95, October 25, 1999.

governing the Single European Sky program was adopted by the European Commission in March 2004. There are four main components of the legislation:[7]

1. Regulation (EC) No 549/2004 of the European Parliament and of the Council of 10 March 2004 provides the framework for the creation of the single European sky. The basic framework proposes that the European Community regulates with assistance from EUROCONTROL in developing the regulations and national authorities have the responsibility for enforcing the regulations.
2. Regulation (EC) No 550/2004 of the European Parliament and of the Council of 10 March 2004 addresses the provision of air navigation services in the single European sky. It requires a functional separation of national regulatory activities and air navigation service provision.
3. Regulation (EC) No 551/2004 of the European Parliament and of the Council of 10 March 2004 addresses the organization and use of the airspace in the single European sky. The goal is to create a European airspace that behaves as a single operating continuum, where common procedures for the design, planning and management of airspace ensure the safe performance of the entire air traffic management network. The regulations define the principles for the organization and use of the airspace, for the co-ordination between civil and military and for the management of air traffic flows.
4. Regulation (EC) No 552/2004 of the European Parliament and of the Council of 10 March 2004 addresses the interoperability of the European Air Traffic Management network. This provision defines the conditions necessary to ensure interoperability in the European Union between the different systems of the air traffic management network and of their upgrading to new technologies as appropriate.

The Basic Framework

The basic framework is a centralized, pan-European approach based on a common master plan to overcome the lack of coordination among the various countries that has plagued European air traffic management in the past. EUROCONTROL is to play a key role in policy formation and guiding research and development, but it is the European Commission who has the binding legal authority. One challenge is that while the notion of a Single European Sky is nearly universally supported at the conceptual level, for every issue to be faced in carrying out the notion, there are numerous and sometime contradictory solutions being proposed. Not surprisingly, the final text of the Single European Sky legislation had to be vague to achieve consensus among the governments, but as a result leaves much open to interpretation.

---

7   *Official Journal of the European Union*, L96, Vol. 47, March 31, 2004.

Separation of Regulation from Provision

A fundamental principle of the Single European Sky is the separation of regulation and oversight of air traffic management from the provision of services to avoid any of the problems possible with having ANSPs self regulate. A total organizational separation into two independent entities is not a requirement of this regulation, but having effective functional separation within the same organization is difficult to achieve. The principle of separation places EUROCONTROL in a difficult and sensitive position, particularly in light of the goal to consolidate airspace. EUROCONTROL purports to have functional separation within the same agency, but their role has become a source of concern to some ANSPs who question its joint position as having considerable influence on regulation but also being a service provider. This dual role could be particularly troublesome should Europe eventually move to consolidate its airspace. As discussed below, such consolidation would almost certainly result in fewer area control centers and most likely in fewer separate ANSPs. The consolidation may well lead to competition among ANSPs to see which will take on more airspace and which will take on less. In such a world, the ANSPs view EUROCONTROL as a competitor but one whose ability to shape regulation gives it an enormous, and arguably unfair, advantage.

The Civil Air Navigation Services Organisation (CANSO) has called for an end to the arrangement where EUROCONTROL is both a regulator and a service provider. CANSO's Secretary General, Alexander ter Kuile, states the position as follows, "We must have a separation of provision and regulation. EUROCONTROL's regulatory tasks can't be combined with provision," adding that while the ANSPs his organization represents are under pressure to reduce costs, EUROCONTROL is still seeking increases in its budget. He goes on to say, "we need a level playing field. Airlines wouldn't accept competing against a carrier that got things free of charge, and neither should Europe's ANSPs." The European Commission recognizes the sensitivity of EUROCONTROL's role in the Single Sky process and vows to continue to asses whether there is sufficient separation between these two roles. The pressure is clearly on EUROCONTROL, given the clear separation between regulation and provision that is developing elsewhere within Europe. Some also see the requirement for a separation of functions likely to see an end to EUROCONTROL's management of the Maastricht centre and perhaps the Central Flow Management Unit.

Organization of the Airspace

The most critical aspect of the Single European Sky program is the organization and use of airspace. The regulations envision the creation of upper airspace Functional Airspace Blocks (FABs), that would be based on air traffic movement needs rather than on national boundaries. The International Air Transport Association (IATA) and others believe all current national boundaries for upper airspace should be replaced by just six FABs.[8] This would allow more efficient traffic flow and would

---

8   "Airline Groups Criticize Slow Pace Of Single Sky Initiative," *Aviation Daily*, Vol. 363 No. 30, February 15, 2006.

dramatically reduce the number of ATC centers required to handle the upper airspace from the current number of 75. Rather than dictate the new airspace boundaries to member states, the Single Sky initiative has left it up to the national governments to decide for themselves how they will combine their airspace with that of neighboring countries. A Member State will be able to designate an organization in another Member State to assume responsibility for air traffic control in its airspace. Together with the establishment of functional airspace blocks, this opens the door to integrated service providers operating over large areas.

However, opening the door and walking through it are two different things. This "bottom-up" approach for the creation of these blocks faces the same basic tension between sovereignty and efficient airspace design that has hampered Europe and EUROCONTROL's efforts since the 1960s. Is there reason to hope that these efforts will be more successful than in the past? The evidence is mixed. On one hand, there are some examples of internationally controlled airspace, notably Switzerland (Skyguide) managing airspace in France, and, of course, EUROCONTROL's long standing center as Maastricht. The airspace which is managed by Skyguide extends beyond Switzerland's national borders into France, Italy, Austria and Germany. In return, part of Switzerland's airspace is managed by Italian air traffic control; and traffic to and from EuroAirport Basel-Mulhouse is handled by France's air navigation service provider. More recently, a series of studies of consolidating airspace into FABs have been started. For example, such talks were started between the UK and Ireland; Bulgaria and Romania; Portugal and Spain; France and Switzerland; and Denmark and Sweden. However, one question that remains is whether proposals coming from these talks would still have airspace boundaries that follow national boundaries or whether airspace efficiency considerations would become dominant.

A discouraging sign is the difficulty in establishing a Functional Airspace Block in Central Europe. In 1997, the Central European Air Traffic Services (CEATS) agreement was signed to manage the combined airspace of Austria, Bosnia and Herzegovina, Croatia, the Czech Republic, Hungary, Slovakia, Slovenia and part of North East Italy. Reaching and implementing an agreement, however, has proven difficult. By 2006, five of the States had ratified the CEATS agreement, but Austria, the Czech Republic and Slovenia had begun working on their own co-operative project and had not ratified the agreement.

A particularly difficult airspace issue in Europe is military use of airspace. Military airspace occupies a significant proportion of the overall European airspace and contributes to the inefficient use of existing civil airspace. Some sharing of airspace occurs, but as civilian traffic grows, the pressures to share airspace more effectively will almost certainly grow. The Single Sky approach is for "flexible airspace" where military airspace is opened to civilian flights, but can be withdrawn in case of a conflict with national military requirements. The plan is that the military will be full partners in the development of any future rules and the preparation of ATM legislation that may affect them as airspace users or as providers of ATM services. Any rules on such things as equipment or airspace organization will need to reflect the requirements and constraints of the military in the same way as those of civilians.

Interoperability

In conjunction with the fourth regulation on interoperability, the Single European Sky ATM Research program (SESAR) was initiated as the modernization program. It is intended to combine technological, economic and regulatory aspects and to use the Single European Sky legislation to synchronize the plans and actions to develop and implement the required improvements in both airborne and ground systems throughout Europe. SESAR is designed to begin with a definition phase which is to deliver a European ATM master plan by 2008. This will be followed by a development phase which is to run until 2013 and will focus on systems design and producing the key systems components. Finally, there will be a deployment phase that is to be completed by 2020.

Financing of this modernization program remains an issue. One suggestion is that the cost of the program (estimated at 2.1 billion Euro) be split three ways, with the EC, EUROCONTROL and industry each contributing one third. For their part, ANSPs warn that neither airlines nor ANSPs can be expected to foot the bill, and certainly not the upfront investment through user charges.

Competition for the Market

There are two basic approaches that might be taken to address the fragmentation and interoperability issues in European airspace. In either case, developing Functional Airspace Blocks based on operational efficiency rather than national political boundaries is a key, but the difference is in how these new airspace blocks would be managed.

One approach might be based on taking advantage of economies of scale and eliminating redundancies by operating a smaller number of larger air traffic control facilities, each responsible for a larger geographic area. With this approach, some area control centers would have to close and some ANSPs would have to merge or stop providing services. Instead, providing services in that airspace would be delegated to another organization and the airspace might well be controlled from a facility located in another country. Some ANSP managers and staff would no longer be needed. While the total number of air traffic controllers might not decrease by more than could be handled by retirement and attrition, some would have to relocate and be retrained for the new airspace configuration they were controlling. It's hardly surprising that those organizations who fear they would shrink or might no longer exist and those people who fear that they might lose their jobs would oppose these consolidations. As discussed in Chapter 17, labor unions have been fiercely opposed to possible plans to reduce the number of air traffic control centers and air traffic controllers held a strike in 2002 to reinforce their opposition to the principle of Single European Sky.[9]

A difficult question with this consolidation by delegation model is how it would be decided which ANSPs would continue to operate and which would delegate their previous responsibilities to other organizations. Air traffic control is not a service that permits competition within the market. Indeed, ICAO standards require that all

---

9　"Out of Control," *Flight International*, June 25, 2002.

aircraft within a given block of airspace be under the control of a single air traffic control operator.[10] But a reduction in the number of ANSPs operating in Europe might well involve some form of competition for the market. There would certainly be pressure from the airlines to select the ANSPs that could operate with the lowest costs, but it seems more likely that some combination of political and economic factors would come into play in making the choices.

A second approach might be characterized as relying on cooperation and interoperability rather than consolidation and delegation.[11] With modern communications, the air traffic controller need not be located directly beneath the airspace being controlled. That's why it's possible to have large consolidated air traffic control centers as discussed above. But that same communication technology also makes it possible to have a series of smaller, more dispersed air traffic control centers so long as there is seamless interoperability among them. With this option, it might not be necessary to close as many air traffic control centers and it might be possible for all or most of the ANSPs to remain in operations. Such an option might be politically more palatable, at least among some stakeholders.

These two different approaches would not only affect existing European ANSPs differently, but they would also likely have different impacts on the vendors of air traffic control equipment. One of the consequences of the fragmentation of the European system was that the different ANSPs often bought equipment from different vendors. Where there was a vendor based in the same country as an ANSP, there was a tendency for the ANSP to buy from that vendor. Under either of the approaches described above for moving toward a Single European Sky, the vendors will have to move to a common interoperable standard. But with the consolidation and delegation approach, there will be fewer ANSPs. Since ANSPs typically prefer to standardize their equipment, a move that results in fewer ANSPs will also increase competition among vendors for a smaller number of larger contracts with the likely eventual result of fewer vendors. With the second approach of cooperation and interoperability, there would likely be room for a larger number of vendors providing air traffic control equipment.

Assessing the relative merits of these two options depends in large part on the extent to which there are scale economies in the provision of upper airspace air traffic control services. If the scale economies were substantial, then the first option could produce markedly lower costs. If the scale economies were minimal, then there might not be much cost differences between the two, although there still might be greater coordination costs with the second approach. It's also important to realize that the choice is not between these two extremes, but rather that there is a whole continuum of options between the two outlined above. The question is not complete consolidation or none, but rather the question is how much consolidation and delegation should there be.

---

10 ICAO, "International Standards & Recommended Practices – Air Traffic Services," Annex 11 to the Chicago Convention, 12th edition, July 1998, at para. 3.5.2 (responsibility for control within a given block of airspace).

11 Francis Shubert, "The Single European Sky Controversial Aspects of Cross-Border Service Provision," *Air and Space Law*, Vol. 28, Issue 1, 2003, pages 32–49.

The Changing World of Air Traffic Management in Europe

While the same basic tension between sovereignty and efficient airspace that existed in the 1960s remains today, that tension operates in a changing world of air traffic management. In the 1960s and 1970s, air traffic management services were provided by government employees working in government agencies. In that world, any agreements for collaboration between ANSPs were by definition agreements between governments. In recent years, as discussed throughout this book, there has been increasing separation between governments and ANSPs. Many ANSPs have become increasingly autonomous and have operated on increasingly commercial principles. As ANSPs become more autonomous with dedicated funding based on user fees, they tend to become more responsive to their customers, the aircraft operators, and less dependent on and controlled by governments. Thus what is different now than in the earlier periods is that there is a mix of ANSPs in Europe in terms of their degree of autonomy. Those more autonomous ANSPs such as NATS are more oriented to dealing directly with other ANSPs to work out cooperative agreements without involving agreements between governments. But the Single Sky program is a European Commission initiative that is built around government to government agreements constructed by bureaucrats. So the tension between sovereignty and airspace efficiency has taken on an added dimension that very different kinds of ANSPs must now work together to strike the balance.

Key Features of Major European ANSPs

Germany

Deutsche Flugsicherung (DFS), the German ANSP was converted from a state-run organization to a corporate form in 1993 and became a commercial, self-supporting government company. Military air traffic control was integrated into the company in the mid-1990s. DFS has reduced costs, partly by consolidating facilities: from three upper-airspace centers to one and from five lower airspace centers to three, plus going from 17 flight service stations to one. The result has been a series of reductions in service fees. The German parliament has passed legislation to permit the sale of 74.9 percent of the company to private investors, thus privatizing DFS. Those plans were delayed in 2006 because of the objection of the German president, Horst Kohler, who has called for the legal and constitutional status of the planned privatization to be examined more closely.

France

DSNA, France's air navigation service provider, has become an autonomous entity under the regulatory oversight of DGAC, France's civil aviation authority. While DSNA remains part of the government, it is self supporting with ATC user charges.

Switzerland

Skyguide, Switzerland's ANSP, is a non-profit making public limited corporation with over 99 percent of the share capital held by the Swiss Confederation. Skyguide is financed through user fees. Swisscontrol had become financially independent from the Swiss Confederation in 1996. In 2001, the military and civil air navigation services were combined into a single authority which was renamed Skyguide.

Italy

ENAV, S.p.A is a publically controlled joint stock company which was formed in 2001. The company is controlled by the Ministry of Economics and Finance and overseen by the Ministries of Infrastructures and of Transportation.

Scandinavia

On January 1, 2005, the Swedish Civil Aviation Authority, Luftfartsstyrelsen, was formed from the Swedish Aviation Safety Department and the Aviation and Public Sector Department. This organization is separate from the LFV Group, a state enterprise which operates and develops State-owned civil aviation airports and also provides peace time air navigation services for civilian and military aircraft. The LFV Group is not funded through government taxes, instead earns its income from services and products available at the airports managed by the LFV Group as well as from the charges for air navigation services. The LFV Group is also required to pay a set dividend to the State. In Norway, Avinor AS is a state owned limited company. Avinor owns and operates 46 airports all over the country, 14 in association with the armed forces and is responsible for air traffic control services in Norway.

Austria

Air traffic control in Austria was first established in 1955, after Austria had regained its independence following the Second World War. On December 28, 1993, the Austrian parliament passed a bill into law, which required the corporatization of the Federal Office of Civil Aviation and the formation of Austro Control GmbH as an independent limited liability company which undertakes all state duties related to civil aviation. It acts on directives from the Civil Aviation Authority (part of the Ministry of Transport, Innovation and Technology) in regulatory or legislative matters. Austro Control is a fully self-funding organization, apart from those duties executed on behalf of the government for which the Ministry of Transport pays on a cost recovery base. Aeronautical charges are calculated in-house but are subject to government approval. Airline stakeholders are kept informed during the process of calculation and approval.

Netherlands

Air traffic control was formally established in the Netherlands in 1945 and, until the beginning of 1993, air traffic services were provided by the Civil Aviation

Administration (CAA) which is part of the Ministry of Transport and Waterworks. On January 1, 1993, Luchtverkeersleiding Nederland (LVNL) or Air Traffic Control – the Netherlands was formed as a corporate entity, independent of the CAA. Military air traffic control remains the responsibility of the Ministry of Defense and is separate from civil air traffic control. LVNL is still fully owned by the state and supervised by a board appointed jointly by the Minister of Transport and the Minister of Defense. There are no shareholders and LVNL is not permitted to make a profit. The supervisory board must approve all proposed tariffs relating to air traffic control provision, which then go to the Minister of Transport for final approval.

How Much Progress?

An assessment of the progress of the Single European Skies initiative was completed by EUROCONTROL's Performance Review Commission in December 2006. The report concludes that little has been achieved to date.[12] Part of the problem stems from the vagueness of the final text of the legislation that was necessary to gain acceptance among the governments. While acceptance was achieved, it came at a cost of providing little guidance about what had to be done, how it was to be done, and when. No methodology has been developed to assess performance so there's been little pressure to move forward. At this point, little of the tension between sovereignty and airspace efficiency seems to have been addressed, much less resolved.

Summary

Europe faces the dual challenges of reducing fragmentation and increasing interoperability in its air traffic control system in a highly confined airspace. In responding to these challenges, Europe will have to confront a long-standing basic tension between national sovereignty, a political consideration, and operationally efficient airspace design, an economic consideration. Much of the rest of the will face these same challenges and this same basic tension as international air traffic grows, so the path Europe ultimately chooses will be watched with interest.

One approach would be to focus on consolidating the current facilities into a much smaller number of air traffic control centers, each of which would oversee a larger, international area. A second approach would be to emphasize greater cooperation and interoperability, thereby retaining a larger number of more facilities that would work more closely together. In practice, these approaches are not mutually exclusive, but strategic choices need to be made. The need is to address the questions of the appropriate timing and degree of consolidation, integration, and delegation.

---

12 Mike Halls, "Official: Single European Sky off course," *Air Traffic Management*, Spring 2007.

SECTION THREE
International Experiences
in Emerging Aviation Markets

Unlike more developed and mature aviation markets, aviation presents different challenges in developing countries. Despite the potential importance of aviation in economic development, limited infrastructure and funding often hinder the performance of the sector. In addition, poor governance structures and inefficiencies often make the performance even worse. Other developing countries face the challenge of managing explosive growth from a small base, frequently in the wake of airline liberalization. This boom in commercial aviation often strains publicly provided airport and air navigation facilities, which lag behind the travel and cargo growth.

Larger developing countries with significant traffic growth and extensive airspace, such as India and China, face the challenge of undertaking major capital programs while trying to make strategic choices in upgrading versus replacing air navigation technologies. Other developing countries, especially in Africa, South Asia, and Latin America face significant investment needs in the context of small national aviation sectors and limited economic and budget resources. As a response to these challenges, some parts of the world, such as southern Africa and Central America, multi-country and regional solutions are beginning to take hold. While these multinational approaches have had some success, they also present dilemmas with respect to governance and sovereignty issues.

Chapter 8 reviews some of the problems in the current operating environment, emphasizing the challenges brought by growth, and alternative strategies to improve air navigation beyond and across national borders.

Chapter 9 discussed the case of Russia and the Former Soviet Union. Russian air traffic management has had to deal with huge challenges in transition from a heavily subsidized, tightly controlled and integrated government-run civil aviation system through a period of disintegration to the current mix of old and new operators, western and Russian technologies, and rapid growth with significant infrastructure limitations.

Chapter 10 examines the moves toward modernization of China's air navigation system. Historically very limited, civil aviation now has experiences more than a decade of incredible growth. China faces the challenge of keeping up with infrastructure, technology, and sufficient technically skilled personnel.

Chapter 11 examines the challenges faced in India. Like China, India faces explosive growth in air travel but lacks sufficient infrastructure. However, the difference in political systems makes the Indian context different. Much more of

Indian airline activity is driven by private parties, but in the context of powerful government organizations controlling airports and air navigation.

Chapter 12 turns to Africa, where aviation in Africa is plagued by poor services, inadequate funding and maintenance, and weak organizational and regulatory frameworks. However, there have been notable successes in air navigation in South Africa and in Cape Verde. Regional agreements and organizations have begun to take hold, and may hold prospects for a model of contracting services across national borders.

Finally, Chapter 13 examines South America. Latin America faces diverse challenges, from small countries trying to manage infrastructure needs to larger countries trying to deal with rapid growth after decades of government control.

Chapter 8

The Challenge of Air Navigation in Developing Countries

Aviation can play a special and critical role in developing countries. In many places, road and other surface transport networks are limited or nonexistent, while limited investment in airstrips and infrastructure can provide access to markets and links to the rest of the world for both passengers and cargo. However, many developing countries and regions face severe economic conditions and public budget constraints that make even rudimentary aviation development a major challenge.

Developing countries face a number of special problems in air navigation: This chapter discusses these issues by reviewing the problems in the current operating environment, the problem of growth, and alternative strategies to improve air navigation.

The Air Navigation Environment in Developing Countries

Managing the turmoil of civil aviation restructuring

The international aviation environment that came into being after the second world war has had dramatic legacy costs for developing countries. In the developed world, the heavily regulated industry protected national carriers and emphasized the role of the state as service provider not only of airlines, but also airports and air navigation. For today's developing world, the situation was worse, as the umbrella of colonial structures created patchworks of civil aviation services with routes and service more tied to the ruling country and to its other colonies than to natural geographic, regional, or economic markets. With the advent of independence in the 1950s and 1960s, the newly established developing countries in South and Southeast Asia and Africa inherited these state-controlled civil aviation systems. The transfer and sustaining of this organizational model was more of a challenge for the newly independent countries, which immediately faced a lack of skilled personnel and limited budgets. To provide support for the sector and to stretch resources, it was common for civil aviation activities to be brought under the control of or with close ties to the military. In the case of many countries in Latin America, independence had come much earlier and the military played a key role in development of aviation activity. The result was typically a state-run civil aviation sector with strong military ties, with in come cases an air navigation system operated by the military, that shared many of the same characteristics as civil aviation in Africa, South Asia, and Southeast Asia.

As civil aviation began to move from the state to the private sector worldwide in the 1970s and 1980s, developing countries struggled to adjust. The legacy of state-owned national, or flag, carriers protected from international and domestic entry created conditions that led to extensive uneconomic services to smaller cities or to remote areas, with the intent of strengthening commercial and political ties. This environment also had few incentives for cost control, resulting in overstaffing and continuing strains to cover operating expenses. A further effect was very limited resources for capital investment, with dramatic consequences for infrastructure, especially air navigation and airports. When resources were available, they were more likely to go to visible face lifts at airports than to largely unseen air traffic control and air navigation facilities. Equipment frequently fell into disrepair, while new or updated technologies simply passed these countries by.

The rise of private sector participation in infrastructure in developing countries in the 1990s spurred a host of organizational reforms, including privatization of many state airlines; the organizational separation of airlines, airports, and air navigation (which was necessary in order to structure private financing); and the development of new legal and administrative structures that moved the government from provider to enabler, monitor, and regulator of civil aviation services.

Not all countries or regions took part in this revolution in civil aviation, and many countries experienced severe problems in adjustment or implementation. For aviation infrastructure, there were more opportunities for landside investments in terminals and concessions that for airside improvements to runways, aprons, and navigation equipment. It also was much more common for airports to be privatized, while air navigation organizations either remained as part of government or were transformed into public enterprise structures that facilitated charging mechanisms (for example, overflight revenues), capital investment, and longer-term dedicated financing.

The surge of private investment into developing country aviation infrastructure was largely concentrated in the capital city or other major commercial center. Secondary airports and en route air navigation equipment proved difficult to finance, so that many countries had improved aviation services in only a few major markets. Moreover, these industry changes frequently were accompanied by sector liberalization, spurring new airlines and rapid growth on the main routes between key cities. The increased competition reduced fares and enabled rapid growth in travel, but also put added pressure on air navigation capacity and tended to reduce the revenues of legacy state airlines and services that helped to support smaller facilities and air navigation facilities. The result is that many developing countries are straining to manage the growth in air travel and cargo activity with older infrastructure built for different traffic patterns and lower traffic volumes.

Meeting international standards

Multilateral organizations, including the International Civil Aviation Organization (ICAO), the United Nations, and a range of multilateral financial institutions, have paid special attention to civil aviation in developing countries. Most of these efforts have been directed at the development of ground-based services for aviation, including airports, air navigation, and communications services. In recent years, however, the growing concern about of security threats in a global industry has shifted resources and attention to aviation security investments.

Because of the interconnectedness of aviation networks, meeting international safety and security standards has become a requirement for all countries. There is no tolerance for poor safety or security performance, in the wake of country reviews and the ability to blacklist travel. Moreover, international airlines are less likely to provide competitive services if infrastructure is deficient, on both efficiency and safety grounds. As a result, economic development is likely to be constrained.

Inadequate or obsolete infrastructure and technology

In many developing countries, air traffic control is procedurally based, with only limited technology support. Radar coverage typically is very spotty, the equipment is often poorly maintained and subject to failure, and it is common to find shortages of skilled technicians to operate and repair the infrastructure. While such limitations may not have posed serious safety risks when air traffic was light, growth in air traffic makes these shortcomings increasingly problematic. Failure to overcome these limitations could sharply constrain economic development in the future.

Inadequate financial resources and financing capability

Air navigation infrastructure requires large capital outlays that are often beyond the capacity of governments to finance. Moreover, most of these technology outlays require hard currency payment, placing addition strains on a country's foreign exchange. Financing also is a challenge, because many developing countries lack the institutions, instruments, or credibility to establish long term capital markets. As a result, most long term financing also requires hard currency borrowing.

Aviation also tends to be viewed as a lower budget priority than other sectors that may affect more of the population, such as education or public health. Even when aviation is able to generate hard currency revenues (for example, from overflight charges or landing fees), these revenues are often not retained in the sector, but revert to other public uses. In some case, these funding shortfalls or diversions are worsened by the prevalence of corruption or other aspects of poor governance.

Organization and governance of civil aviation

The variety of organizational innovations and operating and financial practices in developed economies have not yet reached many developing countries, despite the potential advantages they might bring. Historically, aviation infrastructure had security and defense objectives, so military involvement in civil aviation is widespread. In air navigation, efficiently operated civilian aviation is more difficult to achieve because it is common that large sectors of airspace are frequently set aside for military use only.

Even when civil aviation is distinct from the military, it is common to have integrated aviation sectors in which airports, air navigation, and regulation are part of the same governmental ministry or agency. Growing skepticism over privatization and commercialization has slowed these reform efforts, thus hindering the modernization of air navigation equipment and operations.

Growth Places a New Set of Challenges

As civil aviation has been liberalized worldwide, air travel has increased dramatically, placing new demands on the air traffic control system. In rapidly growing developing countries, rising incomes and global supply chains have put even more pressure on aviation infrastructure. Given the long lead times and the limited budget capacity of the public sector, managing this growth presents a host of safety and efficiency problems.

In particular, both China and India are experiencing explosive growth in domestic air travel along with a lack of sufficient infrastructure to handle this growth without substantial additional investment. In addition, both countries are becoming major international destinations and control significant amounts of airspace in key international travel corridors. As a result, Indian and Chinese civil aviation need to become better integrated with the world's air navigation system, for commercial, safety, and security reasons. Another challenge is that air navigation, as part of state transport ministries, has not been commercially oriented and faces an array of budgetary and political influences in managing existing systems and expanding capacity.

Improving Air Navigation in Developing Countries[1]

Moving from national to regional (to commercial?) structures

Faced with rapid growth and inadequate infrastructure, some developing regions are turning to regional strategies as possible solutions. In addition, economies of scale in managing airspace should help reduce the overall cost of air navigation services. The difficulties lie in developing organizational structures that are autonomous and financially sustainable, and in transitioning from national to multinational governance structures, including issues of performance, oversight, and liability.

While regionalism in air navigation appears economically compelling, the track record of has been somewhat disappointing. There are few examples where countries have ceded control of en route upper air space to a regional organization, let alone lower level traffic and tower operations. In fact, the experience of EUROCONTROL may indicate that alternative organizational approaches are better bets for improving air navigation in developing countries. EUROCONTROL has been most successful in working alongside national ANSPs in coordinating administrative procedures such as centralized collection of charges and coordinated traffic flow management.

---

1   For a more complete discussion of this topic, see C. Schlumberger, "Financing of Essential Air Transport Infrastructure," mimeo, (Washington: The World Bank, 2006), also available at http://www.icao.int/atb/McGill_06/Presentations/Schlumberger_speech.pdf.

EUROCONTROL's operational scope remains limited to selected upper airspace sectors, in the wake of national sovereignty and security concerns. In addition, the task of how to rationalize and restructure facilities and labor in a regionalized European structure has proved daunting on repeated occasions. Strategically, EUROCONTROL initiatives now appear to emphasize "harmonization" and interoperability in managing technology interconnections at national borders.

In contrast, much of the developing world would need regionalization to address a different set of issues. First, the national air navigation systems, technology, and organizations are often absent, inadequate, or obsolete. These significant investment requirements are especially problematic. Ground-based air navigation technology is by definition sited within national borders, although much of its benefit may accrue to surrounding states. Thus, developing multinational organizational and financial structures is required. Second, much of the domestic or regional aviation activity is by airlines which are quite weak financially, at the same time that international airlines are becoming more sensitive to infrastructure charges. Third, in much of the developing world, military aviation often provides significant services to civil aviation, making it harder to move toward multi-country solutions.

If regional, multi-country organizations are unlikely to provide a means to improve air navigation in developing countries, what alternatives might be better? In some airspace, especially in heavily traveled corridors, bilateral agreements might be reached so that one national ANSP might provide more efficient services across a shared border. This has been the case, for example, between France and Switzerland, between the British and Irish, and between Australia and the United States in the Guam airspace.

Another approach that may have the best long-term prospects for the improvement of air navigation in developing countries is the increasing interest in contracting for the provision of air navigation services by the ANSP of another country. This approach enables the host country to retain ownership and physical control of air navigation assets, while having services provided by subsidiaries of other countries. This structure also could extend to investment and lease-type structures, so as to improve air navigation within one's borders. The longer term benefits of this approach is that the ANSPs most likely to provide these contracted-for services will be commercially-oriented, with greater incentive to use standardized or inter-operable technologies, and with commercial structures for charging and managing operations – all of which make it easier to create more seamless airspace over developing countries. In addition, these providers also may have more incentives to implement data- and satellite-based technologies. This would reduce investment needs for ground-based systems in developing regions, many of which present problems of accessibility and coverage. As an outcome, better regional service provision might be best and most rapidly achieved through contracting for air navigation services.

The Financing Challenge

Successful financing of essential air navigation infrastructure in developing countries must meet certain preconditions. Investments and operation must meet ICAO global standards and recommended practices. A *minimum* approach to this problem is to focus on low-cost solutions, including procedural air traffic control in most areas, supplemented by radar in higher density airspace. Traditionally, funding for such infrastructure has come from government funds or from bilateral grants or loans, supplemented to a limited degree by multilateral development banks. However, such a strategy will not work for those developing countries that are growing rapidly, especially if income levels are spurring passenger travel and if the aviation sector is being liberalized.

Public-private partnerships or other forms of private participation in air navigation are much more difficult to design and implement in many developing countries. The difficulty of generating and retaining funds in the aviation sector, described above, represents a major obstacle to private financing. Even if these conditions can be met, marshaling private finance presents additional challenges. First, traffic levels and potential revenue, even in growing economies, can still be quite low relative to the developed world. Second, credit and country risk tend to be higher, so that project finance must seek higher returns. These additional financing costs can be reduce or eliminate the investment's economic viability in the absence of additional insurance or other financial support. Finally, structuring such finance is difficult given poor governance and regulatory structures.

However, there may be alternative options for private participation in air navigation, especially if the air navigation investment and strategy is linked to market conditions in terms of airports and airline activity. There also may be opportunities to finance modernization if a country has access to overflight revenues, which then could be committed to cover financing of such a capital program. In practice, though, these revenues are frequently transferred to the general treasury. Another approach has been to develop securitization structures in which overflight and other aviation charges would be deposited directly into a fiduciary trust. This trust could then issue designated air navigation financial instruments sold in international capital markets, with future revenues pledged as the collateral for such securities (in many cases with additional credit enhancements or guarantees by multilateral institutions). Such structures are beginning to be established, supplemented by increasing opportunities for leasing of more standardized air navigation components.

Conclusions

Air navigation remains a huge challenge in developing countries. Larger developing countries with significant growth and airspace, such as India and China, face strategic choices as well as major investment requirements and upgrading of technical skills in air navigation workforces. Other developing countries face severe financial constraints. In some parts of the world, such as southern Africa and Central America, multi-country and regional solutions are beginning to be put in place. While these regional approaches may help to address the investment and scale aspects of modernizing air navigation, they also present governance and political problems that have tended to prove even more challenging. In the longer term, greater commercial and private participation at the country level might provide better prospects for integrating developing countries into a global aviation network. Doing so would provide huge benefits not only to the developing countries themselves, but also to the world economy through more efficient operations and routes, reduced delays, and lower fuel and environmental costs.

In short, there is much to be done – but we should recognize that much already has been achieved, but needs to be implemented. As Murray Warfield of Qantas has noted:

> Modern technology has transformed aviation and resulted in improvements to flight safety and flight efficiency. There are still many benefits to be realized. It can also result in reduced costs and greater efficiencies for ANSPs.
>
> Unfortunately, this technology has not been adopted in many areas of the world. There are still far too many inefficient practices in operation. These are having a negative effect on aviation.
>
> In these difficult times, the industry cannot afford not to have the available technological advances in place and the challenge is for those ANSPs who have undergone the modernization process to work with those that haven't, to ensure that a truly Global ATM system is in place, sooner, rather than later.
>
> Much of the developmental work has already been completed, the new technology is working, and procedures have been modernized. The industry needs to see more of this work adopted and has to be committed to working in partnership with the ANSPs and Regulators (and governments) to ensure that these outcomes are successfully delivered.[2]

2　Murray Warfield, "Technology and Flight Safety – Benefits to be Realized," in *Essays on Air Navigation: Flying through Congested Skies*, (Montreal: McGill University Center for Research of Air and Space Law and the International Civil Aviation Organization, 2007), p. 45.

Chapter 9

Russia and the Former Soviet Union: Managing the Transition to Market

No other airspace in the world compares with Russia. The country spans eleven time zones and covers an area of 17 million square kilometers – about twenty times the size of the core European airspace. In addition, Russia manages an additional 8 million square kilometers of oceanic airspace.[1]

The country's size and distances between population centers east of the Urals means that air transport is essential. Russia's sheer geography would render it important in any discussion of global airspace, as many dense international air routes overfly the country. But in addition, Russian airspace has begun to serve and could take on an increasingly critical role as a transit corridor for future polar routes connecting North America with the Asia-Pacific region.

But Russian air traffic management has had to deal with huge challenges in transition from a relatively closed, communist system to a market economy. These challenges have taken a variety of forms: the massive macroeconomic adjustments that were more dramatic for aviation than almost any other sector; the disintegration and reconstruction of a vertically-integrated civil aviation system; the need to modernize and integrate with western technology; and the need for newly-established countries to move from the Soviet system to their own national or regional air navigation operations.

The Historical Legacy

In the Soviet Union, civil aviation played a much greater role than it would have in a market economy. Moreover, the aviation system was much different in nature than in Western Europe or North America.

Air travel represented 57 percent of intercity passenger trips in Russia in 1990, a share more than twice as the United States and three times higher than Western Europe.[2] This scale was due to vast distances, extremely low fares (in part due

---

1   "Surveillance on a Grand Scale," *Air Traffic Management*, January/February 2001. The total volume of traffic is much smaller than in western Europe and North America; in 2006 Russian air traffic control handled just under 900,000 flights. See David Hughes, "Russian ATC Reform," *Aviation Week and Space Technology*, Vol. 166 No. 9, February 26, 2007, p. 100.

2   J. Strong et al., *Moving to Market: Restructuring Transport in the Former Soviet Union*, (Cambridge, MA: Harvard University Press for the Harvard Institute for International Development, 1996), p. 136.

to massive fuel subsidies), and the underdevelopment of road and rail passenger transport. Quality of service was notoriously poor, and routes were often linear, and multistop in nature.

The civil aviation system was the responsibility of Aeroflot, and was vertically integrated. Aeroflot was the sole airline and for many years the largest in the world in terms of aircraft and the variety of activities. Aeroflot also operated all aviation infrastructure, including all civil airports and air navigation services. Aeroflot was a Production and Commercial Organization reporting to the Ministry of Civil Aviation, and operated as a holding company with separate subsidiaries for international operations, for domestic operations, and for other operations. In practice, though, Aeroflot worked through a structure of 31 regional directorates, many of which were quite large and operated almost autonomously.

Russia also had extremely close linkages between civil aviation and the military. Much of the airspace was controlled by military air traffic control, with little joint use. This system induced a great deal of circuitous routings along narrow corridors, requiring many more ATC centers and handoffs between them. Another consequence was that, as a strategic industry, workers were subject to military procedures. For controllers, this meant that they were subject to relatively low pay and poorer working conditions than their western counterparts, and were subject to strict discipline and sanctions in the event of an accident.

Aviation and Aeroflot also were viewed as showcases for Soviet technology, so that aircraft and aviation infrastructure technologies shared few commonalities with western technologies. This would lead to problems in transition, as air navigation technologies did not integrate well, both at the borders or with western-built aircraft that were leased and put into domestic service.[3]

The Collapse of the Soviet Union

The collapse of the Soviet Union had shattering consequences for Russian aviation. The massive fuel subsidies and cheap fares that had sustained the sector largely disappeared. The precipitous decline in the economy and in value of the ruble made both business/cargo and personal travel demands fall by 25 percent or more from 1990 to 1992.[4] While large fare increases choked off demand, even greater inflation in fuel prices meant that virtually all domestic aviation operations were making very substantial losses.

The traffic declines were accompanied by organizational disintegration. In the states which suddenly became independent countries (including the Baltics, Ukraine, and Kazakhstan), the local regional Aeroflot directorate became a new, but

---

3   See J. Moxon, "Testing Times," *Flight International*, (December 15–21, 1993), pp.25–29.

4   Data reported by Aerodevco Consultants, Ltd., *Civil Aviation Sector Review*, (London: European Bank for Reconstruction and Development, 1993) and reported in J. Strong et al., *Moving to Market: Restructuring Transport in the Former Soviet Union*, (Cambridge, MA: Harvard University Press for the Harvard Institute for International Development, 1996), p. 138.

still vertically-integrated national aviation organization. Within Russia, the Aeroflot regional directorates devolved into a large number of independent aviation enterprises, each with its own airlines, airports, and air traffic control operations. By the end of 1993, there were 89 registered commercial air carriers, where there previously had been one (Aeroflot). Pressures quickly developed in these organizations to generate revenues, and there was great pressure to operate flights, sometimes to the detriment of safety.

Reforming the System

By 1992 the situation was untenable. More than 40 different organizations had the right to control airspace within Russia, and all of the old Soviet contractual agreements were no longer in effect. In the wake of strike threats by controllers in 1991, the government established two new civil aviation organizations, Rosaeronavigatsia to assume control of a unified air traffic control system, and MAK (Civil Aviation Coordinating Committee), to oversee civil aviation within Russia and the newly independent states. The creation of Rosaeronavigatsia enabled air navigation services to be separated from airport and airline operations to a substantial degree, and to establish a civilian air navigation organization more independent of the military (although still closely linked in practice given the operating environment). The legal structures establishing Rosaeronavigatsia created a financing structure based on overflight charges and user fees for approaches, takeoffs, and landings. This agreement was in basic (if not always detailed) agreement with ICAO standards. However, the government had previously signed a funding agreement that was in conflict with the air navigation agreement, resulting in much confusion and reluctance or refusal of airlines and airports to pay. In addition, many of the newly-autonomous aviation organizations decided that the "home" airline should not pay for such charges, resulting in a patchwork of fee and charging schedules that were often ignored in practice.

A newly-established air traffic controllers union, the FPAD, shifted its attention to signing local or regional agreements. Controllers recognized that privatization efforts would cause financial structures to be examined on a site-by-site basis. While this did facilitate local contracting, it also meant that the controllers union would have a much smaller voice in future discussion about air traffic management strategy.

Faced with uncertain funding, Rosaeronavigatsia attempted to deal with an aviation infrastructure that had much antiquated and unreliable technology, and which did not interface with western technology. Because the system had become so fragmented, initial attention was paid to those air navigation services and investments that could provide hard currency revenues (which in turn could help modernize the rest of the system). In 1993, Russia was receiving about USD 80 million in annual overflight fees, but Rosaeronavigatsia's investment program was estimated at USD 1.3 billion. The investment shortfall was daunting, and the program was only partially implemented. These included Russia-Far East routings that provided better air traffic routes from North America to Japan, and improving system performance in the Europe-Russia corridor. Projects to modernize air navigation at Moscow and

St. Petersburg were supplemented by local efforts to get equipment replaced or upgraded.[5] The modernization program also was delayed by extended discussions with competing western consortia. Air navigation technology has always been a fiercely competitive business with strong national identities. The competition was even more vigorous than usual given the strategic importance of Russia and the fact that the first technology in place was perceived to provide an advantage for future contracts. These groups had different ideas about how best to upgrade and integrate Russian air traffic control with western systems and which supplier technologies should be selected.

In the newly-established countries, organizational reforms began to be implemented to separate air navigation, airports, and airlines. In Latvia, for example, LGS (Latvian Air Traffic Control Services) was established as a newly independent air navigation organization, financed in large part by overflight fees from European flights heading to Moscow. The new Baltic nations were particularly active in changing the airspace structure to facilitate civil (rather than military) aviation, and to adopt policies and procedures consistent with European and ICAO practice. By 2001, the Baltic states had multi-radar tracking, electronic flight strips, electronic coordination between sectors, and conflict alert functions – none of which had been available in the old Aeroflot system. The Baltic states also were quick to cooperate in developing coordinated air navigation procedures to facilitate border transit. The transition also required skills at managing handoffs to two different systems to the east (Europe) and west (Russia).

For much of the 1990s, Russian civil aviation was in turmoil, as the industry was beset by consolidations, bankruptcies, and macroeconomic instability. During that time, air navigation struggled to cope with aging technology, weak and unstable financing, and a volatile industry. But the relative stability following the 1998 financial crisis enabled the industry to begin to establish solid footing by the turn of the century.

In the late 1990s, Russia began a major review of air navigation, setting out a strategy for modernization and growth (as distinct from dealing with the legacy of the air transport sector inherited from the Soviet era.) One of the key problems is that installation and maintenance of traditional ground-based radar was impractical given the distances involved and the extremely harsh climate. This lack of air navigation infrastructure in many remote regions meant that there was minimal surveillance in place; only about 10 percent of Russian airspace was covered by secondary surveillance radar.[6] In addition, the preponderance of Russian aircraft meant that there was little communication between aircraft and the ground-based systems.

The Russian State Research Institute for Aviation System (GosNIIAS), in conjunction with Rosaeronavigatsia and the government, recognized that fundamental improvements could best be made by introduction of new technology. In particular, ADS-B (automatic dependent surveillance) was seen as particularly valuable because it could provide better air navigation information without the extensive ground-based systems. Faced with an air navigation infrastructure that was not only old but

---

5   In 1993, the Moscow Air Traffic Control Center handled about 25 percent of all flights.
6   "Surveillance on a Grand Scale," *Air Traffic Management*, January-February 2001.

increasing hard to maintain, Russia sought to move to CNS/ATM faster than many other parts of the world. Initial experiments proved successful, with a goal of moving toward full ADS-B surveillance of air traffic by 2005. However, the ambitious goals were not realized. Implementation proved more challenging, especially in moving from a ground-based system, in structuring and managing the required investment and financing program, and in getting cooperation between military and civil air navigation.

This last factor, conflicts between civil and military air navigation was particularly problematic. Although Rosaeronavigatsia had been established in 1996 to be the central civil air navigation provider, it had been unable to bring all activities under its control ten years later. Some air traffic centers were operated independently and civil-military sector conflicts remained.

Resolution of these issues was spurred by a widely-publicized civil-military miscommunication incident in 2005. The air defense force told civilian controllers to divert a Vietnam Airlines Hanoi-Moscow flight by a fuel-limited Boeing 777 aircraft. The controllers refused, and cleared the flight to land, which it did with the air defense system on full alert. This conflict, and potential for disaster, pushed the Russian government to establish a Federal Air Navigation Service to develop both short- and longer-terms plans for air navigation throughout the country.

Transition to a Modern System

The Federal Air Navigation Service recognized that a new, more pragmatic approach was required. The new plan had three stages. First, organizational reforms are to be undertaken through the creation of a unified civil-military air navigation organization by 2008. The second stage involves a transition to an advanced ground-based system, supplemented by on-board and satellite technology on main routes by 2015. This stage also aims to upgrade technology for overflight traffic, including gradual implementation of Reduced Vertical Separation Minima (RVSM) to add capacity and to attract more international revenues, especially on flights from Europe and North America to Southeast Asia. The third and final stage intends to achieve a complete transition to advanced satellite technology, linking Russia to global air navigation systems by 2025. The total program was forecast to increase capacity threefold.

This twenty year timetable took into account the need to manage growing air navigation demand while upgrading technology. Unlike the prior strategy, this new approach was incremental in nature and recognized the scale and the current state of air navigation in Russia. However, if fully implemented it would represent a complete change in air navigation service provision.

In 2007, the Russian civil air navigation services include 113 centers and 50 radars to cover the more than 530,000 kilometers of air routes and 25 million square kilometers of air space. The Federal Air Navigation Service had approximately 23,000 staff, including about 7,500 controllers.[7] The proposed plan would consolidate the system dramatically to 13 centers, with unspecified reductions in labor as well. A

---

7   "Control Laws," *Aviation Week and Space Technology*, Vol. 166 No. 3, p. 128.

major prerequisite of this plan is the introduction of ADS-B surveillance, which had not been achieved by 2007.

The cost of the program was estimated at USD 6 billion, or about USD 300 million annually. In comparison, in 2005 total air navigation revenues were approximately USD 600 million. About 90 percent of revenues were required to cover operating expenses, leaving only about 10 percent for capital investment. This is only about 20 percent of the estimated costs of the proposed modernization program. This funding shortfall has led the Federal Air Navigation Service to raise charges to Russian airlines operating on international air routes, and to propose further increase on other en route services and to terminal airspace charges. These proposed increases have been challenged by the airlines, and the situation remained unresolved by mid-2007. The uncertainty is due in part to the lack of an organizational process for oversight of charges, pointing out the need for further administrative restructuring in Russian air navigation. Thus, the ambitious twenty year program has had to confront difficult organizational and financial challenges right from its start.

Conclusions

Russian air navigation has faced perhaps the volatile industry environment of any country. The enormous volumes of air travel during the Soviet era collapsed during the transition, accompanied by a fragmentation of the Aeroflot system. Moreover, the legacy of Soviet technology made Russian air navigation infrastructure hard to integrate with western technology, while the financial situation made maintenance of the old system increasingly difficult, and incapable of modernization.

During the first decade of the transition era, the sheer capacity of the old system enabled Russian air traffic control to cope with the demands it faced. By the late 1990s, though, the need to increase efficiency and capacity became increasingly apparent. While the most recent plans seem sound in concept, the lack of a strong and sustained organizational framework has undercut efforts at modernization. If these structures were more firmly established, other aspects of investment and modernization would be more likely to succeed.

Chapter 10

China:
Moving from Piecemeal
to Comprehensive Modernization

Historically, civil aviation was slow to reach China. Following the 1949 revolution, China's development was largely inwardly focused. The agrarian nature of the country and the predominance of rail transport meant that civil aviation did not serve a significant role in commerce or passenger transport. Chinese airports and infrastructure were quite limited, although in most cases appropriate to the low levels of aviation activity they supported. During this time, the importance of military aviation grew, so that much (if not all) of the air navigation requirements were provided by the defense forces.

Local Response to the Growth in Air Traffic

The opening of the economy to trade, especially in manufacturing, led to increased development of civil aviation in the south, focused on the entrepot of Hong Kong. This growth spurred new airport construction in Shenzhen and Guangzhou, as well as replacement of Hong Kong's Kai Tak with the massive new Chek Lap Kok airport on Lantau Island. The early growth in the south, was quickly followed by growth along the coast, especially in Greater Shanghai. A third wave of development took place in inland, as the government sought to use infrastructure investment to spur growth in interior cities and to take some of the pressure of the teeming coastal areas.

All of this growth put increased pressure on an aviation infrastructure that was not designed to handle the demands of civil aviation, resulting in delays and recurrent operational problems. Throughout the 1980s, Chinese aviation authorities attempted to upgrade existing system through local efforts, with only limited success. By the 1990s, China opened its air navigation market to foreign suppliers, in an effort to modernize its systems as quickly as possible. Recognizing the longer-term opportunity, international suppliers flooded the Chinese market. The Chinese Air Traffic Management Bureau, which was organized on a regional basis, oversaw the program. Each regional office soon embarked on its own deals, resulting in a piecemeal upgrading which added a bit of technology and capacity, but which left China with a patchwork of air navigation systems with little integration.

By 2005, China's airports handled about 100 million passengers and about 20 billion tonne/kilometers of air cargo. Chinese civil aviation has been booming, growing 10 to 15 percent annually since 2000. Over one third of China's airports handle over 1 million passengers per year, with substantial concentrations in flight corridors along the coast. The airspace between Beijing and Hong Kong accounts for about three-fourths of Chinese civil air traffic. Most forecasts estimate continued 10 to 15 percent growth per year for the next decade. Combined cargo and passenger demand is expected to grow at approximately twice the rate of Chinese GDP.

Moving to a Comprehensive Approach

This continued growth and the awarding of the 2008 Olympics to Beijing has prompted China on another massive air navigation initiative, this time with greater emphasis on Chinese participation through joint ventures. When Sydney, Australia hosted the Olympics in 2000, they saw air traffic increase by over 30 percent. Some expect air traffic in China is expected to increase by at least 50 percent by 2008, with the Games generating an additional 15 percent.[1] The Chinese air navigation task of managing this growth is made more difficult by the limitations of existing infrastructure, especially radar systems. There remains an extensive web of airspace restrictions; the Chinese military controls more than three-fourths of Chinese airspace, including some sectors along high density routes.

The General Administration of Civil Aviation of China (CAAC) under China's State Council controls air navigation. The Air Traffic Management Bureau (ATMB) of CAAC governs air traffic affairs in China, is responsible for ATC system planning, funding, and procurement of air traffic control equipment. The ATMB governs: eight Flight information regions; 55 upper or mid airspace control areas; 144 low altitude airspace regions; and over 1200 air routes. The military retains a significant role in the designation and control of flight routings and timing.

China has seen an airport construction boom in the past decade, so that there are now over 130 airports with scheduled services. Air navigation expenditures have also risen, but not as fast as either airport capacity or travel demand. Between 1994 and 2004 over USD 1.2 billion was spent on air traffic control infrastructure and equipment, predominantly primary and secondary radars, VHF communication systems, VOR/DME approach controls, instrument landing systems, and nondirectional beacons for landings. Overall, this capital program has helped modernize Chinese air navigation relative to its previous limited capabilities.

With its penchant for long-term planning, China set out to develop a twenty year plan to modernize and develop its air navigation infrastructure. The piecemeal efforts of the 1980s and 1990s have come to be viewed as necessary steps but inadequate for the future. As part of this process, the government has initiated a process to reform the relevant laws and regulations governing aviation, including the nature and scope of foreign participation.

The centerpiece of this program was the construction of three greenfield area control centers using European technology. Operationally, these three facilities in

---

1   "Getting Airport Ready for the Games," *Financial Times Information Limited – Asia Intelligence Wire* (Chinadaily.com.cn), January 23, 2007.

Beijing, Shanghai, and Guangzhou were established, handling over 70 percent of China's air traffic. The centers included radar and flight data processing, and ADS and datalink capabilities. The centers also retained the ability to interface with the older parts of China's ATM network. In an important illustration of the multinational nature of air navigation, much of the training undertaken by CAAC on the European Eurocat 2000 system was provided by staff from Airservices Australia.

In recent years, China has played an important in regional initiatives to reduce congestion and expand capacity. Reduced vertical separation minima (RVSM) was introduced over a revised South China Sea route structure in November 2001 and was gradually extended to cover more Flight Information Regions across multiple national boundaries. The extension of this program to the Bay of Bengal and the Arabian Sea has enhanced traffic flows between Asia, the Middle East, and Europe.

Choices for the Future

With its relatively underdeveloped infrastructure, China also faces a strategic decision with respect to air navigation: whether to make significant investments in building out a ground-based radar network, or to move more directly to reliance on more satellite-based systems as Australia has done. The latter approach is made more difficult for China because it would require greater cooperation with other countries in automated air traffic control and in the use and governance of satellite technology. China's Air Traffic Management Bureau (ATMB) has made significant progress in modernizing and installing radars along the busiest air routes. This program has replaced procedural control methods which relied on time and space intervals to maintain separation and allowed more capacity as radar safely enables reduced separation between aircraft.

However, ADS-B technology is expected to be preferred to radar in western and interior China, given the greater geographic distances and lower traffic densities. The ADS-B technology is expected to be highly effective and much cheaper than complete radar coverage in the region. This will require a significant role for foreign technology and joint ventures. Once again, this illustrates that a global air navigation system is more likely through commercial rather than political structures.

Chapter 11

India:
The Challenge of Government
Infrastructure in a Booming Market

India has been one of the fastest growing aviation markets in the world, with traffic more than doubling between 1994 and 2006, and forecast to grow by at least ten percent annually through 2011. Aircraft movements have increased more than 60 percent between 2000 and 2006. This growth has been fueled in part by significant airline liberalization and the entry of a number of low-fare carriers operating across all major cities. This growth has placed strains on the air traffic control system, from facilities to equipment to the need for more specialists and trained controllers. This growth in the context of long-neglected infrastructure and oversight has contributed to the below-average safety performance in Indian aviation, ranging from higher accident rates and fatalities to rising rates of near-misses, runway incursions, and delay problems from congested airspace and airside operations.[1]

Background

Indian commercial civil aviation dates back to 1934, with the passage of the Aviation Act of 1934. The state has always played a central role in aviation operations and infrastructure. From the beginning, the central government owned and operated all airports, air navigation services, and the two principal airlines – Indian Airlines (domestic services) and Air India as the international flag carrier. However, for much of the succeeding seventy years, civil aviation was not seen as a high priority and was largely neglected or ignored by successive governments, especially in terms of airport and air navigation infrastructure. As reported in *Air Traffic Management*,

> ... air traffic control systems have often been installed only after the International Civil Aviation Organization (ICAO), or other international organizations have insisted; government-owned airlines have been denied essential funding. As recently as 2000, an Airports Authority of India (AAI) report showed that crucial navigation aids such as the instrument tracking system and the conventional very high frequency omni (radar) were not sufficiently maintained, and that calibration was off because of lack of resources. SS Sidhu, former secretary-general of ICAO, said "sometimes, the problem is that our safety equipment is there, but it is not functional".[2]

---

1   See Alexandra van Marle, "Indian Search for Safety," *Air Traffic Management*, Vol. 13 Issue 4, Winter 2004, pp.19–20.

2   Ibid.

The 1990s

Long a relatively closed economy lagging in development, India embarked on an extensive program of trade, macroeconomic, and financial liberalization in 1991. Subsequently, the restructurings of various government-dominated sectors began to occur. In 1994, the Government ended the domestic monopoly on air services by Indian Airlines, spurring a host of new entrant carriers and unprecedented growth in air travel within the country. The liberalization of international bilateral agreements had a similar effect on international travel, creating new problems of congestion at the main airports.

The industry restructuring also required great separation of infrastructure from the state airlines. Air navigation is run and regulated by the Airports Authority of India (AAI), a state enterprise under the direction of India's Ministry of Civil Aviation. AAI was created in 1995 as a merger of the domestic National Airports Authority with the International Airports Authority, which ran the major airports and air traffic control at Mumbai, Delhi, Chennai, and Kolkata and handled much of the en route and upper airspace traffic. The combined entity has faced huge challenges since its inception, as liberalization of the air market caused unprecedented traffic volumes with airports and air navigation struggling to keep up with these newfound pressures. The legacy of the two separate airport authorities led to the creation of separate domestic and international airports in the major cities (some with shared runways), which makes connecting flights difficult to manage for passengers and controllers alike.

The 1994 reforms and the upheaval in aviation resulted in a period where infrastructure investment and operation could not keep up with the growth in flight operations and passengers. Much attention has been paid to the contentious debate over the privatization of the Mumbai and Delhi Airports, by far the two largest and most profitable in the country. According to AAI, only about 15–20 of the 126 airports are profitable, so that cross-subsidies have always been required. Delhi and Mumbai also present difficult air navigation environments, given the heightened traffic density at both airports and given the severe fogging that pervades Delhi during extended periods each winter.

The Indian Government had long recognized this problem, though, and in anticipation of liberalization had awarded a USD 120 million contract to Raytheon in 1993 to install comprehensive radar coverage and other navigational aids at the key airports and centers. But the program ran into problems almost immediately, including delays in installing hilltop VORs during monsoon season and safety concerns raised about the siting of the control tower at Mumbai Airport. In the wake of these delays, there was growing public discussion of whether the entire project was just too much, that "the sudden jump from an antiquated system to modern, fully automated technology [was] beyond India's ability to handle".[3]

However, the debate took on a different tone altogether in November 1996, when a midair collision occurred between a Saudi Arabian Airlines 747 and a

---

3   Kamlakar Mhatre, "Millennium Facelift for Indian ATC," *Air Transport World*, March 2000, pp. 99–101.

Kazak Airlines IL-76 in the airspace controlled by the Delhi ATC Centre. While the subsequent judicial inquiry did identify aircrew errors and safety standards on Russian-built aircraft, there also was much attention paid to the inadequacies of Indian air navigation.[4] For example, the radars in place at Delhi were unable to provide data blocks associated with individual aircraft that indicated their altitude.[5]

In the wake of the disaster, there was a heightened sense of urgency to modernize air navigation. By 2000, positive control of air traffic over the entire subcontinent had been achieved, backed by fairly comprehensive radar coverage. The initial steps were taken to make sure the program would be able to more easily make transitions to satellite and datalink technologies. The new ATC systems were up and running in 1999 at Mumbai and Delhi. Subsequent to the 1996 midair collision, transponders were made mandatory on all aircraft, so that the new radar displays can now receive and show complete flight data and notify controllers when potential conflicts are detected. Ground radars also were upgraded to have minimum safe altitude warning systems.

Other air navigation improvements also were adopted in the late 1990s. Controller training was changed from one standard program to separate certification for tower, approach, and area control centers, enabling controllers to work to international standards for the first time. Communications infrastructure was upgraded throughout the country using various technologies, with older systems being put in place in lower traffic areas. The new systems also enabled new designations for air routes. Many routes were made unidirectional to increase capacity by allowing reductions in longitudinal separation from 15 minutes to 10 minutes. Overflight traffic from Southeast Asia to the Middle East no longer needed to transit Mumbai airspace.

However, by 2000, gaps still remained in the radar coverage between some major cities, and along the Pakistan border. Although India shares a long border with China, there was no common Flight Information Region boundary there, given the remote geography on both sides and the mountainous terrain. As a result, India-China traffic transited through Pakistan or Myanmar.

Problems also remained in connecting domestic airports within the air traffic control system. This situation was complicated by large amounts of Indian airspace explicitly reserved for use and control by the military. Military controllers did not have direct communications with their civilian counterparts, so that in some cases the airspace was closed to commercial traffic. For example, at the important tourist destination of Goa, airspace was restricted to military aviation during extended parts of the day. Military control of air navigation at Pune, near Mumbai, was said to have contributed to a number of near-misses in the area.

The boom in flight operations and the massive investment in infrastructure also spurred more discontent among the country's 900-plus controllers. Part of the problems came from the claim that reduced separation standards had increased

---

4   John D. Morrocco and Pushpindar Singh, "Tragedy Hits Just Prior to Indian ATC Upgrade," *Aviation Week and Space Technology*, Vol. 145 Issue 21, November 18, 1996, pp. 34–36.

5   Perry Bradley and Gordon A. Gilbert, "Assessing International ATC," *Business and Commercial Aviation*, Vol. 80 Issue 3, March 1997, pp. 27–28.

controller workloads and that updated systems compromised safety because they were inconsistent with historical operating and departure practices. The controllers also felt they had been mistreated within the AAI structure – and that air navigation was seen as not as important as airports. This led to increasing calls for further organizational separation, which continued for more than a decade amidst occasional labor actions by controllers.

Since 2000: The Second Growth Surge

By 2003, a renewed boom in new airlines and flight operations led to new strains on the system. The growth in the 1990s had been driven by new airlines that had little experience or financial capacity, who tried to fly only on the main routes – all of which led to a spate of failures within two years. By 2003, the main private carriers (such as Jet Airways) had become well-established, so the new entrants tended to concentrate on underserved routes and segments, including a surge in low-fare capacity.

The upgrades and modernization of the late 1990s were now proving inadequate in the wake of this next generation of growth and development. By 2004, there were about 4,000 flights per day in India, an increase of 2,500 since 1994.[6] Since 2000, AAI had concentrated on improving air navigation performance at the busiest airports, Mumbai and Delhi, including upgraded radars and enhanced datalink communications. However, AAI had not hired any new controllers since 1999, and some staffing models indicated that the country may have been as much as 50 percent understaffed.[7] AAI's own analysis indicated that they were short more than 100 controllers, or about 15 percent understaffed.[8] This situation led to ongoing tensions between the ATC Guild (the controllers union) and AAI about the risks of staffing levels and hours worked.

The worsening situation increased calls for a new comprehensive civil aviation policy. The policy was based largely on a 2003 Naresh Chandra committee report, *A Road Map for the Civil Aviation Sector*. The report encouraged more extensive participation of the private sector in airport development and operation, but recommended that air navigation remain under governmental control and operation, for security reasons. The report recommended unbundling of air navigation services from AAI through creation of a separate ATC government corporation, with safety oversight by the Director General of Civil Aviation within the Ministry of Transport, and economic regulation through a newly-created Aviation Economic Regulatory Authority (AERA).

Much of the report was well-received, although AAI was opposed to many of the proposed changes. Most of the attention was paid to the greenfield concession airports at Bangalore and Hyderabad in 2005, along with the compromise plan to create a public-private joint venture for Mumbai and Delhi Airports, which was finally

---

6   Alexandra van Marle, "Indian Search for Safety," *Air Traffic Management*, Vol. 13 Issue 4, Winter 2004, p. 19.

7   Ibid.

8   "Crisis what crisis?" *Air Traffic Management*, Vol. 14 Issue 4, p. 31.

enacted in 2006. After having their own airport improvement plan rejected by the Government in 2004, AAI sought to become part of the joint venture in Mumbai and Delhi, and was able to obtain a 26 percent share. (Mumbai and Delhi combined were estimated to represent 60 percent of AAI revenues.) The Government has announced plans to continue seeking private participation in the operation, financing, and investment in airports, continuing with Kolkata and Chennai and then proceeding to secondary cities.

The new laws fundamentally changed airport policy – and practice – in India, yet did little to change the organizational or financial capabilities of AAI in air navigation. But by 2004, it was again apparent that the air navigation system was struggling to keep up and the air traffic control centers were nearing effective capacity at levels that were far below international norms. For example, Mumbai was averaging 25–30 aircraft movements per hour, far below the 40 or more movements in Europe in similar situations. This shortage of takeoff and landing slots resulted in routine delays of 15–20 minutes. Pilots reported continuing problems with radio and telephony contact with controllers, despite AAI's efforts to install national VHF coverage and contract for additional satellite communications capacity.[9] The number of air miss incidents grew each year from 2003 to 2006. Similarly, the number of runway incursions also was increasing over the period.

In the wake of this situation, another select committee was established to make recommendations on air traffic management. The Roy Paul Committee, as it was known, was to suggest ways to alleviate problems and risks in the short-term while also enabling better capacity management and expansion in the longer term. The Committee cited the consequences of extensive delay costs imposed by constrained air traffic management, and was sharply critical of the acute manpower shortages – especially of controllers.[10] The Committee also recommended that a flexible joint-use model of military-civilian airspace be adopted, as major cities were faced with restricted airspace and flight routings that restricted capacity and imposed higher operating costs on airlines. Recommendations also were made and were being studied with respect to reducing take-off separation and to make greater use of simultaneous operations on existing runways.

The Roy Paul report was well-received, but progress in implementation continued to be slow. By 2007, continuing concerns about air safety led to further reviews of the air traffic management system, with AAI recommending an accelerated timetable for implementation of enhancements and upgrades to the existing system. The AAI plan treats each of the four Flight Information Regions (FIRs) as a separate entity, and has favored the lower-cost option of upgrading each of the four systems' functionality through expanded use of instrument landing systems (ILS) and secondary surveillance radar (SSR). In contrast, some airline officials and analysts believe that that long-run effectiveness requires an integrated solution that approaches Indian ATM as a single system rather than four interconnected systems.

In the meantime, Raytheon (who supplied the 1990s ground based radar technology), has been working with AAI and the Indian Space Agency to develop

---

9   Ibid, pp. 30–33.
10 Ibid, p. 33.

the next generation satellite based technology and to try to assure that it would be compatible with the current ground-based system. India has been developing its own satellite-based technology. The country has made extensive commitment to upgrading its ground-based navigation system (known as Geo-Augmented Air Navigation, or GAGAN), spending over USD 100 million. GAGAN is intended to be coupled with the Indian GPS satellite system that is being developed. The air navigation system under development would allow more precision approaches at major airports and more flexible and efficient routes. Given the major travel corridors between Europe and Southeast Asia, the system also could help to bridge the gap in airspace coverage provided by the European system to the west and the Japanese system to the east. However, implementation is moving slowly, due in part to the many demands on AAI and the lack of commercial orientation in this integrated structure. There have been persistent and growing calls for organizational and functional restructuring of AAI.

Looking Ahead

By 2007, Indian air traffic management struggled to keep pace with industry growth and dynamics. Many problems remain: air navigation related delays are widespread, there are severe staff shortages of controllers and technicians, and safety issues, including loss of separation, are a persistent challenge. The Indian military forces control significant parts of the airspace, with only limited agreements on its flexible use. In addition, there remains sizeable uncovered airspace – gaps in Indian skies where aircraft do not have any link with radar.

India's economic growth and liberalization of the airline sector has put much strain on air navigation. There seems to be a cycle of crisis and response, which buys only a bit of breathing room before the next surge of growth threatens to overwhelm the system. The legacy of lackluster state enterprise performance has resulted in a variety of reform initiatives, but they have been somewhat more effective in dealing with airports than air navigation – although even there progress has been slow. While there has been much preliminary and discussion of satellite navigation and ADS-B communications technology, progress by 2007 had been limited in moving toward new technologies.

Overall, further organizational reforms are likely to be needed to help India manage the challenge of growth.

Chapter 12

Africa: Searching for Solutions

The operating environment for African aviation is the most difficult in the world. With less than four percent of the world's flights, Africa experiences about 27 percent of all accidents. Pilots must often use High Frequency Radio because VHF or Radar is nonexistent. Growing numbers of flights over the continent sometimes result in wait times of 5 to 10 minutes to find a moment for pilots to send messages. At other times, pilots talk over each other, so that communication in often lost or unheeded. Much air traffic control is procedural, based on 10-minute longitudinal standards, rather than positive control based on radar or satellite systems. Aviation in Africa is plagued by inadequate maintenance of navigational facilities resulting in frequent failures, poor safety oversight, and lack of skilled technicians to operate and repair the infrastructure.

The small size and limited traffic of most of the countries in sub-Saharan Africa means that developing effective civil aviation organizations is a continuing challenge. Airlines and airports struggle to cover operating costs. Regional agreements and organizations have tended to be limited in scope and subject to a lack of political and economic support from their member states, even when financially supported by multilateral organizations or through aid programs. At the same time, colonial legacies have created air networks that often focus on long-haul connections with Europe based on former colonial ties, rather than being built to enhance economic linkages with neighboring countries or within regions.

The fragmented nature of Africa has led to many efforts to develop large-scale multinational projects. Enthusiasm for these initiatives has waned, though, as continued political instability and limited financial resources make even modest modernization efforts daunting. Devalued currencies make it even more difficult to finance investments that are priced in hard currency. Weak government fiscal positions have made public investment scarce, and a lower priority than other social needs. As a result, suppliers have tended to focus on installation of navigation aids along key routes rather than more comprehensive approaches.

Some regional efforts have been modestly successful. In Southern Africa, satellite-based approach and departure procedures were implemented in 2002 at 37 airports in the 14 Southern Africa Development Community (SADC) States as well as in Kenya and Cape Verde. The project is an excellent example of cooperation between States and IATA to improve navigational procedures, enhance air safety and significantly improve the regularity, efficiency, and cost-effectiveness of air transport in Southern Africa.

In 2003, a major air navigation meeting was held between the Angola, Botswana, Congo, Côte d'Ivoire, the Democratic Republic of Congo, Gabon, Ghana, Namibia, Nigeria, Sao Tome and Principe, Senegal, South Africa, Zambia, and Zimbabwe to improve coordination and investment programs. While there were some improvements in airspace management and operations as a result, the summit predominantly highlighted the many shortcomings and needs of the region's air infrastructure. Overall, governmental and multilateral efforts at improving air navigation have had only limited success. In contrast, there are at least two case studies within Africa that may hold lessons for the future: Cape Verde and South Africa.

Cape Verde

Cape Verde is a relatively isolated set of islands 500 kilometers off the coats of West Africa. In terms of air navigation, Cape Verde sits at the center of two key trade routes – Europe to South America, and the United States to west and southern Africa. This favorable geography has enabled Cape Verde to undertake a massive USD 22 million investment in air navigation, as part of a USD 100 million program to upgrade airports and aviation infrastructure in the archipelago.

The project was developed in 1996 in response to a review of the existing air navigation technology, which had been installed in 1980 and was becoming obsolete. The islands provide air traffic control for the SAL Oceanic Flight Information Region, which covers a large part of the Atlantic Ocean between the west coast of Africa and Brazil. The project evolved to its current objective of becoming a regional aviation hub serving West Africa, as well as an intermediate stop on longer-haul international flights. In addition, the growing volume of overflight revenues provided a ready source of financing.

The project involved three major radar installations and the construction of a new air traffic control center. The project was intended to meet the latest ICAO standards, including full communications and datalink technologies. When it became fully operational in 2005, air navigation benefited from the growing overflight traffic, from increased tourism, and from the development of the oil industry in West Africa (for which Cape Verde is a good staging point). Now that it is in place, however, the technological capability means that it could begin to serve a regional role as West Africa's air navigation center, leaving individual countries to focus on tower and approach operations while contracting en route operations with Cape Verde.

South Africa

South Africa presents an example of dramatic improvements in air navigation organization and operation in a relatively short period of time.[1] Air Traffic and Navigation Services Company of South Africa (ATNS) controls 22 million square kilometers of airspace and has becoming the leading air navigation organization in

---

1   More extensive discussions of ATNS and South African air navigation can be found in "Southern Star," *Air Traffic Management*, Spring 2005, and in W. Stander, "Lessons from the Commercialization of Air Navigation Services in South Africa," in *Essays on Air Navigation: Flying through Congested Skies*, (Montreal: McGill University Institute of Air and Space Law and the International Civil Aviation Organization, 2007), pp. 21–24.

Africa. Since 1994, the number of air traffic movements has grown by more than 150 percent, totaling about 600,000 movements and 20 million passengers in 2003. This traffic represents about half of all traffic in southern Africa.

The current South African air navigation system dates from 1993, when ATNS was created by the government. The legislation established ATNS as a provider of air traffic control and related services on a commercial "user pay" basis. ATNS has, since the 1995/96 financial year, operated entirely from revenue generated from its customer base. ATNS is a state enterprise that is subject to both economic and safety regulation by the government. The government is also the sole shareholder, as represented by the South African Minister of Transport.

ATNS' structure and operational autonomy has enabled it to marshal significant resources for capital modernization and improved operations. The most significant was the South African Advanced Air Traffic System (SAAATS), which covered spending of 600 million rand on major projects between 1993–2005. Three new air traffic control centers were developed. These included strengthened VHF communications, an improved VOR/DME network, an increase in the number of air traffic controllers by 30 percent from 2003 to 2005, and greater efficiencies through the reduction in Flight Information Regions (FIRs) from five to three. Full radar coverage was planned and completed, with new initiatives on Automatic Dependent Surveillance (ADS) and controller Pilot Data Link Communications (CPDLC).

ATNS provides an example of a large developing country that made an overall strategic commitment to improving air navigation performance and safety, and executes this strategy by creation of an independent and self-sustaining organizational structure. ATNS also shows that the use of modern technology such as satellite and datalink communications are a very cost-effective and operationally sound way to upgrade air navigation and the management of African airspace. This is especially true when compared to the cost of installing and maintaining ground-based systems in a fragmented and geographically challenging continent. ATNS has continued to stay abreast of new technologies, such as the trialing of multilateration technologies at Cape Town, and upgrades to satellite systems.

The other major aspect of ATNS' strategy involves regional leadership in air navigation. ATNS chief executive Wrenelle Stander has stated,

> One role of ATNS in the future is to assist the rest of the continent in achieving the development objectives – in effect both as a leadership model and also as a provider. Across Africa each country has its own air traffic control operations, but, because of airlines' drive to push down costs, and improvements in technology, air traffic control is increasingly going to happen more on a regional basis than on a national basis. At ATNS we are positioning ourselves to become one of these regional service providers.[2]

For Africa, the capacity of ATNS creates an opportunity to manage air navigation through contracting, and enables South Africa to amortize the air navigation costs over a larger geographic and traffic market. This commercial version of regional cooperation has begun to be realized, as ATNS has signed commercial agreements to facilitate regional service provision. ATNS provides a host of aeronautical services

---

2 "ATNS: The Next Step Forward," *Air Traffic Management*, Spring 2006.

and training to other African countries. ATNS also has taken the lead in developing and managing VSAT networks across the 14 Southern African Development Community (SADC) countries, linking air traffic control centers and making reliable communication possible across these centers for the first time. ATNS also was working to extend these centers further across northeast Africa and to better connect air navigation in French- and English-speaking countries.

Chapter 13

South America:
Facing a Full Range of Challenges

South America is the fourth largest land mass in the world, after Asia, Africa, and North America, with 17,840,000 square kilometers and has the fifth largest population, after Asia, Africa, Europe, and North America. As with Africa, most of the countries were colonies at one point, in the case of South America mostly colonies of either Spain or Portugal. Most South American countries gained their independence in the early 19th century, so the period of colonization did not have an important impact on the pattern of air service that was established in the latter part of the 20th century.

An Array of ANS Challenges

The countries in South America face a wide array of air navigation challenges. It is a region with relatively little radar coverage, in part because of much of the continent has mountainous terrain and large tracts of jungle but also in part because of the responsibilities for large blocks of oceanic airspace. The Andes, the world's longest mountain range, run down the western edge of the continent and present a geographical challenge to establishing and maintaining radar coverage. Much of the land to the east of the Andes comprises the vast Amazon River basin, largely a tropical rainforest and again an area where establishing and maintaining radar coverage is difficult. These same factors make surface transportation difficult to establish, so in South America, as in many developing countries elsewhere in the world, aviation has the potential to play a large role in economic development. South America's maritime countries provide air navigation services for large blocks of airspace in the western Atlantic and eastern Pacific oceans. Brazil for example is responsible for an oceanic area almost twice its territorial area. Argentina, Chile, Peru and Colombia have similar obligations.

South America also has a large number of independent countries which encompass a wide array of levels of economic development and investment capabilities. For example, the International Monetary Fund estimates that for 2007, Argentina and Brazil, two of the most prosperous countries in the region, have Gross Domestic Products (GDP) per capita of USD 6,549, and USD 5,518 respectively. Bolivia, one of the less prosperous countries, has a GDP per capita of only USD 1,151. As points of comparison, Canada has a GDP per capita of USD 41,348, the United Kingdom has GDP per capita of USD 41,960, Australia has a GDP per capita of 37,982, and the United States has a GDP per capita of 46,082.[1]

For many South American countries, there are little or no financial means to invest in air navigation facilities, equipment, and personnel training. Moreover, most South American airlines are not financially strong, so that structuring a commercially viable and sustainable air navigation system is a challenge. Air transportation services in these countries may be primarily provided by foreign airlines bringing tourists from abroad rather than from a dynamic domestic air transportation industry. Airport fees will barely cover the maintenance of their present facilities, and air navigation fees will hardly pay for the salaries of controllers, let alone the needed capital investments. Within these States, it may be very difficult to justify the investment in new air navigation or air traffic control facilities when these projects may be competing for resources against a new medical equipment needed for a hospital or improved education.

In most South American countries, air traffic control is run by the military, typically the air force. Elsewhere in the world, where there is a strong military influence on air traffic control, such as China, a principal effect is that large blocks of airspace are reserved for the military and closed to civilian operations. In South America, the main problem with military control is that the military has different needs from an air navigation and air traffic control system than does civilian aviation. The military also has different incentives with respect to air navigation than a civilian organization would. For example, should civilian aviation activity grow rapidly while military aviation activity grew more slowly or remained constant, the military who operates the air traffic control system would likely have less of an incentive to invest their resources to keep up with civilian aviation growth than might a civilian operated air traffic control system would. Indeed, facilitating rapid growth in civilian aviation might well increase pressure to remove restrictions on airspace reserved for the military.

Brazil

Brazil, with one of the strongest economies in the region, illustrates the air navigation challenges throughout South America. The September 29, 2006 mid air collision between a Gol Airlines B737-800 and a Legacy 600 private jet, which killed all 154 people aboard the B737, focused attention on Brazil's air traffic control system. Soon after the crash, Brazil military officials said actions of controllers at Brasilia Center resulted in the aircraft traveling in opposite directions along the same airway and at the same altitude. Later, Brazil's lead accident investigator also said that the controllers were partially responsible. The International Federation of Air Traffic Controllers Associations (IFATCA), which represents 50,000 members in 125 countries, said blame is not to be placed on controllers, but on outdated equipment in Brazil's ATC system. IFATCA added, "the air traffic management system in Brasilia

---

1   http://www.imf.org/external/pubs/ft/weo/2006/02/data/weorept.aspx?sy=2005&ey=2 007&scsm=1&ssd=1&sort=country&ds=.&br=1&c=213%2C193%2C218%2C223%2C156 %2C112%2C111%2C299&s=NGDPDPC&grp=0&a=&pr.x=73&pr.y=12.

airspace did not register or correctly detect the true altitude of the Legacy aircraft" when crossing the Brasilia VOR.[2]

In the investigations in the wake of this accident, Brazilians discovered that their airspace is pocked with blind spots, that equipment is faulty and lacks backups, and that pirate radio stations were interfering with communications between controllers and pilots. One underlying problem was that the air force runs air traffic control and the Ministry of Defense, which is responsible for the air traffic control system in Brazil, had failed to keep up with booming civilian traffic, which grew at 15 percent a year or more from 2004 through 2006. The government ignored repeated calls for more air traffic controllers and investment. While control towers lacked essential equipment, and there were shortages of air traffic controllers, airports received expensive facelifts.[3]

Perhaps not surprisingly, Brazil also faces some labor unrest among its air traffic controllers. For example, in December 2006, air traffic controllers staged a work slowdown, protesting alleged poor working conditions and demanding the end of military control of their employment.[4] Such slowdowns have been a recurring theme in recent years.

Shortcomings in Brazil's air navigation system appear to be beginning to affect its economic development. Problems with air traffic control hampered tourism in Brazil in December 2006 as flight delays became more frequent and longer. A consumer survey at the time showed consumers who have bought all-inclusive tour packages in advance are particularly concerned about not being able to travel – sales of the packages were down 45 percent from previous estimates. Travel agents say they are not responsible for delays and cancellations and point the finger at airlines, which, in turn, blame the government for not supplying more trained air traffic controllers at understaffed facilities. These problems have prompted Brazil's President to characterize the air traffic control system as being in crisis and not prepared for tourism increases.[5]

Argentina

Argentina, another country with a strong economy, presents a similar set of challenges to those in Brazil. The aviation industry in Argentina comes under the jurisdiction and management of Argentine Air Force's Air Regions Command. The Argentine Air Force has sole responsibility to provide technical and operational infrastructure for commercial and private operators including air traffic control, landing and navigational aids, communications, meteorology reports, and fire fighting services.

Argentina faced problems reminiscent of those in Brazil in the wake of a lightening strike on March 1, 2007 that damaged Argentina's primary radar facility.

---

2   "Who's To Blame?; Finger-pointing continues in Brazilian midair collision probe," *Aviation Week & Space Technology*, January 29, 2007.

3   "Grounded: Aviation in Brazil," *The Economist*, US Edition, December 16, 2006.

4   "Congested Airports, Delays Will Hamper Brazil Holiday," *Aviation Daily*, December 22, 2006.

5   "Brazil's President Admits Govt. Role in ATC Woes," *Aviation Daily*, March 30, 2007.

While there is a manual (procedural) backup system, many regard it as inadequate and having to rely on it has reduced capacity substantially. In much the same way as the mid-air collision in Brazil highlighted a broader set of air navigation problems in that country, this lightening incident has highlighted a broader set of problems in Argentina. Since reverting to manual control methods, unions and associations of air traffic technicians and professional controllers have reported at least six "near collision" situations involving planes on the ground or in the air.[6] The pilots of Austral, Argentina's largest domestic airline, conducted a brief strike in March 2007 over the radar problem.[7]

But the problems go beyond the loss of a single piece of equipment. Air traffic in Argentina increased four fold between 2002 and 2006, largely because of a growth in tourism. Criticism of air traffic control as operated by the air force prompted the government to order a gradual transfer of air control to a new National Civil Aviation Authority, in September 2006. But both the installation of the new radar and the transfer of air traffic control authority have been delayed, and many believe the risks are increasing. "We are very concerned, the system has deteriorated and the authorities are just denying that there are any problems," said Pablo Biro of the Argentine Air Line Pilots' Association.[8] In Spring 2007, the International Federation of Air Line Pilots' Associations (IFALPA) issued a recommendation to pilots flying in Argentine airspace to be extremely vigilant and alert. Shortly after that, a similar warning was issued by the Federation of Air Traffic Controllers' Associations (IFATCA). In response, the Argentine government raised the pay for air traffic controllers in May 2007.[9]

Looking to the Future

From a technological standpoint, a Global Navigation Satellite System (GNSS) would seem ideally suited to both the challenge of both mountainous and large tracts of rainforest terrain and to the challenge of large blocks of oceanic airspace. But the availability of such technology is not enough. Such systems would likely require a level of cooperation among South American countries that would be easier to achieve with commercialized ANSPs than with the military control that prevails in the region.

Another concern for some countries is reliance on a satellite system provided by another country for both their civilian and military needs. Only one system is currently operational, the GPS system provided by the United States. While the United States has indicated that it will continue to provide GPS at no cost to users, several countries are concerned about the consequences of adopting it as the standard navigation means. Either for strategic reasons, or for more practical legal rules,

---

6   http://ipsnews.net/news.asp?idnews=37836.

7   "Airline News – Latin America," *AirGuide Magazine & AirGuide Online*, March 19, 2007.

8   http://ipsnews.net/news.asp?idnews=37836.

9   "Argentina Raises Air Traffic Controller Pay Amid Safety Fears," *Dow Jones Newswires*, May 23, 2007.

many countries are concerned about the use of the GPS as the needed GNSS for the CNS/ATM systems. Some countries have expressed concern about approving GPS widespread use because, if one accident occurs that can be attributed to a failure in the GPS system, they could be made legally responsible for having approved the use of a system that is beyond their control.[10] While it may be possible to overcome these and other concerns, it's clear that simply having suitable technology in existence may not be enough to get it implemented.

---

10 "Caribbean and South America Regional Air Navigation Plan," IBAC Technical Report Summary, www.ibac.org/Library/ElectF/iran/CAR_SAM_3.pdf.

SECTION FOUR
Air Traffic Management in the United States

This section of the book, Chapters 14 through 16, turns to the situation in the United States, the last major country in the world where air traffic services are still provided by a government agency and funded by excise taxes and general tax revenues. Chapter 14 reviews the history and evolution of the provision of air navigation and air traffic control services in the United States starting with the first night flights guided by bonfires in 1921. The problems facing the FAA today are not new problems and have their origins years, or even decades ago. FAA has had repeated difficulty with its modernization and has always had problems with uncertain and unstable funding. Congress has frequently become involved in detailed FAA management decisions, usually to prevent job losses in specific congressional districts. A series of independent commissions dating back to the 1980s have all concluded that air traffic control be funded by user fees instead of taxes and that the organization that provided air traffic control services have greater independence.

Chapter 15 reviews the changes made to FAA's organizational structure with the formation of the Air Traffic Organization (ATO) in 2004 and examines the challenges that remain for the FAA, if it is to be able to accommodate the expected growth in air traffic. The ATO faces three fundamental challenges as it seeks to modernize and operate an efficient air traffic management system that can handle the expected future growth in air travel.

The first challenge is the disconnect between the cost drivers and the revenue drivers of the air traffic management system. The second challenge is diffused accountability which has lead to continuing poor performance and high costs of its capital investment programs. The third challenge is the lack of organizational independence which has hampered FAA throughout most of its history.

Chapter 16 examines the possible alternatives for reform of the FAA and how well these potential reforms might do in confronting FAA's major challenges. While, the formation of the Air Traffic Organization (ATO) within the Federal Aviation Administration (FAA) has been an important step in improving the management of the air traffic control system in the United States, three fundamental challenges still remain. The first challenge, the disconnect between the cost drivers and the revenue drivers, could be most easily addressed by changing the manner in which the ATO is financed from a system of taxes unrelated to the cost of providing air traffic control services to a system of user fees that more closely matched the cost drivers. To address the second challenge, diffused accountability, the ATO would have to have its funding determined independently from the federal budget process which would probably require having the ATO removed from FAA. The third challenge – the lack of organizational independence – can best be addressed by removing the ATO from the FAA. To avoid potential problems of self regulation, most other countries have established their ANSP as organizationally independent from their civil aviation regulator and the United States needs to do the same thing.

Chapter 14

The Evolution of Air Traffic Control in the United States

Although Federal Aviation Administration (FAA) was not created until the Federal Aviation Act of 1958, the federal government role in civil air transportation began much earlier. This chapter traces the evolution of the government's role in air traffic management. As will be seen, the major problems facing FAA today are not new but are recurrent themes that date back for years or in some cases decades. The chapter then turns to the various calls to reform how air traffic management services are provided that have arisen in response to recognition of these problems.

Prior to 1930

The aviation era began on December 17, 1903 with the Wright Brothers' first flight. At the time, newspapers took little notice, either not believing the reports of the flight or not thinking it significant. Few believed that the aircraft of this era could ever evolve into a useful form of transportation.

Federal government involvement with civil aviation began with the US Post Office. Funds for the carriage of airmail were provided as early as 1916 from monies appropriated for "Steamboats or Other Power Boat Service." Using aircraft and pilots supplied by the US Army, the US Post Office began airmail service on May 15, 1918, and assumed full control of that service by August. Passenger air transportation was rarely successful in these early years because the aircraft of the day could barely compete with surface transportation in terms of either speed or safety. Air travel was still considered a novelty and was largely limited to a few short routes to island destinations. The St. Petersburg-Tampa Airboat Line offered the world's first regularly scheduled airline service using heavier-than-air craft in early 1914, but the service lasted for only three months.

It was only with the advent of transcontinental airmail service that the potential advantages of airplanes began to become apparent. A key to this service was the ability to conduct night flights. The first experimental night flights started in 1921 using bonfires for navigation. The bonfires were soon replaced by electric and gas lighting and by 1924, a portion of the transcontinental airway between Chicago, Illinois and Cheyenne, Wyoming was lit and routine night flights were being conducted along this section. By 1925, the Post Office had completed a transcontinental system of night lighting and landing fields from New York to San Francisco. The Contract Air Mail Act of 1925 (commonly knows as the Kelly Act) was the first major piece of US civil aeronautics legislation.

On May 23, 1926: Western Air Express (WAE) became one of the first US airlines to offer regular passenger service, flying from Los Angeles to Salt Lake City via Las Vegas. In the East, the Philadelphia Rapid Transit Company inaugurated the first daily passenger air service between Philadelphia and Washington, D.C., although this service lasted only five months. In both cases, the fledgling airlines carried both passengers and mail under contracts with the Post Office.

President Calvin Coolidge signed the Air Commerce Act of 1926 on May 20, which instructed the Secretary of Commerce to foster air commerce; designate and establish airways; establish, operate, and maintain aids to air navigation (but not airports); arrange for research and development to improve such aids; license pilots; issue airworthiness certificates for aircraft and major aircraft components; and investigate accidents. The Aeronautics Branch (renamed the Bureau of Air Commerce in 1934) was formed within the Department of Commerce to take on these responsibilities. The first airway light beacon erected by the Aeronautics Branch began operation in December 1926. This type of beacon reached its peak in 1946, when 2,112 were in service. Their number declined during the 1950s, and, despite tremendous technological advancement, the last was not decommissioned by FAA until April 1973.

On May 21, 1927, Charles Lindbergh completed the first nonstop, solo, transatlantic flight, flying 3,610 miles from Roosevelt Field, Long Island, N.Y., to Le Bourget Field, Paris, France, in 33 hours 29 minutes. There had been several other transatlantic flights prior to Lindberg's, one as early as 1919, but they had been conducted by multi-person crews and often in stages. Lindberg's flight captured the public's imagination and raised the public awareness of aviation. Only a few weeks later, in early June 1927, Charles Levine became the first passenger to cross the Atlantic by airplane when he flew nonstop between New York and Germany in a plane he sponsored that was piloted by Clarence Chamberlin. In the wake of Lindberg's flight, this one attracted little attention.

In October, 1927, the International Radio Convention met in Washington, DC to secure international agreements on which radio frequencies would be used by aircraft and airports. In 1929, fifteen airlines formed Aeronautical Radio, Inc. (known as ARINC), to serve as the single coordinator of communications for the air transport industry.

The 1930s

Throughout the 1920s, there was little need for a system of air traffic control to keep aircraft from running into each other. With the exception of transcontinental air mail service, most flights operated during daylight hours under the practice of "see and be seen," an approach that evolved into today's visual flight rules. As aircraft technology improved, planes were increasingly able to fly at night and under worse weather conditions. The need for air traffic control first arose at airports. Early airports rarely had designated runways but consisted instead of large fields covered with sod or cinders. On windy days, pilots all tended to take off and land facing into the wind, but on calm days, planes could take off and land in any direction and collisions became more of a risk. The earliest method of air traffic control was to have someone stand in a prominent location on the air field and communicate with pilots using a system of colored flags. In 1929, St. Louis hired the nation's first air traffic controller, Archie League. Throughout the 1930s, other airports hired air traffic controllers and the system of colored flags was replaced with light guns with colored lenses. These early air traffic controllers operated from control towers which were usually placed on top of the highest structure at the airport to give controllers an unobstructed view.

In 1930, Cleveland, Ohio became the first airport to establish radio control of airport traffic. During the next five years, 20 other cities followed Cleveland's lead. Initially, airlines were reluctant to install radio equipment, in part because the weight would displace revenue producing space and in part because the electrical systems of early aircraft provided insufficient power to operate the radios. There was also little agreement in the early years about the phraseology that would be used in these communications.

On July 1, 1933, the Aeronautics Branch assumed sole responsibility for constructing and maintaining airways, ending the prior arrangement under which this function had been part of the Bureau of Lighthouses. Under the Aeronautics Branch, the first organizational consolidation took place when the number of districts in which this function was organized was reduced from eight to six.

The Federal Aviation Commission submitted its report to the president on January 22, 1935, and recommended the establishment of an independent Air Commerce Commission that would eventually be absorbed, along with agencies regulating other forms of transportation, into an overall transportation agency. The idea garnered considerable support, but it took over 30 years, until 1967, for the Department of Transportation to be formed.

On November 1, 1935, increased commercial air traffic caused the Bureau of Air Commerce to impose the first restrictions on general aviation, restricting their operations along the routes and at the airports used by air carriers. On December 1, 1935, American, Eastern, TWA, and United Airlines formed the first experimental airway traffic control center at the Newark, New Jersey airport. Its purpose was to separate air traffic operating on the airway during instrument flight rules weather. On July 6, 1936, the Bureau of Air Commerce took over operation of the airway traffic control centers at Newark, as well as ones these airlines had been encouraged to establish at Chicago, and Cleveland, signaling the beginning of federal government operation of air traffic control. Up to this time, these centers had been operated by private airline companies, air traffic controllers had not been federally certified, and pilots had not been legally required to use their services. In the fall of 1936, the Bureau of Air Commerce solidified its grip on air traffic control and began commissioning additional air traffic control centers elsewhere in the country. In 1937, the Bureau of Air Commerce launched the first of what would become many air traffic control modernization and extension programs, allocating $5 million to modernize the existing airways and $2 million to extend the airways system.

A major development in the government's role in civil aviation came on June 23, 1938, when President Roosevelt signed the Civil Aeronautics Act of 1938. This law created the Civil Aeronautics Authority, or CAA, as a new kind of federal agency that assumed the responsibilities of the old Bureau of Air Commerce. The administrator of the CAA was appointed by the president with the concurrence of the Senate, giving Congress an explicit role in the management of the air traffic control system for the first time. The administrator's functions under the law were the encouragement of civil aeronautics and commerce, establishment of civil airways, provision and technical improvement of air navigation facilities, and the protection and regulation of air traffic along the airways. Airports were not excluded from the facilities that the administrator could establish and maintain, as they had been under the Air Commerce Act of 1926, although the administrator was prohibited from acquiring any airport by purchase or condemnation.

The 1940s

On November 1, 1941, the CAA began operating air traffic control towers at airports. Prior to this time, towers were operated by local airport authorities, except at CAA-managed Washington National Airport.

In November, 1944, the Chicago Convention brought together delegates from 52 nations to consider issues critical to the future of international aviation. The Chicago Convention established the privileges and restrictions of all contracting states and provide for the adoption of Standards and Recommended Practices (SARPs) regulating international air transport. The Convention accepted the basic principle that every State has complete and exclusive sovereignty over the airspace above its territory and provides that no scheduled international air service may operate over or into the territory of a Contracting State without its previous consent. The Chicago Convention also established the International Civil Aviation Organization (ICAO), as a specialized agency of the United Nations and charged with coordinating and regulating international air travel.

On August 15, 1946, CAA instituted the first user charges by requiring a fee of $5 for registering and recording aircraft titles, with an additional fee of $5 for titles involving liens or other encumbrances. Later in 1946, CAA began providing air traffic control over the North Atlantic in conjunction with the establishment of the North Atlantic Region of ICAO.

On June 30, 1948, Bell Telephone Laboratories made the first public demonstration of the transistor, developed by Bell scientists John Bardeen and Walter Brattain. Another Bell scientist, William Shockley, invented a simpler and improved amplifying device, the junction transistor, which was announced in 1951. Great advances in electronics followed the introduction of first the transistor and then integrated circuits, which quickly replaced the vacuum tube. As had been the case with light beacons, however, FAA was slow to replace vacuum tubes with more advanced technologies. Indeed, it wasn't until 1982 that FAA developed a plan to replace all vacuum tubes in navigational aids with solid state equipment. And, even when the plan was released, the replacement wasn't scheduled to be completed for another 20 years.

By the late 1940s, the growth in air travel began to put pressure on the air traffic control system. The combination of procedures carried over from the 1930s and the higher speeds of aircraft of the 1940s meant that aircraft were being separated by between 50 and 100 miles in the airways. With the growing traffic, there wasn't enough airspace to allow this kind of separation and on busy days controllers were forced to hold aircraft in flight or delay their departures.

The 1950s

In the development of air transportation, the 1950s saw two milestones. 1951 was the first year that passenger miles traveled by air exceeded passenger miles traveled in Pullman railroad cars and 1958 was the first year that the total number of transatlantic passengers traveling by air exceeded the number traveling by sea.

The Civil Aeronautics Authority first experienced budget instability in 1954 when the Eisenhower administration's retrenchment cut CAA's budget to $115.9 million, $20 million less than the agency received in fiscal 1953 and the lowest amount since 1949. The reduction forced the elimination of 1,500 positions, discontinued control tower operations at airports with light commercial traffic, decommissioned nonessential communications stations, and curtailed services to private fliers. The CAA attempted to reduce costs by closing interstate airway communication stations, first established in the early 1940s and no longer needed. The move was met by opposition from Congressmen who wanted to avoid even very small job losses in their districts. Congressional pressure forced CAA to withdraw the plan for these closures. This was the first case of Congress preventing a consolidation of facilities to achieve greater efficiency. It set a pattern that continues to the present.

As the airlines operated more flights and with the general aviation fleet growing by about 5,000 aircraft a year, the congestion and delays that had begun to emerge in the late 1940s continued to grow and the air traffic control system became overloaded. On September 15, 1954, air traffic controllers in the New York area were faced with a combination of a record number of flight plans files and approaching bad weather. On that day, called "Black Wednesday" in the media, over 45,000 airline passengers and hundreds of private aircraft experienced substantial delays. As traffic continued to grow throughout the 1950s, delays grew in major metropolitan areas even during clear weather. In 1956, the first surveillance radar was purchased by the CAA for use in air traffic control centers and the first air traffic control computer was installed at Indianapolis center.

On June 30, 1956, a TWA Super Constellation and a United Air Lines DC-7 collided over the Grand Canyon, Arizona, killing all 128 occupants of the two airplanes. The collision occurred while the transports were flying under visual flight rules (VFR) in uncongested airspace. The accident dramatized the fact that, even though US air traffic had more than doubled since the end of World War II, little had been done to expand the capacity of the air traffic control system or to increase safeguards against midair collisions. Indeed, 65 such collisions had occurred in the United States between 1950 and 1955. This was partly because the ATC system did not have the ability to segregate VFR traffic from instrument flight rules (IFR) traffic, or slow-moving flights from faster ones.

On August 14, 1957, President Eisenhower signed the Airways Modernization Act, which established the Airways Modernization Board charged with "the development and modernization of the national system of navigation and traffic control facilities to serve present and future needs of civil and military aviation." This was the second major modernization initiative, following the initial one in 1937.

By the late 1950s, air traffic controllers were increasingly dissatisfied with their working conditions and pay and began leaving the profession at increasing rates. As a result, CAA was forced to try to hire as many has 400 new controllers per month. The lack of experienced controllers put more pressure on the remaining controllers to work longer hours without breaks. In response to these conditions, a group of controllers formed the Air Traffic Control Association to push for increased pay and better working conditions.

On August 23, 1958, President Eisenhower signed another major piece of aviation legislation, the Federal Aviation Act of 1958. The new statute repealed the Air Commerce Act of 1926, the Civil Aeronautics Act of 1938, the Airways Modernization Act of 1957, and those portions of the various presidential reorganization plans dealing with civil aviation, and assigned the functions to two independent agencies – the Federal Aviation Agency (FAA), which was created by the act, and the Civil Aeronautics Board (CAB), which was freed of its prior administrative ties with the Department of Commerce. The new FAA focused on air traffic management and safety regulation while the CAB focused on the economic regulation of the airlines.

The 1960s

On December 16, 1960, a TWA Super Constellation and a United Airlines DC-8 collided over New York City, killing 128 people aboard the two aircraft and eight people on the ground. The accident was caused by an error by the United Airlines pilot when, perhaps in part because of a problem with his navigation receiver, he flew outside his assigned holding pattern into the path of the TWA plane. However, the accident report also concluded that if the controllers had had surveillance radar available, they might have detected the problem and issued instructions to avoid the accident. This accident increased the pressure to install radar equipment at busy airports.

On March 8, 1961, President Kennedy requested FAA to conduct a scientific, engineering review of aviation facilities and related research and development and to prepare a long-range plan to ensure efficient and safe control of all air traffic within the United States. The review was completed in September and found that the air traffic control system was "being expertly operated by a highly skilled organization," but concluded, in language that would be repeated by numerous studies over the next 40 plus years, that substantial improvements were needed to meet the future challenge of aviation's projected growth. FAA urgently needed an overall systems plan. In effect, the recommended improvement involved a major reorientation of the modernization effort that had been launched only four years earlier.

In January 1962, President Kennedy signed Executive Order 10988, which gave federal workers the right to be represented by trade unions. At the time, FAA Administrator Halaby argued without success that air traffic controllers should be excluded from the provisions of the order because they served a national defense function. In January 1968, a group of New York controllers, with the help of well-known attorney F. Lee Bailey, formed the Professional Air Traffic Controllers Organization (PATCO). Within six months, PATCO had over 5,000 members.

On February 4, 1964, as part of a continuing effort to modernize the National Airspace System, FAA announced the first phase of a long-range plan to gradually reduce the number of flight service stations in the contiguous 48 states from 297 to 150. By now, aviation was a strong and growing commercial and political force in the United States. Whereas earlier consolidations had proceeded without interference, this plan encountered strong resistance from general aviation organizations, individual private pilots, and Congress, reflecting the concerns of communities where facilities were scheduled to be closed. In view of this opposition, Congress attached a rider to the fiscal year 1965 Independent Offices Appropriations Act restraining FAA from closing any flight service stations during fiscal 1965. After restudying their plan, FAA in August 1965 informed Congress that it would not implement the consolidation program; instead, it would evaluate the service needed in each flight service station area on a case-by-case basis.

On April 1, 1967, the Department of Transportation began operations in the same basic form that had first been recommended in 1935. As part of the formation of DOT, FAA ceased to be the independent Federal Aviation Agency and became the Federal Aviation Administration, a modal agency within the new department.

In response to growing congestion, FAA implemented a rule on June 1, 1969, placing quotas on instrument flight rule (IFR) operations at five of the nation's busiest airports between 6 a.m. and midnight. Originally implemented for a six-month period, this so-called "High Density Rule" was subsequently extended to October 25, 1970. At that point, the hourly limitations on operations were suspended at Newark Airport, but retained at New York LaGuardia, New York Kennedy, Washington National, and Chicago O'Hare. Today, nearly 40 years later, these four airports remain among the most congested airports in the United States.

Relations between FAA and PATCO deteriorated quickly. While PATCO was not allowed to strike, PATCO organized a work stoppage in the form of a sickout on June 18 to 20, 1969 that resulted in widespread delays. Not surprisingly, the sickout coincided with Congressional hearings on controller pay and benefits. FAA suspended 80 of the participating controllers and terminated it's agreement with PATCO to withhold dues from paychecks. In October, FAA denied PATCO's request for formal recognition because of the sickout. Two days later, however, President Nixon signed a new executive order which gave the Department of Labor the authority to grant recognition to federal unions.

The 1970s

The Airport and Airway Trust Fund was created on May 21, 1970, when President Nixon signed Public Law 91–258, of which Title I was the Airport and Airway Development Act of 1970 and Title II was the Airport and Airway Revenue Act of 1970. Airport and airway development programs had been inadequately funded from the General Fund and had failed to keep pace with the growth in aviation activity, resulting in a severe strain on the air traffic control system. By establishing an Airport and Airway Trust Fund modeled on the Highway Trust Fund, the hope was that airport and airway development would not have to compete for general Treasury funds. The Airport and Airway Trust Fund would receive new revenues from aviation user taxes levied by the Airport and Airway Revenue Act, plus other funds that Congress might appropriate, to meet authorized expenditures. Questions, and disagreement, about how much of the trust fund could be used for operating expenses as opposed to capital expenditures emerged the following year and continue to this day. The hope that airport and airway development would not have to compete with general Treasury funds has not been realized.

In February 1970, PATCO filed a petition with the Federal Labor Relations Council requesting certification as the exclusive bargaining agent for non-supervisory air traffic controllers. PATCO organized another sickout between March 24 and April 10, 1970 in response to an FAA decision to reassign three controllers, but also in response to an atmosphere of widespread controller discontent. The sickout was ruled an illegal strike and FAA suspended 1,000 controllers and fired 52. On January 29, 1971, the Department of Labor stripped PATCO of its status as a labor organization because of the strike. PATCO posted notice that it would not engage in illegal strikes and on June 4, 1970 was allowed to petition once again to be the bargaining unit for air traffic controllers. In February 1972, FAA announced that the fired controllers could apply for re-employment and 46 of the 52 fired controllers were eventually rehired. On October 20, 1972, the Federal Labor Relations Council once again certified PATCO as the sole bargaining unit for air traffic controllers. On May 17, 1973, the first labor contract was signed between the FAA and PATCO. In August 1974, the Air Transport Association (ATA) decided to withdraw from the flight familiarization program whereby air traffic controllers could have up to eight free flights a year as cockpit observers. In response, PATCO organized a work slowdown until the ATA reversed its decision in October.

On September 26, 1973, DOT submitted to Congress a cost allocation study on how the federal costs of the airport and airway system should be shared among the various users. The report concluded that the proportion should be about 50 percent for air carriers, 30 percent for general aviation, and 20 percent for the military and the public sector. The study also concluded that taxes at the time failed to recover more than 55 percent of the total costs, with the general aviation sector accounting for the largest shortfall. The study recommended that at least a high percentage of the shortfall be recovered through user fees. The issues in this study – the share of costs that should be covered by general aviation and the use of user fees to pay for the airport and airway system – continue to be controversial today.

Between July 28 and July 31, 1976, a PATCO slowdown disrupted air traffic throughout the country. The slowdown was in response to the US Civil Service Commission's delay in completing a pay reclassification for controllers. The Civil Service Commission agreed to expedite the review. In November, in response to PATCO threats of more slowdowns, the Civil Service Commission reversed an earlier decision and upgraded controllers in 8 of the nation's busiest airports.

In January 1978, FAA submitted to Congress a new master plan for the long-delayed modernization of FAA's 292 flight service stations. The first stage involved the installation of semi-automated computer equipment at the 43 busiest stations. The second stage involved a choice between the eventual consolidation of all 292 stations into 20 large ones, co-located at the 20 Air Route Traffic Control Centers, or modernization of up to 150 of the existing stations at their present sites. The decision on this stage was not anticipated until 1982. The third stage would add the capacity for pilot self-briefings, thus completely automating the most important flight service station function.

As with earlier consolidation plans, these proposed consolidations were opposed by general aviation groups and by Congress. Two years later, in 1980, the plan was revised to consolidate the flight service stations into 61 automated stations instead of the original 20 and not to co-locate flight service stations with air route traffic control centers. In 1981, FAA announced a planned regional consolidation that would reduce the number of regional headquarters from 11 to six. That plan also aroused political opposition, and FAA agreed to review the decision. Later that year, FAA announced a revised regional consolidation plan under which the number of regions would be reduced from 11 to nine.

On May 25, 1978, PATCO began slowdowns in response to the refusal of some foreign flag carriers to provide overseas familiarization flights to controllers. The slowdowns lasted two days in May and were repeated for two days in early June. On June 21, PATCO agreed to obey a federal court injunction against such slowdowns. PATCO also agreed to pay a $100,000 fine to the Air Transport Association for violating the permanent injunction against such slowdowns that had been imposed in 1970.

The 1980s and Later

On August 15, 1980, PATCO conducted a one-day slowdown at Chicago O'Hare airport that caused over 600 delays and cost the airlines over $1 million in wasted fuel. The slowdown was to protest FAA's decision not to award O'Hare controllers an annual tax-free bonus of $7,500.

On March 15, 1981, the labor contract between FAA and PATCO expired. Under the provisions of that contract, virtually all the contract provisions were to remain in effect until agreement on a new contract was reached. On April 28, PATCO broke off formal negotiations with FAA and on June 17, PATCO broke off informal talks. The next day, the US District Court rejected PATCO's motion to lift the injunction against PATCO engaging in illegal job actions or strikes. On June 22, DOT and PATCO reached a tentative contract agreement, thus averting a PATCO strike threatened to begin that day. However, PATCO's executive board unanimously recommended rejecting the tentative contract and on July 29, 1981, PATCO membership rejected the contract. PATCO then announced that a nationwide strike would begin on August 3.

Nearly 12,300 members of the 15,000-member Professional Air Traffic Controllers Organization (PATCO) went on strike, beginning at 7:00 a.m., EST, grounding approximately 35 percent of the nation's 14,200 daily commercial flights.

President Reagan issued the strikers a firm ultimatum to return to work within 48 hours or face permanent dismissal. Even before the 7:00 a.m. walkout, a US District Court for the District of Columbia signed an order directing the controllers to return to work. Late in the evening on August 3, another judge of the same court found the union in contempt for failing to obey the first order and imposed an accelerating schedule of fines totaling $4.7 million if the controllers failed to report to work. Approximately 875 controllers returned to work during the 48 hour grace period granted. After expiration of the grace period, about 11,400 controllers were dismissed. Most of those fired appealed the action, and 440 were eventually reinstated as a result of their appeals.

The firings reduced the number of controllers at the full performance or developmental level from about 16,375 to about 4,200. To keep the airways open, approximately 3,000 ATC supervisory personnel worked at controlling traffic. FAA also assigned assistants to support the controllers, and accelerated the hiring and training of new air traffic personnel. Military controllers arrived at FAA facilities soon after the strike began, and about 800 were ultimately assigned to the agency. The combined force was sufficiently large to handle traffic without activating the National Air Traffic Control Contingency Plan, which called for FAA itself to establish rigid, severely curtailed airline schedules and to prescribe routes and altitudes.

The day the strike began, FAA adopted Special Federal Aviation Regulation (SFAR) 44, establishing provisions for implementing an interim air traffic control operations plan. That plan allowed FAA, among others things, to limit the number of aircraft in the national airspace system. The agency implemented a plan knows as "Flow Control 50," under which air carriers were required to cancel approximately 50 percent of their scheduled peak-hour flights at 22 major airports. FAA increased en route horizontal spacing between aircraft under instrument flight rules and kept planes on the ground, as necessary, to maintain this spacing. Medical emergency flights, Presidential flights, flights transporting critical FAA employees, and flights dictated by military necessity were given priority. General aviation flights operated under the most severe restrictions. Aircraft with a gross takeoff weight of 12,500 pounds or less were prohibited from flying under instrument flight rules and aircraft flying under visual flight rules were prohibited from entering terminal control areas. Other general aviation aircraft were served, as conditions permitted, on a first-come-first-served basis.

On October 2, 1981, FAA announced a $10 million contract with the University of Oklahoma to help train new air traffic controllers to replace those fired for participating in the illegal strike. The University would provide FAA-certificated instructors as supplemental staffing for the FAA Academy. The agreement proved to be the first in a series of controller training contracts with the University.

Through the training programs FAA established with the University of Oklahoma and others, FAA was eventually able to rebuild the number of controllers to the point where the last of the special flight restrictions were lifted in 1984. One important legacy of the strike, however, is that the large number of controllers hired during this rebuilding period would all become eligible for retirement at about the same time, creating another potential shortage of controllers.

On January 28, 1982, FAA released a National Airspace System Plan, a comprehensive 20-year blueprint for modernizing the nation's air traffic control and air navigation system. That plan called for consolidation of 20 air route traffic control centers into 16, but was revised a year later to retain all 20 of the centers.

On September 3, 1982, President Reagan signed the Tax Equity and Fiscal Responsibility Act, general tax legislation that increased aviation user taxes. These taxes provided renewed funding for the Airport and Airway Trust Fund, which had received no tax revenues for nearly two years. This was the first interruption in funding for the trust fund. In 1996, there was a second interruption of funding for the Airport and Airway Trust Fund when, on December 31, 1995, the authority to collect aviation user taxes expired at midnight. Loss of this revenue quickly reduced the amount of money in the Airport and Airway Trust Fund. Legislation enacted on August 20, 1996, temporarily reinstated these taxes, but they expired again at the end of 1996. The taxes were reinstated in March 1997 to remain in effect until September 2007. However, the original hope from the 1970s that the trust fund would provide stability in funding for modernization was not realized.

On March 22, 1983, FAA presented to Congress another approach to facility consolidation that was to be reflected in a revised National Airspace System (NAS) Plan. The number of Air Route Traffic Control Centers (ARTCCs) in the continental US was to be reduced from 20 to 16, and the 188 existing terminal radar approach control (TRACON) and terminal radar approach control in the tower cab (TRACAB) facilities were to have been consolidated into about 30 regional or hub TRACONs. Again, the proposed consolidations were not well received by Congress, and eventually, on April 19, 1993, FAA modified its consolidation plan to continue to operate all of the existing ARTCCs and to operate 170 to 175 standalone TRACONs and five consolidated TRACONs.

In 1983, FAA started a small pilot program to contract out the operations of a few airport towers that had low volumes of traffic and that handled only visual flight rule (VFR) operations. The pilot program produced cost savings and was expanded to 17 locations by 1987. FAA concluded that significant cost savings could be achieved with this program and developed a plan to expand it in 1989. By 2002, the operations of 219 towers had been contracted out at an estimated annual savings of $60 million.

By the mid-1980s, the nation's air traffic controllers became increasingly dissatisfied with their relations with the FAA. New equipment was slow to become operational and existing equipment was becoming increasingly difficult to maintain. In 1987, controllers voted to form a new union, the National Air Traffic Controllers Association (NATCA).

On March 30, 1994, another outside factor had an important effect on FAA operations when President Clinton signed the Federal Workforce Restructuring Act of 1994. The act targeted a reduction of 272,900 federal employees between 1993 and 1999 through a program of buyouts of up to $25,000 to personnel willing to leave federal service. The buyout was offered in conjunction with an early retirement option. FAA initially offered the buyout to its personnel between March 31 and May 3, 1994. Some employees received subsequent buyout offers, some with a deferred retirement option, during 1994 and 1995. Eventually, more than 3,000 FAA employees received buyouts.

These buyouts were a major factor in the reduction of FAA's full-time equivalent workforce, which fell from 52,352 in fiscal 1992 to 47,738 at the end of fiscal 1996. Thus, much of the decline in employment was not due to efficiency gains or a careful assessment of FAA needs, but because FAA was caught up in a broad-brush government-wide effort to reduce federal employment.

History and Background: Major Themes

Several themes seem to run through the evolution of FAA. One is that new modernization initiatives have been a recurrent theme since 1936. FAA has not been quick to replace old technology, using light beacons into the 1970s and vacuum tubes well into the 1990s. Concerns about being able to upgrade and expand the air traffic control system to accommodate anticipated growth in air traffic have been almost continual since the early 1960s. Indeed, many of the conclusions of the reports written over the last 40 years all sound as if they could have been written today.

A second theme is that both FAA and its predecessor agencies have been subject to uncertain and unstable funding. Indeed, the Airport and Airway Trust Fund was formed because of concerns about the inadequacy of funding from general Treasury funds. However, the trust fund hasn't worked out to be the funding solution its originators had hoped. In every year but one since 1970, a portion of FAA's funding has had to come from general Treasury funds and even the trust fund revenues have had to go through the congressional budget process. In addition, the taxes that feed the trust fund have been allowed to expire on two separate occasions.

A third theme is that Congress, often at the urging of aviation special interest groups, has become involved in FAA management decisions. In the clearest example, Congress has repeatedly blocked, in one way or another, virtually every attempt FAA has made to improve the efficiency of their operations through facilities consolidation.

Calls for Reform

Concerns about FAA's persistent difficulties in modernizing and expanding the nation's air system to accommodate growth in air travel have given rise to a series of calls for reform of FAA. While the most far-reaching proposals have not been enacted nor have all of FAA's major problems been addressed, some important changes have been made as a result of these calls for reform.

The first presidential commission to call for substantial reforms for FAA was the Aviation Safety Commission, which released its report in April 1988. Among its conclusions was that instability and uncertainty in the level of resources available to FAA contribute to many of the problems observed in field operations including uneven flows of new hires, particularly among safety inspectors, airways facilities technicians, air traffic controllers, and support staff. The commission also found that throughout the budget cycle, as much as one-fourth of FAA management time that could have been devoted to operations in the field was devoted instead to contingency planning for possible budget cuts. Personnel, procurement, budget, and appropriations practices were found to be major obstacles to implementing the necessary changes in air traffic control. Among the Aviation Safety Commission's recommendations was that FAA be removed from the Department of Transportation and established as an independent organization funded by user fees that would cover all capital and operating costs including the provision of navigational aids, with the exception of those services provided to the military. The Commission also recommended that FAA be allowed to develop its own personnel and procurement rules. Finally, the Aviation Safety Commission was concerned about the frequent turnover among FAA administrators and recommended a fixed seven-year term.

On August 19, 1993, the National Commission to Ensure a Strong Competitive Airline Industry released its recommendations. The commission focused primarily on the economic health of the commercial airline industry, but its report called for FAA to become an independent federal corporate entity with its expenditures and revenues removed from the federal budget. The new body was proposed to be exempt from the rigidities of government procurement and personnel rules, and to maintain accounting practices that were consistent with best practices in the private sector. It would also be granted the right to raise capital in the manner of a private firm by issuing long-term bonds. This commission pointed out that one of the difficulties faced by FAA under its structure as an agency within DOT and under governmental budgeting rules was that the Airport and Airway Trust Fund's budget surplus was used to count against or mask the federal government's general deficit in the same way the Social Security surplus was used, rather than being available to support investments in air travel infrastructure. The unified budget concept forced all government fiscal operations to share a common bottom line, and so encouraged the reduction of services and capital spending throughout government in response to deficit concerns. One of the commission's goals was to remove the provision of air traffic management services from this constraint.

About a month later, on September 7, 1993, Vice President Gore released the report of the National Performance Review, a study of the operations of the federal government. The report's most far-reaching recommendation concerning FAA was its proposal for creating a government-owned corporation to provide air traffic control services. Following up on that recommendation, on March 3, 1994, Vice President Gore and Transportation Secretary Federico Peña announced the Clinton administration's proposal to create a new Air Traffic Services Corporation to operate, maintain, and modernize the air traffic system. Under the proposal, 38,000 FAA employees involved in providing air traffic services would become part of a new not-for-profit government corporation. Financial support for the corporation would be derived from user fees levied upon commercial aviation, subject to approval by the Department of Transportation.

Almost immediately, aviation leaders in Congress objected to the proposal. The chairmen of the House and Senate aviation subcommittees at that time, Representative James Oberstar and Senator Wendell Ford, issued a joint statement arguing that Congress should retain a role in overseeing air traffic control, but that under this proposal they would have none. Similarly, the chair of the Senate Commerce Committee, Senator Fritz Hollings, stated that instead of creating an air traffic control, or ATC corporation, the "real" problems in FAA needed to be addressed.

While the proposal to create the United States Air Traffic Services Corporation did not succeed in overcoming this opposition, the mounting pressure to address FAA's problems did have some results. On August 23, 1994, as part of the Federal Aviation Administration Authorization Act of 1994, which provided fiscal year 1994–1996 funding and authorization for FAA's programs, a fixed five-year term of office for the FAA administrator was established to counter concerns highlighted by the Aviation Safety Commission about frequent turnover in the job. In August 1997, Jane Garvey was sworn in as the first FAA administrator appointed for a fixed term.

On April 1, 1996, reforms were enacted that gave FAA new flexibility on personnel and procurement policies, a change made possible by legislative relief from various statutory requirements passed the previous year. The new acquisition management system aimed at reducing the time and cost of acquiring systems and services while making the acquisition workforce more accountable. The new personnel system was intended to speed recruitment and to reward outstanding employees while dealing effectively with substandard performance.

On February 12, 1997, the White House Commission on Aviation Safety and Security released its final report. Among its recommendations were that the users of the National Airspace System should fund its development and operation. The commission found that the system of funding air traffic control through the excise taxes operating through the trust fund provided little direct connection between the excise taxes paid and services provided or the amount made available to FAA through the budget and appropriations process. This commission recommended replacing the traditional system of excise taxes with user fees so that revenues and spending might be more closely matched.

The Mineta Commission and the Air Traffic Organization

In December 1997, the National Civil Aviation Review Commission, chaired by former Congressman Norman Mineta, issued its report. The so-called Mineta Commission was blunt in its three major criticisms of FAA's situation. The first was that federal budget rules were found to be "crippling." They concluded that federal budget procedures were "inappropriate for a system controlling commercial operations that needs to be driven by demand for services." The second criticism was that there were "too many cooks" involved in air traffic management decisions, which made authority and accountability too diffused. They stated that while FAA, DOT, the aviation industry, the administration, and Congress all wanted to make the system work efficiently, there were simply too many different groups who viewed themselves as in charge. Finally, they found that increasing operational costs were "freezing out" capital investments under federal budget caps. None of these criticisms were new, but they reflected the belief that the fixed term for the administrator and the personnel and procurement reforms were not going to be sufficient to solve FAA's problems.

The Mineta Commission's recommendations were not as dramatic or far-reaching as those of earlier commissions and studies. They recommended neither a corporatization of FAA nor removing air traffic control activities from FAA or from DOT. Instead, they recommended that services related to the air traffic system be placed in a Performance-Based Organization (PBO), which would be managed by a chief operating officer and overseen by a board of public interest directors. In addition, they recommended that FAA should institute a cost accounting system and be given authority to implement innovative programs involving leasing and borrowing authority. They also recommended, in line with their major criticisms, that the revenue stream funding air traffic control activities become cost based and that it be shielded from federal budget caps. These recommendations were not nearly as objectionable to some of the established aviation interests as earlier commissions' recommendations had been.

The PBO proposal didn't take Congress, the administration, the secretary of transportation, or the FAA administrator out of the loop, nor did it remove air traffic control from FAA, thereby leaving FAA dramatically smaller in terms of budget and employment. The Mineta Commission recommended that the FAA be primarily funded through cost-based user fees for commercial passenger and air cargo carriers and a fuel tax for general aviation. The commission acknowledged that the current general aviation fuel tax did not cover the costs general aviation imposed on the system and recommended that the magnitude of the fuel tax be re-evaluated. Even so, the general aviation and business aviation communities did not feel nearly as threatened that this proposal would lead to substantially increased costs for them, as had been the concern with some of the earlier proposals.

The PBO proposal was generally well received and in December 2000, President Clinton signed an executive order and Congress passed supporting legislation that, together, provided FAA with the authority to create the performance-based Air Traffic Organization, or ATO, to control and improve FAA's management of the modernization effort. Working out the details of what the ATO would include and finding a chief operating officer took some time. It wasn't until February 2004 that FAA reorganized, transferring 36,000 employees, most of whom worked in air traffic services and research and acquisitions, to the ATO. Russell Chew, a highly respected former pilot and executive at American Airlines, was appointed as the first Chief Operating Officer.

While the ATO faces substantial challenges, some encouraging steps have been taken since February 2004. One major aspect of the ATO organizational structure is that capital investment and operations were brought more closely together. In principle, this should allow the ATO to improve overall program management, including areas such as on-time delivery of modernization programs and management of program costs. Historically, FAA capital projects were geared to introduce newer technology and more reliable services. But FAA developed capital and operating budgets separately, with success for capital investments defined simply as completing the capital programs. It has always been striking that FAA's justification for new capital projects virtually never included what might be called the business case for capital investments resulting in operating cost savings. While the business case was sometimes examined quietly within FAA, it was rarely used as a justification for choosing one potential project over another. The result has typically been higher operating costs even when capital projects were completed. The ATO is now changing investment priorities to also emphasize operating cost efficiencies.

A second important change with the formation of the ATO has been a new emphasis on developing a cost accounting system and a labor distribution system. There had been attempts to develop cost accounting systems prior to the formation of the ATO, but they had been more in the nature of demonstration projects applied to a limited portion of FAA's activities rather than an operational system designed to support management decision making. Such systems are difficult to develop and implement and are not yet complete, but as they improve, they should allow the ATO to do a better job of managing costs and focusing resources in line with their business plan.

A third change with the ATO has been the development of performance metrics and operational goals based on those metrics. ATO's management believes that much of their success will depend on how effectively performance is measured and how well those measurements are used to reinforce individual and organizational accountability and improvement. As a further step to improve accountability, the ATO has reduced the layers of management from eleven to six. The metrics also reflect ATO 's move to more of a customer focus than has governed air traffic control decisions in the past.

Many in the aviation community are hopeful that the ATO can result in some improvements both in how the air traffic management system is operated and in the capital investment program. However, the ATO has only been in operation for about two years, and it's clearly too soon to tell how successful the changes the ATO is trying to implement will be. The ATO also faces a culture of resistance to change among many of its employees. A panel of air traffic control experts assembled by GAO concluded that FAA is an environment where multiple stakeholders with entrenched interests struggle to preserve their interests and to retain control or influence. There are also concerns that the ATO still faces at least three fundamental challenges to effective long-term management of the air traffic management system.

Summary

The major problems facing FAA today are not new but are recurrent themes that date back for years or in some cases decades. FAA has had repeated difficulty with its modernization programs continuing to use light beacons into the 1970s and using vacuum tubes into the 1990s. FAA has always been subject to uncertain and unstable funding and the hope that the Airport and Airway Trust Fund would resolve these problems has not been realized. Congress has frequently become involved in detailed FAA management decisions, usually to prevent job losses in specific congressional districts.

In response to these recurring problems there have been a series of independent commissions examining the FAA dating back at least to the late 1980s. While the recommendations of these commissions have varied in their details, all have been consistent with their recommendations that air traffic control be funded by user fees instead of taxes and that the organization that provided air traffic control services have greater independence. In 2004, the ATO was formed within the FAA to bring all the air traffic control related functions together. While the ATO has been able to make some important improvements in how air traffic control is managed, the fundamental challenges that have hampered air traffic control in the United States for decades remain to be addressed.

Chapter 15

Fundamental Challenges
that Remain for FAA

Introduction

The formation of the Air Traffic Organization (ATO) in 2004 has both streamlined decision making and brought decisions about capital investment and operations more closely together in FAA's organizational structure. ATO has placed greater emphasis on developing a cost accounting system and has emphasized developing performance metrics and operational goals. These could be important improvements in air traffic management in the United States, but the challenges the ATO faces are enormous and the changes made thus far won't be enough to meet those challenges. Since 1995, GAO has designated the ATC modernization program a high-risk information technology initiative because of its size, complexity, cost, and problem-plagued past.[1] Under the best of circumstances, the ATO would face a difficult task in its capital projects because they tend to be complex and often push the edge of available technology.[2] But the ATO does not face the best of circumstances. Instead, three fundamental barriers, which can also be viewed as challenges, remain that severely impede the ATO from building and operating an efficient air traffic management system to handle the anticipated growth in air traffic:

1. Disconnect between the cost drivers and the revenue drivers.
2. Diffused accountability.
3. Lack of organizational independence.

Disconnect Between Cost Drivers and Revenue Drivers

FAA, including ATO, is financed primarily from specific excise taxes that go into the Airport and Airway Trust Fund with some contribution from the general fund. Table 15.1 shows the current aviation excise tax structure. Table 15.2 shows the revenue from these taxes, broken down both by the type of tax and by how much is paid by each industry segment. The vast majority of the tax revenue comes from commercial passenger travel. As can be seen at the bottom of the table, taken together the four

---

1 In 1999, FAA's Financial Management was also designated as High Risk by GAO, but because of improvements in FAA's cost accounting system, it was removed from this designation in 2005. High-Risk Series: An Update, GAO–05–207.

2 National Airspace System, Transformation Will Require Cultural Change, Balanced Funding Priorities, and Use of All Available Management Tools, GAO–06–154.

Table 15.1   United States aviation excise tax structure
(Taxpayer Relief Act of 1997, Public Law 105–35)

Aviation Taxes	Comment	Tax Rate
PASSENGERS		
Domestic Passenger Ticket Tax	Ad valorem tax	7.5% of ticket price (10/1/99 through 9/30/2007)
Domestic Flight Segment Tax	"Domestic Segment" = a flight leg consisting of one takeoff and one landing by a flight	Rate is indexed by the Consumer Price Index starting 1/1/02 $3.40 per passenger per segment during CY2007
Passenger Ticket Tax for Rural Airports	Assessed on tickets on flights that begin/end at a rural airport.	7.5% of ticket price (same as passenger ticket tax). Flight segment fee does not apply
International Arrival and Departure Tax	Head tax assessed on pax arriving or departing for foreign destinations (and US territories) that are not subject to pax ticket tax	Rate is indexed by the Consumer Price Index starting 1/1/99 Rate during CY2007 = $15.10
Flights between continental US and Alaska or Hawaii		Rate is indexed by the Consumer Price Index starting 1/1/99
		$7.50 international facilities tax + applicable domestic tax rate (during CY07)
Frequent Flyer Tax	Ad valorem tax assessed on mileage awards (for example, credit cards)	7.5% of value of miles
FREIGHT / MAIL		
Domestic Cargo/Mail		6.25% of amount paid for the transportation of property by air
AVIATION FUEL		
General Aviation Fuel Tax		Aviation gasoline: $0.193/gallon Jet fuel: $0.218/gallon
Commercial Fuel Tax		$0.043/gallon

Source: http://www.faa.gov/about/office_org/headquarters_offices/aep/aatf/media/
Simplified_Tax_Table.xls.

taxes on passengers amount to 86.5 percent of all tax revenues. The far right column of Table 15.2 shows the share of total taxes paid by each segment of the aviation industry. US commercial passenger carriers flying large jet aircraft pay 64.5 percent; regional jets taken together pay 9.9 percent, and general aviation taken together pays 3.3 percent. If all segments of commercial passenger operations including air taxis (Part 135 non-scheduled passenger) are taken together, commercial passenger operations pay 88.5 percent of the total taxes.

Most of the trust fund revenues are determined by two factors: the number of passengers traveling and the prices these passengers paid for their tickets. The costs of operating the air traffic control system, however, are driven primarily by entirely different factors – the number of aircraft using the system and which specific services within the system these aircraft use. This disconnect between revenue drivers and cost drivers creates two types of potential problems. The first is that the share of the revenue contributed by each segment of the industry may not reflect the share of the costs that segment imposes on the air traffic control system. The second is that even if each segment of the industry happened to be paying its appropriate share at a given point in time, which doesn't appear to ever have been the case, changes in how the industry operated could have much different impacts on revenue than it did on costs.

FAA cost allocation studies

Starting in 1973, FAA has sponsored a series of cost allocation studies that have attempted to determine the share of FAA's costs that could be allocated to each major sector of aviation. Table 15.3 summarizes the principal findings of these studies. As can be seen in the table, the studies have all reached remarkably similar conclusions. The reasons for the differences in the 1995 study are discussed below. The first study, in 1973, found that air carriers were responsible for 50 percent of the costs while general aviation was responsible for 30 percent with the remaining 20 percent attributed to public use which includes military use of the airport and airways system. Through subsequent studies in 1978, 1985, and 1991, the air carrier share steadily increased from 50 percent to 62 percent while the general aviation share dropped from 30 percent to 26 percent and the public use share dropped from 20 percent to 12 percent. These changes in shares between 1973 and 1991 are to be expected since during that period, air carrier traffic nearly doubled while both general aviation and military flights, a primary component of public use, declined.

The 1995 study shows a markedly higher share for air carriers and much lower shares for both general aviation and public use than the earlier studies. There are several reasons for these changes. One, of course, is the continued growth in air carrier traffic and continued declines in general aviation and military traffic. A second reason is that Part 135 nonscheduled service, commonly known as air taxis, were considered part of air carriers in the 1995 study whereas they had been considered part of general aviation in all of the prior studies. In 1995, air taxis accounted for only 3 percent of the costs, so without this change, the general aviation share would have been 3 percent higher and the air carrier share would have been 3 percent lower. However, this change would have made a greater difference in 1991 and earlier years since air taxi traffic had declined by 36 percent between 1991 and 1995.

Managing the Skies

Table 15.2   Taxes by type and by industry segment (millions)

Industry Segment	Passenger Ticket Tax	Segment Tax	International Passenger Tax	Alaska-Hawaii Passenger Tax	Waybill Tax	Commercial Fuel Tax	GA Turbine Fuel Tax	GA AvGas Tax	Total User Tax	Total User Tax (%)
US Commercial Passenger Carriers	$3,772.5	$1,319.4	$724.5	$57.2	$24.8	$281.7	$0.0	$0.0	$6,180.1	64.5%
Foreign Carriers	$64.3	$21.0	$746.1	$11.5	$1.1	$9.0	$0.0	$0.0	$853.1	8.9%
Regional Airlines-T-prop/Piston	$105.7	$58.7	$14.4	$0.0	$0.1	$12.3	$0.0	$0.0	$191.2	2.0%
Regional Airlines- Jets<60 seats	$483.3	$205.6	$9.2	$0.0	$1.2	$51.0	$0.0	$0.0	$750.3	7.8%
Regional Airlines- Jets 61+ seats	$126.2	$49.2	$5.9	$0.0	$0.5	$19.0	$0.0	$0.0	$200.8	2.1%
Charter Flight on US Carrier	$36.5	$11.8	$34.3	$1.2	$0.2	$3.9	$0.0	$0.0	$88.0	0.9%
Passenger Subtotal	**$4,588.4**	**$1,665.8**	**$1,534.4**	**$69.9**	**$28.0**	**$377.0**	**$0.0**	**$0.0**	**$8,263.5**	**86.3%**
US Commercial Carrier Freight	$0.0	$0.0	$0.0	$0.0	$397.9	$46.5	$0.0	$0.0	$444.4	4.6%
Foreign Carrier Freight	$0.0	$0.0	$0.0	$0.0	$9.4	$4.2	$0.0	$0.0	$13.6	0.1%
Regional Airline Freight	$0.0	$0.0	$0.0	$0.0	$20.0	$9.7	$0.0	$0.0	$29.8	0.3%
Freight Subtotal	**$0.0**	**$0.0**	**$0.0**	**$0.0**	**$427.4**	**$60.4**	**$0.0**	**$0.0**	**$487.8**	**5.1%**
Fractional Ownership Programs	$51.9	$7.2	$1.1	$0.1	$0.0	$8.0	$0.0	$0.0	$68.2	0.7%
Non-Scheduled Part 135 Passenger	$179.8	$13.0	$3.9	$0.0	$0.0	$17.0	$0.0	$0.0	$213.8	2.2%
Non-scheduled Part 135 Freight	$0.0	$0.0	$0.0	$0.0	$28.2	$17.4	$0.0	$0.0	$45.6	0.5%
Fractionals / Non-Sched Part 135 Subtotal	**$231.6**	**$20.2**	**$5.0**	**$0.1**	**$28.2**	**$42.4**	**$0.0**	**$0.0**	**$327.6**	**3.4%**

Continued – Table 15.2 Taxes by type and by industry segment (millions)

Industry Segment	Passenger Ticket Tax	Segment Tax	International Passenger Tax	Alaska-Hawaii Passenger Tax	Waybill Tax	Commercial Fuel Tax	GA Turbine Fuel Tax	GA AvGas Tax	Total User Tax	Total User Tax (%)
General Aviation-Turbine	$0.0	$0.0	$0.0	$0.0	$0.0	$0.0	$140.2	$0.0	$140.2	1.5%
General Aviation-Piston	$0.0	$0.0	$0.0	$0.0	$0.0	$0.0	$0.0	$17.7	$17.7	0.2%
General Aviation-Rotor	$0.0	$0.0	$0.0	$0.0	$0.0	$0.0	$0.1	$0.0	$0.1	0.0%
General Aviation Subtotal	**$0.0**	**$0.0**	**$0.0**	**$0.0**	**$0.0**	**$0.0**	**$140.3**	**$17.7**	**$157.9**	**1.6%**
Government/Military	$0.0	$0.0	$0.0	$0.0	$0.0	$0.0	$0.0	$0.0	$0.0	0.0%
Tax Exempt	$0.0	$0.0	$0.0	$0.0	$0.0	$0.0	$0.0	$0.0	$0.0	0.0%
Not Classified by User Type	$0.0	$0.0	$0.0	$0.0	$0.0	$0.0	$0.0	$0.0	$0.0	0.0%
ETMS Subtotal	**$4,820.1**	**$1,686.0**	**$1,539.4**	**$70.1**	**$483.6**	**$479.7**	**$140.3**	**$17.7**	**$9,236.8**	**96.4%**
Commercial	$109.0	$60.9	$0.0	$0.0	$0.1	$12.5	$0.0	$0.0	$182.5	1.9%
Military	$0.0	$0.0	$0.0	$0.0	$0.0	$0.0	$0.0	$0.0	$0.0	0.0%
General Aviation	$0.0	$0.0	$0.0	$0.0	$0.0	$0.0	$139.0	$20.5	$159.4	1.7%
Non-ETMS Subtotal	**$109.0**	**$60.9**	**$0.0**	**$0.0**	**$0.1**	**$12.5**	**$139.0**	**$20.5**	**$341.9**	**3.6%**
Total	**$4,929.1**	**$1,746.9**	**$1,539.4**	**$70.1**	**$483.7**	**$492.2**	**$279.2**	**$38.1**	**$9,578.7**	**100.0%**
Total (%)	**51.5%**	**18.2%**	**16.1%**	**0.7%**	**5.0%**	**5.1%**	**2.9%**	**0.4%**	**100.0%**	

Note: Calculated taxes are adjusted to IRS-certified total amounts for each tax type. Totals may not add due to rounding.

Source: http://www.faa.gov/about/office_org/headquarters_offices/aep/aatf/media/Revised_Data_Detail.xls.

A third reason is that in 1995 the Airport Improvement Program grants were allocated to users according to the legislative requirements of the grants whereas in the 1985 and 1991 studies, they were allocated based on the airport activities funded by the grants. A fourth reason is that common costs were allocated somewhat differently in the 1995 study than in prior studies.

Table 15.3   Summary comparison of FAA cost allocation results

Percentage Allocation of FAA Costs By User Group

Year	Air Carrier	General Aviation	Public Use	Overflights
1995	81	12	7	1
1991	62	26	12	
1985	60	27	13	
1978	58	27	15	
1973	50	30	20	

Note: Overflights were not considered in FAA cost allocation studies prior to 1995. Air Taxis were considered part of General Aviation in 1991 and prior studies. Air Taxis are included in Air Carriers in the 1995 study and accounted for 3 percent of total costs. The 1991 study was an update of the 1985 study.

Sources: A Cost Allocation Study of FAA's FY 1995 Costs, Final Report, March 19, 1997, GRA, Incorporated. http://www.faa.gov/library/reports/cost_allocation/.

With both air traffic control and other services that FAA provides, there are substantial joint and common costs. For example, commercial air carriers, general aviation, and military flights all make use of towers, TRACONs, and En Route Centers. While the operating costs of those facilities may vary with the amount of traffic they handle, the cost of the buildings and hardware are fixed. The same is true of many navigational aids. It is relatively straightforward to allocate the incremental operating costs to various user groups based on the activities at the facilities and the cost allocation studies have done so using activity data and statistical cost models. The approaches used have been widely accepted. Allocating the fixed costs that are common to providing services to more than one user group is both more complicated and subject to more disagreement among user groups.

There are three basic approaches that might be considered for allocating common costs to user groups. One would be simply to allocate all of the costs to a single group and have the other groups bear none of the costs. This approach would be valid if there was a single dominant user group and all of the common costs would have been incurred even if this dominant user group were the only users of the system. Some general aviation interests have argued that commercial air carriers should pay all of the common costs of the air traffic control system and general aviation should pay none because the system was designed to meet the needs of air carriers and none of the fixed costs are needed to serve general aviation's needs. As will be seen later in this chapter, the volume of general aviation activities at various air traffic control facilities is simply too large to allow this to be a credible argument. Were there no general aviation activities, these facilities either would not have been needed or could have been made significantly smaller and thus less costly.

A second approach would be to allocate the common costs in direct proportion to the direct costs. Under this scheme, if a user segment was responsible for 20 percent of the direct costs of a type of facility, that segment would be allocated 20 percent of the common costs of that type of facility. Such an approach has the virtue of being simple and seeming intuitively fair. Unfortunately, the proportional approach has some drawbacks when applied to air traffic control. There are no user charges for air traffic control in the United States, so the patterns of facilities use that are seen are based on a price of zero. Thus the patterns of use don't reflect the value the users place on the use of the facilities. By allocating the fixed costs in proportion to the direct costs, the implicit assumption is that all users place the same value on the services, an assumption that seems unlikely at best.

A third approach is to allocate the common costs in a way that reflects the value the various users place on the use of the facilities. This technique, known as Ramsey pricing, was used in both the 1985 and 1995 studies. Ramsey pricing techniques are often used to allocate fixed and common costs in large networks, such as electrical utilities and telecommunications. Under Ramsey pricing, a commercial air carrier which places a higher value on air traffic control services than would be typical for a general aviation piston-engine aircraft would be allocated a higher share of the fixed and common costs. From the perspective of economic efficiency, Ramsey Pricing, which assigns common costs to users in inverse proportion to their elasticities of demand, results in the least distortion from an economically efficient outcome because it minimizes the degree to which users alter their consumption from what would have occurred under marginal cost pricing. The fundamental advantage of Ramsey Pricing is that it allows the service provider to achieve cost recovery with minimal departure from economic efficiency. For the FAA, this would allow the agency to fully recover its costs while eliminating as few customers as possible due to increased taxes/user fees. In other words, Ramsey Pricing would charge higher taxes/fees to those consumers who are least likely to change their behavior based on higher costs. From a practical perspective, Ramsey pricing as applied in the 1995 cost allocation study assigns a much smaller share of common costs to general aviation than would be the case with a proportional allocation, but obviously a larger share than allocating all of the common costs to commercial air carriers.

The network nature of air traffic control will always result in a high percentage of fixed and common costs. However, the improved cost accounting system implemented by the ATO should reduce the percentage of common and fixed costs by assigning more of the FAA's costs directly to beneficiaries through improved activity based costing. Telecommunications companies, which are often used for benchmarking against the FAA, typically show fixed and common cost between 15 percent and 30 percent of total costs. The FAA, with its cost structure, could be expected to reduce its fixed and common costs from 55 percent found in 1995 to perhaps 40 percent of total costs through cost accounting, and some believe this can be reduced further.[3]

ATO cost allocation study

The most recent cost allocations study differs from the previous ones in two important respects. First, it is concerned with allocating the costs incurred only by the newly formed ATO and not the entire FAA. Second, it benefits considerably from dramatically improved cost data that FAA and ATO have developed. In addition, of course, the aviation industry has changed considerably in the past 10 years. Because of these differences, this study isn't comparable to the earlier ones.

Table 15.4 summarizes the results of the 2005 Air Traffic Organization cost allocation study. Commercial aviation is almost entirely provided in high performance turbine powered aircraft. As the study found, commercial aviation accounted for 73.5 percent of the ATO's costs, in contrast to the 97.6 percent of the trust fund revenues it contributes (Table 15.2) In contrast, business and general aviation account for 15.6 percent of the costs yet contribute only 3.3 percent of the trust fund revenues. There would appear to be considerable cross-subsidy of business and general aviation's use of the air traffic control system by commercial aviation.

Table 15.4   ATO cost allocation summary (FY 2005)

	Cost Allocation	
	Amount (millions)	Share
High Performance Commercial	$6,745	73.0%
Piston Commercial	$50	0.5%
High Performance General Aviation	$896	9.7%
Piston General Aviation	$546	5.9%
High Performance Exempt	$433	4.7%
Piston Exempt	$11	0.1%
Flight Services	$564	6.1%
Total	$9,245	100.0%

Source: Federal Aviation Administration, Cost Allocation for Reauthorization: Air Traffic Organization FY05, February, 2007.

Current patterns of use

The cost allocation summarized in Table 15.4 seems consistent with the patterns of use of air traffic control facilities by various segments of the aviation industry. Table 15.5 shows the usage of en route center air traffic control facilities by industry segment. The table shows not only usage by industry segment but also

---

3   http://www.faa.gov/ncarc/whitepaper/costallo.doc.

usage by "High Performance" aircraft, basically jets, and "Piston" aircraft, the bulk of which are small general aviation aircraft. Not surprisingly, the segment making the greatest use are the large US commercial carriers who account for 47 percent of the activity. The next largest segment, again not surprisingly are regional jets. General aviation turbine aircraft, basically business jets, account for the third largest group and account for 8 percent of en route center activity. Overall, general aviation accounts for 11 percent of en route air traffic control activity.

Table 15.6 shows the use of terminal operations at airports and TRACONS. Operations are broken down both by industry segment and by airport size. Large hubs are airports and their associated control facilities that enplane 1 percent of more of US scheduled enplanements. There were 37 such facilities in the 2005 study and they included the busiest airports like Atlanta Hartsfield, New York LaGuardia, Washington Reagan, and Chicago O'Hare. Middle terminals are those with less than 1 percent of enplanements but more than 100,000 enplanements per year. There were 179 airports in this category that included such places as Nashville, Cleveland, Indianapolis, Pittsburgh, St. Louis, and Tucson. Finally, low activity towers are those with fewer than 100,000 enplanements per year. These 287 airports have FAA towers but typically have very little commercial activity and are used primarily by general aviation aircraft.

Since over 90 percent of commercial service is concentrated in Large Hubs and Middle Terminals, they were combined in Table 15.6. The first thing to notice in the table is that general aviation accounts for 27 percent of operations at Large Hubs and Middle Terminals and 52 percent of all terminal operations at all airports. General aviation's share at the Large Hubs and Middle Terminals is only slightly smaller than the 29 percent attributed to US Large Commercial Carriers. The figures in Tables 15.5 and 15.6 seem quite consistent with the cost allocation studies that find general aviation's share of the costs imposed on the air traffic control system to be far greater than the 3.3 percent of revenues they were seen to contribute in Table 15.2. Similarly, regional jets which account for 17 percent of en route operations and 18 percent of terminal operations at large hubs and middle terminals would seem to impose greater costs on the air traffic controls system than the 9.9 percent of revenues they were seen to contribute.

Some argue that figures such as these are misleading and overstate the load general aviation places on the air traffic control system and that the cost allocations studies are flawed. Their argument is that the air traffic control system was designed and sized for commercial passenger carriers and that general aviation should only be charged the marginal cost placed on the system, which would be far lower than suggested by the figures in the preceding tables. Indeed, the National Business Aviation Association goes so far as to say, "Business users of private jets and turboprops pay more in federal aviation user fees than the total costs borne by the federal government to provide them with aviation services."[4] Referring back to Tables 15.2, 15.5, and 15.6 finds that the kinds of operations they are referring to

---

4   National Business Aviation Association, "Costs Incurred and User Fees Recovered by the Federal Government for Services to Business General Aviation," October 2004.

Table 15.5   En route activity by industry segment

Industry Segment	Great Circle Miles			
	High Performance	Piston	Total	Share
US Large Commercial Carriers	3,880,928,353	743	3,880,929,096	47%
Foreign Passenger Carriers	426,514,589	8,312	426,522,901	5%
Regional Turboprop/Piston	220,322,773	11,046,258	231,369,031	3%
RJ < 60 seats	1,143,437,480		1,143,437,480	14%
RJ 61+ seats	273,078,559		273,078,559	3%
US Large Commercial Freight	350,744,182		350,744,182	4%
Foreign Carrier Freight	30,451,132		30,451,132	0%
Regional Airline Freight	69,986,090	1,193,081	71,179,171	1%
Charter Flight on US Carrier	50,676,576	146,044	50,822,620	1%
Non-scheduled Part 135 Passenger	292,089,106	28,146,894	320,236,000	4%
Non-scheduled Part 135 Freight	78,298,546	1,891,334	80,189,880	1%
Fractional Ownership	211,937,688		211,937,688	3%
Commercial (Non-ETMS)			-	
Commercial Subtotal	**7,028,465,074**	**42,432,666**	**7,070,897,740**	**85%**
GA- Turbine	627,764,840		627,764,840	8%
GA - Piston		295,032,440	295,032,440	4%
GA - Rotor		491,115	491,115	0%
GA (Non-ETMS)			-	0%
GA Subtotal	**627,764,840**	**295,523,555**	**923,288,395**	**11%**
Tax Exempt	101,840,140	15,065,058	116,905,198	1%
Government/Military	195,983,427	6,311,354	202,294,781	2%
Non ETMS Military			-	0%
Not enough information to classify	28,304,988	3,084,213	31,389,201	0%
Exempt Subtotal	**326,128,555**	**24,460,625**	**350,589,180**	**4%**
Total	**7,982,358,469**	**362,416,846**	**8,344,775,315**	**100%**

Source: Feferal Aviation Administration, FY 2005 Cost Allocation Report, January 2007, Appendix B.

– general aviation turbine – contribute 1.5 percent of revenues, account for 8 percent of activities in the en route centers, and account for 4 percent of terminal operations in Large Hubs and Middle Terminals. These numbers seem quite consistent with the cost allocations study finding that these aircraft account for 9.7 percent of air traffic control costs.

The argument that the air traffic control system was designed for large commercial passenger flights and that general aviation is only a marginal user imposing few if any costs cannot be dismissed on conceptual grounds. If there is excess capacity in a system, the marginal cost of one additional use of the system can be well below the average cost. However, a look at the data casts considerable doubt on this argument in the case of air traffic control. First, one of the major concerns about the air traffic control system in the United States is that it's approaching or in some areas at capacity. Where there isn't excess capacity, there is no reason to believe that the marginal cost of additional use is low. Indeed, to the extent that it contributes to congestion, the cost of additional use could be quite high. Second, and more importantly, general aviation is such a major user of the system that it's clear that the system was designed to accommodate both commercial and general aviation use.

Changes in industry structure

A second problem with the mismatch between revenue drivers and cost drivers is that changes in how major segments of the industry operate may change costs differently than revenues. Consider, for example, the large increase in the use of regional jets between the late 1990s and 2003. In 1995, for example, there were no regional jets flying that were affiliated with domestic mainline carriers. By 2000, 16 percent of aircraft departures from major hub airports were made by affiliated regional jets and by 2003, that figure had more than doubled to 38 percent. Some of that growth in regional jet flights was to communities previously served by commuter carriers in turboprop aircraft. Much of the growth, however, was airlines substituting more frequent flights in smaller regional jets for less frequent flights in larger traditional jets.

There has also been dramatic growth in business jets and twin turboprop aircraft commonly used in business aviation. Figure 15.1 shows the growth in the number of aircraft in the fleet for business jets, twin turboprops, airline jets, and regional jets. The growth in regional jets since the late 1990s has been widely observed. Less notices has been the even more dramatic growth in business jets and twin turboprops. At the time the Airport and Airway Trust Fund was established there were substantially more aircraft operated by the airlines than there were business aircraft. Taken together there are now nearly three times as many high performance business aircraft as there are airline jets and regional jets combined.

Such substitutions of regional jets for larger jets and the dramatic changes in the mix of aircraft using the air traffic control system highlight the mismatch between cost drivers and revenue drivers. Table 15.7 shows the estimated excise tax contributions from different aircraft flying on the same route. The first example in the table shows the impact of substituting three regional jet flights for a single B737 flight in the Los Angeles to San Francisco market. Both alternatives carry the same

Table 15.6   Terminal operations by industry segment

Industry Segment	Large Hubs and Middle Terminals			
	High Performance	Piston	Total	Share
US Large Commercial Carriers	10,490,016	2	10,490,018	29%
Foreign Passenger Carriers	575,707	27	575,734	2%
Regional Turboprop/Piston	2,019,470	116,125	2,135,595	6%
RJ < 60 seats	5,565,439	-	5,565,439	15%
RJ 61+ seats	1,042,373	-	1,042,373	3%
US Large Commercial Freight	870,759	-	870,759	2%
Foreign Carrier Freight	45,024	-	45,024	0%
Regional Airline Freight	408,552	3,833	412,385	1%
Charter Flight on US Carrier	97,418	759	98,177	0%
Non-scheduled Part 135 Passenger	714,245	116,832	831,077	2%
Non-scheduled Part 135 Freight	516,147	9,032	525,179	1%
Fractional Ownership	493,595	-	493,595	1%
Commercial (Non-ETMS)	553,815	704,855	1,258,670	3%
Commercial Subtotal	**23,392,559**	**951,466**	**24,344,025**	**68%**
GA- Turbine	1,340,812	-	1,340,812	4%
GA - Piston	-	714,245	714,245	2%
GA - Rotor	-	2,790	2,790	0%
GA (Non-ETMS)	1,720,717	6,030,262	7,750,979	21%
GA Subtotal	**3,061,529**	**6,747,297**	**9,808,826**	**27%**
Tax Exempt	274,118	53,442	327,560	1%
Government/Military	354,497	26,611	381,108	1%
Non ETMS Military	1,058,177	74,775	1,132,952	3%
Not enough information to classify	52,926	8,219	61,145	0%
Exempt Subtotal	**1,739,718**	**163,047**	**1,902,765**	**5%**
Total	**28,193,806**	**7,861,810**	**6,055,616**	**100%**

Continued – Table 15.6 Terminal operations by industry segment

Low Activity Towers				All Terminals			
High Performance	Piston	Total	Share	High Performance	Piston	Total	Share
13,758	-	13,758	0%	10,503,774	2	10,503,776	17%
8,424	20	8,444	0%	584,131	47	584,178	1%
294,954	40,521	335,475	1%	2,314,424	156,646	2,471,070	4%
83,893		83,893	0%	5,649,332	-	5,649,332	9%
4,739		4,739	0%	1,047,112	-	1,047,112	2%
46,707		46,707	0%	917,466	-	917,466	1%
1,592		1,592	0%	46,616	-	46,616	0%
169,133	1,706	170,839	1%	577,685	5,539	583,224	1%
7,005	600	7,605	0%	104,423	1,359	105,782	0%
480,148	85,062	565,210	2%	1,194,393	201,894	1,396,287	2%
221,930	9,188	231,118	1%	738,077	18,220	756,297	1%
296,668		296,668	1%	790,263	-	790,263	1%
333,805	424,842	758,647	3%	887,620	1,129,697	2,017,317	3%
1,962,756	**561,939**	**2,524,695**	**9%**	**25,355,315**	**1,513,405**	**26,868,720**	**43%**
979,392		979,392	4%	2,320,204	-	2,320,204	4%
	994,017	994,017	4%	-	1,708,262	1,708,262	3%
	3,719	3,719	0%		6,509	6,509	0%
4,589,941	16,085,470	20,675,411	77%	6,310,658	22,115,732	28,426,390	45%
5,569,333	**17,083,206**	**22,652,539**	**85%**	**8,630,862**	**23,830,503**	**32,461,365**	**52%**
197,889	42,660	240,549	1%		96,102	96,102	0%
171,718	26,969	198,687	1%		53,580	53,580	0%
1,087,115	76,820	1,163,935	4%		151,595	151,595	0%
20,940	4,881	25,821	0%	73,866	13,100	86,966	0%
1,477,662	**151,330**	**1,628,992**	**6%**	**3,217,380**	**314,377**	**3,531,757**	**6%**
9,009,751	**17,796,475**	**26,806,226**	**100%**	**37,203,557**	**25,658,285**	**62,861,842**	**100%**

Source: Federal Aviation Administration, FY 2005 Cost Allocation Report, January 2007, Appendix B.

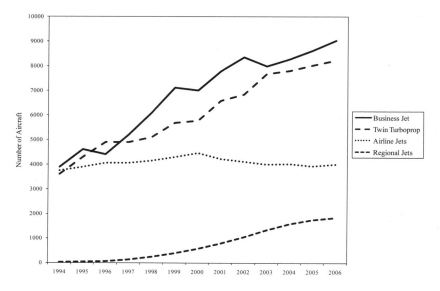

Figure 15.1   Changes in the aircraft fleet

number of passengers at the same ticket price, so both contribute the same amount of ticket tax and also segment tax. The three regional jets consume more fuel, so pay slightly more in fuel tax. The net effect is that the three regional jet flights generate about 3 percent more revenue for the trust fund. However, from an air traffic control standpoint, handling a regional jet flight requires the same effort as handling a B737 flight, so the regional jet alternative places three times the workload on the air traffic control system in exchange for only slightly more revenue.

The second example in the table shows the different tax contributions to the trust fund of three different flights, each of which would place about the same workload on the air traffic control system. A B767 places the same workload on the air traffic control system as a B737, yet has the capacity to generate substantially more tax revenue. By contrast a Learjet 35 business jet also places the same workload on the air traffic control system yet can be expected to generate only about one twentieth the revenue of a B737 flight and yet might generate only about one fortieth the revenue of a B767.

Another recent trend that has highlighted the mismatch between revenue drivers and cost drivers is the steady growth of low-fare carriers lead by Southwest. In 1999, Southwest operated 15 percent of the major jet airline passenger flights. By 2005, Southwest's share of flights had increased to 20 percent. If Air Tran and Jet Blue are also considered, the share of flights by these three carriers had reached 26 percent by 2005. The spread of these low-fare carriers has resulted in more passengers traveling on low fares, with the result that the tax revenue per passenger has declined. A jet aircraft operated by Southwest Airlines will generate less ticket tax than the same-sized jet operated by a legacy airline charging higher fares. However, the Southwest jet will impose the same workload on the air traffic control system, even though it contributes less revenue to the operation of the system. Thus, the growth of low-

Table 15.7   Estimated excise tax contributions from various flights
(Approximately 300-mile flight from Los Angeles to San Francisco)

	Example #1		Example #2		
	One 737 flight	Three CRJ-200 flights	One 767 flight	One 737 flight	One Learjet 35 flight
Number of seats	132	144	231	132	a
Number of passengers	105	105	180	89	a
Average fare ($)	$100	$100	$82	$84	a
Fuel consumed (gallons)	937	1,797	1,646	937	190
Ticket tax	$788	$789	$1,100	$565	$0
Passenger segment tax	$348	$348	$544	$270	$0
Waybill tax	$2	$0	$27	$2	$0
Fuel tax	$40	$78	$71	$40	$41
Total Revenue	$1,178	$1,215	$1,742	$877	$41

Notes: a – not applicable.
Source: GAO analysis of FAA data (GAO–06–1114T, page 13).

fare airlines has resulted in less revenue per aircraft operation but has not reduced the air traffic control costs of handling those operations. The effects of lower fares were not confined to the traditional low fare carriers such as Southwest. As part of the competitive response to the growth of low fare carriers, other carriers lowered their fares as well. The DOT inspector general's office found that although air traffic levels continue to show improvement from the sharp declines that began early in 2001, expected trust fund revenues have not materialized. Their analysis showed that in March 2000, the average cost of a ticket for a 1,000-mile flight was $149, while in March 2005, it was about $118, a drop of over 20 percent.[5]

Figure 15.2 shows the Airport and Airway Trust Fund receipts over the life of the trust fund and FAA appropriations over the same period. With the exception of a single year, trust fund receipts have not been sufficient to cover FAA's budget. More importantly, the trust fund has not been a stable source of funding. On two occasions, taxes have been allowed to lapse, interrupting the flow of revenue into the trust fund. Also, the impacts of the structural changes as the industry moved to rely more heavily on regional jets between 2000 and 2003 can be seen in the decline in trust fund revenues – a decline aggravated by the growth in low-fare carriers.

---

5   *Perspectives on the Aviation Trust Fund and Financing the Federal Aviation Administration*, Statement of the Honorable Kenneth M. Mead, Inspector General, US Department of Transportation, Before the Committee on Transportation and Infrastructure, Subcommittee on Aviation, United States House of Representatives, May 4, 2005.

Figure 15.2   Airport and Airway Trust Fund receipts and FAA appropriations 1971–2006

The growth of low-fare carriers and the spread of regional jets is not the first structural change in the airline industry, but it's the first one that has resulted in a drop in revenues per commercial aircraft operation. Throughout the first two decades of the trust fund, average aircraft sizes were increasing, particularly with the spread of wide-body aircraft. This trend worked in favor of helping trust fund revenues keep pace with the cost of providing air traffic control service. So the mismatch between cost drivers and revenue drivers has been there from the beginning of the trust fund. It's only these most recent structural changes that have reduced revenues relative to costs rather than helped revenue. Future structural changes will also have a different impact on revenues than on costs so that the disconnect between cost drivers and revenue drivers will continue to complicate air traffic control funding. So long as there is a mismatch between revenue drivers and cost drivers, ATO funding will be vulnerable to such changes in the industry.

Diffused Accountability

A second challenge ATO faces is diffused accountability which has lead to continuing poor performance and high costs of its capital investment programs. As the Mineta Commission reported, "There are 'too many cooks' making authority and accountability too diffused."[6] FAA modernization projects have a long record of (1) promising more capability than they ultimately deliver, (2) being completed later than promised, and (3) costing far more by the time they are completed than

---

6   National Civil Aviation Review Commission, Executive Summary, December 11, 1997.

the initial cost estimates. As GAO reported in 2004, "Initially FAA estimated that its ATC modernization efforts would cost $12 billion and could be completed over 10 years. Now, two decades and $35 billion later, FAA expects to need another $16 billion through 2007 to complete key projects, for a total of $51 billion."[7] The DOT inspector general concurred in 2005: "We found that cost growth, schedule delays, and performance shortfalls with FAA's major acquisitions continue to stall air traffic modernization. Overall, 11 of the 16 projects we reviewed will experience a total cost growth of about $5.6 billion, and 9 of the 16 will have schedule slips from 2 to 12 years, based on current estimates."[8]

From time to time, both Congress and the administration have exerted considerable influence over FAA's actions and, on occasion, have simply imposed their decisions on FAA. In some cases, FAA has been prevented from doing things they would like to do, such as consolidating facilities, and in other cases, they have been forced to do things they would not otherwise have chosen, such as budget cuts or reducing employment to meet administration-imposed targets. Such control is part of the oversight roles of Congress and the administration and may well be appropriate. However, one effect of others exerting control over FAA is that FAA is much less accountable for its actions. Instead, accountability is shared with both Congress and the administration. As the Mineta Commission also reported, "Because there is so much dispersed power and authority in making budget decisions, FAA managers, industry, and the Congress can always point fingers when something goes awry."[9]

The nature of the budget process for the ATO contributes to diffused accountability. As mentioned earlier, the funds to support the ATO come from two sources, the Airport and Airway Trust Fund and the General Fund. The various tax rates that determine the flow of money into the Airport and Airway Trust Fund are determined by Congress with input from FAA and various constituent groups. The decisions about how much money is available to support the operations of the ATO and the investment in capital are determined through the standard federal budget process. The US federal budget process involves both many steps and many different actors. Figure 15.3 presents a highly simplified flowchart of how that process works when it works smoothly and assumes no presidential vetoes or continuing resolutions. The budget request for the Air Traffic Organization becomes part of FAA's budget request, which in turn becomes part of DOT 's budget request, which in turn becomes part of the President's budget request. This request goes to Congress, where there are separate authorization, appropriations, and budget committees in both the House and the Senate, all of whom have an opportunity to influence the resources available to the ATO, as do individual members of Congress who are not on any of these committees.

---

7   Air Traffic Control, FAA's Modernization Efforts – Past, Present, and Future, Statement of Gerald L. Dillingham, Director, Physical Infrastructure Issues, GAO–04–227T.

8   Status of FAA's Major Acquisitions: Cost Growth and Schedule Delays Continue to Stall Air Traffic Modernization, Federal Aviation Administration, Report Number AV–2005–061, date issued: May 26, 2005.

9   National Civil Aviation Review Commission, Section III, December 11, 1997.

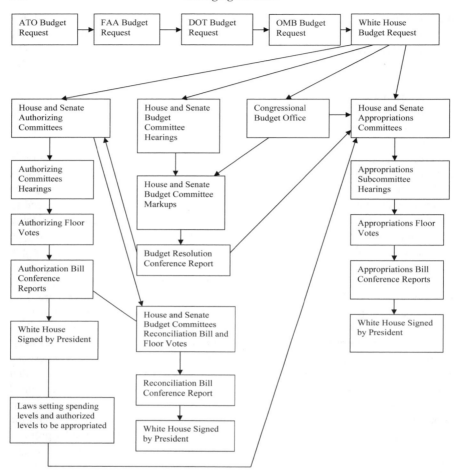

Figure 15.3   Simplified flow chart of the budget process to which the ATO must adhere

Note: The House and Senate have parallel processes that are represented as a single process on this flow chart and that the flow chart assumes that there are no Presidential vetoes. It is further assumed that no Continuing Resolution is needed.

Source: Adopted from the Senate Budget Committee, March 2005.

The problems of diffused accountability are inherent in the structure of ATO's relationship with other agencies and with Congress. There may be periods of time when the specific individuals involved are able to work well together to minimize these problems, but the structure will allow them to crop up again in the future, as they have cropped up periodically in the past.

Diffused accountability can result in inadequate incentives for financial discipline. Differences in financial discipline are among the most striking differences between

FAA and both NAV CANADA and NATS. It manifests itself in at least two ways: (1) the types of capital projects undertaken and (2) the pressure to complete those projects. Both NATS and NAV CANADA must project the impact of investment programs on future user charges. Users see and judge the "worth" of investments in very tangible terms: Do the services that users are going to get justify the cost in terms of the impact on future user charges? A major difference between FAA and NAV CANADA is the type of capital projects undertaken. With NAV CANADA, a strong "business" case has to be made to users before a project is undertaken. Given NAV CANADA's board structure, representatives of the people who will ultimately pay for the project – the users of the ATC system – must agree that the project will provide benefits that are worth the cost. Perhaps as a result, NAV CANADA undertakes projects that are more incremental in nature, of a more modest scale, and with a shorter time horizon than the projects typically undertaken by FAA. FAA, in contrast, tends to look much farther into the future in designing its projects and undertakes larger-scale projects that are a greater technological leap. By looking so far into the future, some of these projects have had unrealistic expectations or turn out to be much more complex than anticipated.

Looking into the future is critical for developing ATC improvements, but the question is how far into the future to look with any given project. NAV CANADA, by taking on more incremental improvements, is looking into the future, but in any one step, they aren't looking as far into the future. This incremental approach has some advantages for a system that has to operate on a continual basis with an extraordinarily high degree of reliability and accuracy. Incremental improvements to equipment are less likely to bring on unanticipated technological challenges than great leaps and are likely to require less dramatic adaptation by the workforce. Indeed, the motivation behind some incremental changes may well come from the controller and maintenance technician workforce. Even if the motivation for change comes from outside the workforce, it's easier to solicit and incorporate feedback from the workforce for incremental changes than it is for great leaps.

Incremental projects also come with inherently more financial discipline than projects requiring great technological leaps. It's easier to estimate both the costs and the benefits of a project using technology that's already been developed than for a project requiring new technology. It's also easier to hold project managers accountable on shorter-term projects. These projects can be completed while the cost and benefit estimates are still remembered and are still applicable. If costs are underestimated or benefits are overestimated, it's easier to hold the people who developed those estimates and the project managers accountable. There's a quick feedback loop, and managers who "low ball" cost estimates, overstate benefits, or underestimate the time it takes for completion to get a proposed project approved will quickly lose credibility, and perhaps their jobs. That environment creates a very strong incentive, not only to make the best possible cost and benefit estimates, but also to bring the project in on time, within budget, and up to the promised performance.

Longer-term projects that rely on unproven or yet to be developed technology present a much different environment. With such projects, the longer the time between making the initial cost, benefit, and timing estimates and the completion of the project, the less relevant those initial estimates are. In part, that's because it can be more difficult to estimate the costs of developing new technology than of implementing existing technology in a new application. Also, with a long-duration project, there is more of a temptation to change the specifications, and therefore the costs and benefits, of the project as it progresses than with a shorter project. When the specifications are changed, the original estimates must be updated to reflect the changes, reducing the accountability for those original estimates. With such projects, there may well be a temptation to make "optimistic" estimates to improve the chances of the project being selected, and there is much less penalty, or more likely no penalty at all, for estimates that prove to be inaccurate. Perhaps it shouldn't be surprising that the history of FAA ATC modernization projects has a nearly universal pattern of projects being over budget, under performing, and late.

With NAV CANADA and NATS, the financial discipline comes primarily from the role of aircraft operators in approving and overseeing capital investment decisions. NAV CANADA has four directors nominated by air carriers and one nominated by business aviation. NATS currently has 42 percent of its stock owned by the Airline Group, with only the government owning a larger share. The use of private capital markets may also add some financial discipline to NAV CANADA and NATS to the extent that these markets closely review investment plans.

However, were FAA to use private capital markets, it wouldn't necessarily bring added financial discipline to their capital investment programs. To the extent that the private debt was guaranteed by the government, there is no reason for private financial markets to be concerned about potential risk of the proposed project. Indeed, even if the debt isn't formally guaranteed, the markets might assume that there is an implicit guarantee by the government and behave as if the debt were guaranteed. The Tennessee Valley Authority, for example, has the right to issue private debt that is not guaranteed by the government, but because of TVA's role as a government entity, the markets still treat that debt as if it were guaranteed. Thus, simply using private financial markets to finance capital investments would not necessarily bring added financial discipline to FAA's capital investment program.

Unfortunately, the challenge of diffused accountability extends to the planning for the so-called Next Generation Air Transportation System (NGATS). In 2003, Congress created the Joint Planning and Development Office to coordinate the transformation of the current air traffic control system to a system capable of handling a tripling of air traffic by 2025. JPDO has a senior policy committee made up of representatives of seven different organizations: Department of Transportation, Department of Commerce, Department of Defense, Department of Homeland Security, Federal Aviation Administration, NASA, and the White House Office of Science and Technology Policy.

In July 2006, GAO reported to Congress that JPDO faced a series of problems.[10] At that time, JPDO had not had a permanent director for six months and the senior

---

10 United States Government Accountability Office, *Next Generation Air Transportation System: Preliminary Analysis of Progress and Challenges Associated with the Transformation of the National Airspace System*, Statement of Gerald L. Dillingham, Ph.D., Director, Physical Infrastructure Issues, Testimony Before the Subcommittee on Aviation, Committee on Commerce, Science, and Transportation, US Senate, GAO–06–915T, July 25, 2006.

policy committee had been without a head since the resignation of the Secretary of Transportation. Moreover, three years after the formation of JPDO, it still did not have formal signed agreements with the member agencies about their respective roles and responsibilities. JPDO tries to incorporate interests of nonfederal stakeholders as well as the expertise of private industry, state and local governments, and academia through the NGATS Institute. JPDO has also created eight integrated product teams that bring together federal and nonfederal experts to plan and coordinate the technologies to address JPDO's strategies. These integrated product teams include more than 190 stakeholders from over 70 different organizations. One clear problem is that many of the people who staff these integrated product teams work for partner agencies and thus work only part-time for JPDO. Those agencies have other missions and priorities besides NGATS which could limit the commitment of the individuals assigned to these integrated product teams. In much the same way that diffused accountability has been a barrier to successful modernization projects in the past, it may also be a barrier to successful planning for the next generation air transportation system.

Lack of Organizational Independence

The lack of independence from congressional concerns has hampered FAA throughout most of its history, as described in the previous chapter. From time to time members of Congress may base funding decisions on how jobs in their districts will be affected by proposed FAA actions, rather than on how reasonable the business cases for actions may be.[11] The National Commission to Ensure a Strong Competitive Airline Industry expressed concern about a reluctance to spend out of the trust fund because trust fund balances counted against federal budget deficits, but the problems go beyond any one specific situation.

For example, FAA has been caught up in government-wide programs that have nothing to do with FAA's particular situation. The lack of organizational independence made FAA vulnerable to the Federal Workforce Restructuring Act of 1994, which targeted a reduction of 272,900 federal employees between 1993 and 1999. In response to that act, more than 3,000 FAA employees eventually received buyouts, which were a major factor in the reduction of FAA's full-time equivalent workforce from 52,352 in fiscal 1992 to 47,738 at the end of fiscal 1996. Beyond this one specific example, there can often be pressure on government agencies to reduce their number of full-time employees, or head count, as it's often known. These pressures are not intended to necessarily save money, nor do they typically stem from a belief that the employment level in any specific agency is too high, but instead reducing the number of government employees is regarded as an end in itself.

Two problems emerge from this pressure on head count. One is that instead of saving money, it often ends up costing more. When the head count is reduced, the agency's responsibilities are not lessened, so that the agency has to increasingly

---

11 National Airspace System, Experts' View on Improving the US Air Traffic Control Modernization Program, GAO–05–333SP.

turn to contracting with outside companies for activities that were previously done in house. There are many cases where turning to outside companies can result in substantial savings for government agencies, such as when highly specialized expertise is needed. However, doing it for what had been normal functions of the agency prior to the head count reductions is likely to end up costing more rather than less. For example, an investigation by DOT's inspector general revealed that the contractor's work may not differ from work FAA employees do but that it may be at substantially higher costs to the government.

The second problem from pressure to reduce head count is that opportunities for FAA employees to do the same work for higher pay for contractors can lead to a loss of technical expertise within FAA. Indeed, one of the concerns that a panel of air traffic control experts assembled by GAO found was that a shortfall in technical expertise needed to design, develop, or manage complex air traffic systems had developed in FAA and, as a result, FAA has to rely on contractors, whose interests may differ from its own.[12]

Another, perhaps larger, problem related to a lack of organizational independence is that FAA both operates the air traffic control system and regulates itself in its operation of that system. In other aspects of US aviation, such as the design and manufacture of aircraft and aircraft components, the training and certification of pilots and mechanics, the procedures used to maintain aircraft, and the procedures under which airline operations are conducted, FAA provides independent regulatory oversight. FAA has no operational responsibilities in any of these areas. Instead, the operations are left to other organizations completely independent from FAA, and FAA's responsibility is to develop and approve the rules and procedures under which these organizations operate and to make sure that the rules and procedures are followed properly.

Air traffic control is different. As with other aspects of aviation, FAA has the responsibility to develop the rules and procedures for air traffic control and has the enforcement responsibility to ensure that these rules and procedures are followed. Unlike other aspects of aviation, however, FAA also has operational responsibility for the air traffic control system. The rules FAA develops are for itself, and the enforcement of those rules is enforcement of itself. In other words, FAA self-regulates air traffic control.

Self-regulation of air traffic control creates long-recognized potential conflicts of interest when there are decisions to be made about trade-offs between safety and capacity. As the Aviation Safety Commission stated in their 1988 report, "Both safety and public confidence in the safety of the system might be enhanced if greater separation existed between the functions of regulating the ATC system and operating it."[13] FAA has two goals in operating the air traffic control system, and these goals can often pull in different directions. One goal is to operate the air traffic control system safely. The other is to provide enough capacity to avoid excessive and persistent delays. Some of the potential ways of improving safety can reduce capacity and

---

12 Ibid.

13 *Aviation Safety Commission: Final Report and Recommendations* (Washington, DC: Government Printing Office, 1988), p. 25.

increase delays, and some potential ways of increasing capacity can reduce safety. Currently FAA, as both regulator and operator of the air traffic control system, makes the capacity versus safety trade-offs internally. If excessively conservative standards are imposed, capacity is reduced, delays increase, and FAA faces the capacity penalty in the form of dissatisfied airlines and passengers. Alternatively, if FAA shades its procedures too much toward enhancing capacity, safety may be reduced and passengers and crews could be placed at greater risk.

The trade-offs between safety and capacity are inherent in air traffic control, and they are often subtle. To be sure, many forms of capacity enhancements do not reduce safety, and others may even increase safety. These decisions are relatively straightforward. However, other capacity-related decisions such as aircraft separation standards and the conditions under which various runway configurations are used can pose a trade-off between safety and capacity that FAA must make. These trade-offs are difficult because while it may be easy to determine the capacity enhancement implications of a even impossible to determine how much that proposal might degrade safety or if, indeed, it would degrade safety at all.

Were the air traffic control system to be reorganized to place air traffic control operations into one organization and air traffic control regulation into a separate organization, the situation would change. The same trade-offs between safety and capacity would remain and be just as technically difficult, but the regulatory tensions that are now internal to one organization would become external and between two different organizations. Decisions that are now made internally within FAA would become external in a manner similar to safety regulatory decisions in other aviation sectors. The debate about trade-offs between safety and capacity would be more public and open to outside scrutiny. The air traffic control operating organization would have to consider carefully any changes to the minimum safety standards they propose and clearly state the justification for that proposal. The regulatory organization would have to consider, specify, and defend the criteria it used for selecting one standard over another, and for accepting or rejecting any proposed changes.

Following the formation of the ATO, FAA has attempted to place greater separation between the regulation of air traffic control and its operation. Starting in 2005, FAA's Office of the Associate Administrator for Regulation and Certification established a separate Air Traffic Safety Oversight Service, which has the responsibility to establish, approve, and/or accept safety standards for the ATO. The ATO itself also has a separate safety unit directed by a vice president. This restructuring has added more separation between operations and regulation. However, all of these units are still within FAA, so there remains a degree of self-regulation.

Self-regulation is widely believed to be less effective than arms-length, independent regulation in many areas, including air traffic control. Throughout the world, when air traffic control organizations have been reorganized along commercial principles, countries have consistently taken the step of separating regulation of the air traffic control system from its operation. Indeed, of the major countries in the world, only the United States continues to have the organization responsible for operating the air traffic control system also regulate it.

The issue of the effectiveness of self regulation came to the forefront in the wake of the August 27, 2006 crash of a Comair regional jet on takeoff from Lexington, Kentucky. ATO's procedures for staffing the tower at Lexington called for two controllers to be on duty. However, at the time of the crash, only one controller was on duty. Obviously, there is no way of knowing whether or not a second controller in the tower would have prevented the accident. The point is that FAA operated in violation of its own regulations on staffing the Lexington tower. Moreover, the Lexington airport wasn't alone. At the time of the Lexington crash, airports in Duluth, Minnesota and Fargo, North Dakota were also operating with one controller when two were required.[14]

The controller staffing issue is not the first time that concerns have been raised about FAA and self-regulation. FAA came under criticism for failures in self-regulation surrounding the crash of a flight inspection aircraft in Fall 1993. In its investigation of that accident, the National Transportation Safety Board (NTSB) said it was concerned "that the basic elements of flight operations and flight safety management that the FAA expects of air carrier and commuter operators are not presently established in the FIAO flight operations mission. The Safety Board is further concerned that these same basic elements of flight operations safety management may not be present in the other FAA regional and headquarters units that conduct flight operations utilizing over 55 public-owned aircraft and a variety of leased assets." NTSB further stated that "timely corrective actions are necessary to ensure that flying missions of the Office of Aviation System Standards operate at a level of safety equivalent to that of the aviation industry."[15] NTSB was concerned that the FAA has allowed itself to shortchange safety in ways it would not tolerate in air carrier, commuter and corporate flight operations.[16] In response to the accident and the NTSB report, FAA revamped the management structure of its internal flight operations to bring them up to Part 135 standards.[17] The specific problems may have been solved, but the concern remains that a pattern of self-regulation allowed the conditions to exist that led to that accident.

Another problem that could be viewed by some as a failure of self-regulation was the 1993 finding of the U.S. Department of Transportation Inspector General that the FAA's own fleet of 62 aircraft contained as many suspected unapproved parts as any other U.S. certificated fleet of airplanes.[18] Approximately 39 percent of the $32-million parts inventory of spares for the fleet stocked at the FAA Logistics Center, Oklahoma City, were not approved parts, according to FAA regulations, the Inspector General audit team reported. The parts were not produced by FAA-approved manufacturers

14 Minnesota Public Radio, September 1, 2006, http://minnesota.publicradio.org/display/web/2006/09/01/obestar/.

15 "NTSB Issues Scathing Report on Deficiencies in FAA Flight Operations," *The Weekly of Business Aviation*, November 29, 1993, Volume 57, Number 22, p 226.

16 "When No One Watches the Watchers," *Business and Commercial Aviation*, January 1994, Volume 74, Number 1, p 90.

17 "FAA Reorganizing Agency Flight Operations in Wake of Crash," *The Weekly of Business Aviation*, April 18, 1994, volume 58, Number 16, p 168.

18 Suspect Parts Found in FAA Aircraft," *Aviation Week and Space Technology*, March 15, 1993, Volume 138, Number 11 p 34.

or traceable to the approved manufacturers, as required by FAA regulations. In a hands-on inspection of three FAA aircraft, eight of thirty sample parts on the aircraft were determined to be unapproved by FAA standards. Three parts were produced by manufacturers that had no FAA approval, and five lacked proper documentation for repair work or could not be traced to approved manufacturers. Auditors faulted the quality of FAA inspection procedures related to spares. Agency officials failed to report suspected unapproved parts for investigation as they were required, ignoring the agency's own directives, according to the report.

The specific problems with FAA flight operations or with suspected unapproved aircraft parts that emerged in 1993 haven't reoccurred. Similarly, it seems likely that controller understaffing problems in towers won't emerge again any time soon. Specific problems that emerge from self-regulation can always be corrected once they are identified, but they are only identified once self regulation has failed. Such problems are endemic to self-regulation. As long as there is self-regulation, problems will continue to emerge.

Summary

The ATO faces three fundamental challenges as it seeks to modernize and operate an efficient air traffic management system that can handle the expected future growth in air travel.

The first challenge is the disconnect between the cost drivers and the revenue drivers of the air traffic management system. The current system of funding the FAA with a series of excise taxes supplemented by monies from the General Fund means that the number of passengers, the price of airline tickets, and the fees to ship air cargo are the primary determinants of the revenue available to FAA. However, the number of aircraft that use the air traffic control system and the way in which they interact with the system are the primary determinants of the costs of running the system. Because these cost and revenue drivers are different, changes in the costs of running the system due to changes in service patterns or the structure of the aviation industry are not matched by changes in revenues to cover these costs. In addition, the current system has substantial cross subsidies inherent in it which result in some users paying far more than the costs they impose on the system while other users pay far less. Virtually all other countries in the world use some form of user fees that is more closely matched to the costs incurred on behalf of the user.

The second challenge is diffused accountability which has lead to continuing poor performance and high costs of its capital investment programs. Both Congress and the administration have exerted considerable influence over FAA's actions from time to time and, on occasion, have simply imposed their decisions on FAA. One effect of others exerting control over FAA is that FAA is much less accountable for its actions. Diffused accountability can result in inadequate incentives for financial discipline and may result in decisions that are less in tune with the needs of the users of the system.

The third challenge is the lack of organizational independence which has hampered FAA throughout most of its history. In some cases, the result has been decisions made more on the basis of the job impacts in Congressional districts and in other cases FAA has been caught up in government wide ceilings or caps that are unrelated to the needs of air traffic management. Perhaps the largest problem related to a lack of organizational independence is that FAA both operates the air traffic control system and regulates itself in its operation of that system. Virtually every other country in the world has separated the regulation of the air traffic control system from its operation. The United States is the only major country that still self-regulates its air traffic management system.

Chapter 16

Alternatives for Reform
in the United States

Introduction

The formation of the Air Traffic Organization (ATO) within the Federal Aviation Administration (FAA) has been an important step in improving the management of the air traffic control system in the United States, but the three fundamental challenges identified in the previous chapter still remain. Unless or until these challenges are addressed, ATO will be severely limited in how much progress it can make in modernizing its system to accommodate the expected future growth in air traffic. Further reforms will be needed to address these three challenges:

1. Disconnect between the cost drivers and the revenue drivers.
2. Diffused accountability.
3. Lack of organizational independence.

Disconnect Between the Cost Drivers and the Revenue Drivers

As seen in the previous two chapters, the evidence on the disconnect between cost and revenue drivers is clear and has been recognized for some time. Recall that every major independent group or commission to study air traffic control in the United States since the late 1980s has called for financing air traffic control with a system of user fees that more closely mirror the costs of providing services than the current system of taxes. The FAA itself has recognized both this disconnect and that a change in the air traffic control funding mechanism needs to be made. As FAA states, "FAA needs a consistent, stable revenue stream that is not tied to the price of an airline ticket but rather reflects our actual cost to provide service."[1] The Air Transport Association also recognizes the disconnect and goes further when they state, "Congress must determine and impose a specific schedule of mandatory user charges – directly and proportionally linking system use with system costs – which are fair, equitable and simple."[2] However, general aviation interests, including business aviation are adamantly opposed to user fees when they state, "All GA groups are united in the belief that user fees equate to bad government …"[3] The GA

---

1   http://www.faa.gov/airports_airtraffic/trust_fund/media/Trust_Fund.pdf.

2   http://www.airlines.org/government/issuebriefs/Statement+of+Principles+Airport+and+Airway+Trust+Fund+Reauthorization.htm.

3   http://web.nbaa.org/public/govt/GA_United_200609.pdf.

groups go on to say, "Any system of user fees, even one that excludes all or some segment of general aviation is unacceptable ..."[4]

To put the issue of the disconnect between cost and revenue drivers in a broader context, it's useful to consider how air navigation service providers (ANSPs) are financed throughout the world. There are four basic revenue structures for ANSPs:

1. Government funding. In a few countries, general government revenues are used to provide and support air navigation services. Historically, this has been most common when the public sector retains substantial ownership and control over civil aviation activities. Government funding typically provides little if any autonomy for ANSPs. As more countries throughout the world have switched to a commercialized approach, this method of funding has become far less common.

2. Indirect charges or taxes which are not closely related to the cost drivers of air traffic control such as aircraft activity. An example is the passenger ticket tax in the United States, the revenue from which is a function of fare paid and the number of passengers in the aircraft rather than the costs the aircraft imposes on the air traffic control system. These taxes are generally collected by the government, and then appropriated in some form to the ANSP. These amounts, even when earmarked, may or may not be sufficient to operate the air navigation system. These structures typically provide somewhat more budget autonomy than annual appropriations from general tax revenues, but far less autonomy than most systems of user charges.

3. User charges based on an established formula, most commonly aircraft weight and distance traveled in the airspace.

4. User charges supplemented by additional revenues, typically from general tax revenues, user charges for other specific services, or from charges to specific classes of users. Examples include the use of fuel taxes on general and some business aviation or the use of a fixed annual fee for general aviation aircraft in lieu of weight and distance charges.

In considering any funding mechanisms for ANSPs, there are a series of issues that need to be confronted, the most important of which are identified below.

Cost recovery from users

FAA currently has four distinct and separate responsibilities:

1. Providing air traffic control services.
2. Aviation safety regulation and oversight.
3. Airport infrastructure development.
4. Commercial space licensing and oversight.

Governments routinely provide a wide array of safety regulation and oversight services in many sectors of the economy and fund these activities with general revenues. There is no compelling argument why aviation safety and oversight should not be provided and funded in the same way.

---

4   http://web.nbaa.org/public/govt/GA_United_200609.pdf.

Airport infrastructure development, operations, and funding in the United States have traditionally been the responsibility of local governments or special authorities. Airport infrastructure includes elements such as runways and taxiways that can impact air traffic control operations but also includes much more such as terminals, gates, and parking. Some money from the Airport and Airway Trust Fund has gone to the Airport Improvement Program, primarily on the rationale that it aided economic development. However, AIP funding accounts for only about 16 percent of total capital spending at large hub airports where congestion is most often found, so the impact of AIP on relieving congestion by adding capacity to the air traffic system is minimal. Indeed, the FAA contends that "Large and medium hub airports generally operate with surpluses and can finance their capital needs without Federal assistance."[5] Even before the formation of the ATO, the AIP program has always been separate from air traffic control operations and it seems reasonable that it might be funded with a separate revenue stream.

The same is true for the limited costs of commercial space licensing and oversight. In sum, three of the four FAA functions – aviation safety regulation and oversight, airport infrastructure, and commercial space activities – are clearly separate functions from the function of constructing, maintaining, and operating an air traffic control system. In each case the government's role is different and in each case, those factors that drive the costs are different as well. There is no reason why funding for these three activities should be linked to or intermingled with funding for air traffic control.

With air traffic control, another issue is who should pay for the costs imposed on the system by military aircraft and by government-owned aircraft. There seems to be widespread agreement that the government should cover these costs from the general fund and, indeed, that has always been part of the rationale for a general fund contribution to the FAA budget. As seen in Tables 15.5 and 15.6 in the previous chapter, government and military aircraft do not constitute a large portion of activities in the air traffic control system. As seen in the cost allocation study in Table 15.4, government and military aircraft account for only 4.8 percent of ATO costs.

Structural changes in the aviation industry

ANSPs that are completely funded by government general funds are not vulnerable to structural changes in the aviation industry in the sense that none of their funding is driven by aviation industry activity. However, because these systems must compete for funds with other government activities, they are vulnerable to changes in priorities in government spending completely unrelated to air navigation or air traffic control needs. Should the demands for spending on something completely unrelated to aviation increase, such as health care, national defence, retirement programs, or education, the pressure on resources could easily lead to a reduction in funding for air traffic control, with little regard for air traffic control's financial needs. Having to compete for funds with all other government activities is different kind of funding vulnerability and one that can be just as big a problem. Indeed, in the United States, it was the experience with

---

5   FAA, *Airports Data Package for Stakeholders*, September 2, 2005, http://www.faa. gov/about/office_org/headquarters_offices/aep/aatf/media/Airports%20Data%20Package.pdf.

and concern about just this sort of vulnerability that lead to the creation of the Airport and Airway Trust Fund in 1970 as an attempt to provide a dedicated sources of funding.

Funding through taxes or indirect charges, as is the case with the FAA and ATO, leaves the ANSP vulnerable to structural changes in the industry, as has been evident in recent years and discussed in the previous chapter. Indeed, in part because of changes in the structure of the industry, notably an increase in the use of regional jets and rapid growth of low-fare carriers, the Trust Fund's uncommitted balance decreased by more than 70 percent from the end of fiscal year 2001 through the end of fiscal year 2005.[6] While it's difficult to forecast future structural changes in aviation, potential future changes such as a large and growing use of very light jets (VLJs) could easily worsen the implications of the mismatch between cost and revenue drivers.

One of the attractions of user fees cited by their proponents is that they reduce this vulnerability. Historically, the International Civil Aviation Organization (ICAO) has supported user-charge systems as the best mechanism to achieve full cost recovery and thus greater fiscal autonomy. Recent commercialization and organizational reforms of ANSPs have led more countries to adopt or extend user fee based systems. A widely held view is that such systems have less vulnerability to industry changes than indirect-tax systems because they tie revenues more closely to aircraft activities and thus to costs imposed on the air navigation system. Clearly, user charges have the potential to achieve this, but they must be carefully designed or they may not do as well linking charges to underlying cost drivers as one would hope.

The success of user fees in matching revenues to costs depends critically in how the user fees are designed and implemented. The key economic attraction of user charge systems is the potential to have charges and thus revenues match the costs of provision of services. The most commonly used fees charge aircraft a fee based on the distance traveled in the air traffic control system and the weight of the aircraft. The distance component of such charges may be a reasonable proxy for the amount of "handling" in the en route portion of the air navigation system, but aircraft weight has little if any connection to air traffic control costs. The only possible connection is that some very large aircraft may create larger wake vortices that require additional separation from aircraft following them, thus taking up more space, and thus capacity, in the system, but this effect doesn't apply to all aircraft and is likely to be minor. (Weight is typically used as a basis for landing fees at airports, but that can be justified because heavier aircraft require greater runway load bearing and length capabilities.) In practice, the weight component of air traffic control charges is more of a proxy for ability-to-pay and is thus a source of cross-subsidy in the charging scheme. The ability-to-pay principle is a concept in the theory of taxation that states that taxes should be levied in proportion to an individual's ability to pay. Basically, those with higher income or greater wealth should pay a larger share of taxes even if they don't use or benefit more of the service provided by the tax receipts. Of course, it's an open question whether commercial air carriers and their passengers automatically have a greater ability to pay than other civil aviation users.

---

6   United Stated Government Accountability Office, Report to Congressional Committees, Aviation Finance: Observations on Potential FAA Funding Options, GAO–06–973, September 2006.

It's important to realize that all weight and distance user charge formulas currently in use aren't the same. Table 16.1 summarizes the en route weight and distance formulas for NAV CANADA, Airservices Australia, and EUROCONTROL. In each case, the formula is of the form: Charge = Rate x Distance Factor x Weight Factor. The rates are different for each organization. More importantly, the relative emphasis given to weight compared to distance is also different. Whereas Canada uses the great circle distance itself, both Airservices Australia and EUROCONTROL divide the great circle distance by 100 and each adjusts the distance by a different amount to account for approach and terminal control services. Both NAV CANADA and Airservices Australia use the square root of the maximum takeoff weight, but EUROCONTROL divides the maximum takeoff weight by 50 before taking the square root. Thus, none of the three organizations places the same relative emphasis on distance versus weight.

Table 16.1   Comparison of weight and distance formulas for en route fees

Basic Formula: Charge = Rate x Distance Factor x Weight Factor

NAV CANADA

Distance Factor is the great circle distance measured in kilometers between the origin and destination. For flights between most major airports where approach and terminal services are provided at the airport, the distance is reduced by 65 kilometers for each airport.

Weight Factor is the maximum takeoff weight measured in metric tonnes raised to a power of 0.5. In other words, it is the square root of the weight.

Airservices Australia

The rate is substantially lower for aircraft weighing less than 20 metric tonnes than for aircraft weighing more than 20 metric tonnes.

Distance Factor is the great circle distance measured in kilometers between the origin and destination airports divided by 100. For flights between most major airports where approach and terminal services are provided at the airport, the distance is reduced by 55 kilometers for each airport.

Weight Factor is the maximum takeoff weight measured in metric tonnes raised to a power of 0.5. In other words, it is the square root of the weight. If the aircraft weights less than 20 metric tonnes, the weight is raised to a power of 1.0. In other words, it is the weight and not the square root of the weight.

Eurocontrol

Distance Factor is the great circle distance measured in kilometers between the origin and destination airports divided by 100. The distance factor is reduced by 20 kilometers for each takeoff and landing.

Weight Factor is the maximum takeoff weight measured in metric tonnes divided by 50 and then raised to a power of 0.5. In other words, it is the square root of one fiftieth of the weight.

For terminal charges are calculated by a formula of the form: Charge = Rate x Weight Factor. For NAV CANADA, the weight factor is the maximum takeoff weight raised to the power of 0.85; for EUROCONTROL the weight factor is the maximum takeoff weight raised to the power of 0.95, and for Airservices Australia the weight factor is the maximum takeoff weight raised to the power of 1.0. Thus even in terminal charges, weight is included in the formula in a way that larger aircraft pay a greater charge than lighter aircraft.

Table 16.2 shows the impact of these differences on user charges that NAV CANADA, Airservices Australia, and EUROCONTROL would impose on three different aircraft for the same flight. The table also shows the taxes that those same flights would pay in the United States. When an ANSP goes beyond a simple weight and distance formula and supplements it with other user charges or taxes it has more flexibility to more closely match user charges to the costs imposed on the air navigation system by the flight. In addition to the en route charges, NAV CANADA, Airservices Australia, and EUROCONTROL all use terminal charges. In addition, Airservices Australia assess a charge to cover the cost of fire and rescue services.

**Table 16.2   Taxes and charges in the United States, Canada,
            Australia and Europe (US$)**

(Based on a 300-mile flight between two large cities)

(US Dollars)	B737-300	CRJ-200	Learjet 35
US Taxes	$1,178.00	$405.00	$41.00
US ATO Portion	$777.48	$267.30	$27.06
NAV CANADA Charges	$674.10	$319.01	$139.31
Airservices Australia Charges	$451.40	$199.03	$70.74
Eurocontrol Charges	$481.70	$285.99	$161.62

(Ratios)	B737-300	CRJ-200	Learjet 35
US Taxes	100%	34%	3%
US ATO Portion	100%	34%	3%
NAV CANADA Charges	100%	47%	21%
Airservices Australia Charges	100%	44%	16%
Eurocontrol Charges	100%	59%	34%

Note: ATO is about 66% of the FAA budget, so the ATO portion of the US Taxes is calculated as 66% of the US Taxes. For Eurocontrol, Rome's terminal charges were used.

As can be seen in the upper portion of the table, each of the three systems charges a different amount whether it's for a large commercial jet such as a B737-300, a regional jet such as a CRJ-200, or a business jet such as a Learjet 35. Each of these planes traveling the same route would impose about the same workload on the air traffic control system, yet in each of these three systems using weight and distance user charges, the smaller aircraft pay less than the larger aircraft. The charges are most nearly equal with EUROCONTROL, but even here the regional jet pays less than 60 percent the amount paid by the B737 and the Learjet pays only 34 percent. Of the three ANSPs, the differences are greatest in Airservices Australia where a regional jet pays only 44 percent as much as a B737 and where a Learjet 35 pays only 16 percent. Thus, in all three of these systems that have user charges, there is still significant cross-subsidy from large commercial jets to smaller commercial jets and private aircraft.

The system of indirect taxes used in the United States gives smaller aircraft a much bigger break than any of the three user charge systems shown in Table 16.2. In the United States, a CRJ-200 regional jet pays only 34 percent as much as a B737 and a Learjet 35 pays only three percent as much. Thus of the four systems shown in the table, the cross subsidies to smaller aircraft are by far the largest in the system of taxes and fees used in the United States.

It's critical to realize that there is significant variation in the relationship among charges to various aircraft within these three user charge systems. All too often, the debate about taxes versus user charges in the United States presents the choice as a binary one – either taxes or a user charge system that charges everyone the same to use the air traffic control system. In reality, none of the user charge systems used by the major ANSPs charges every user of the system the same. All retain some degree of cross-subsidy in the form of reduced charges for smaller aircraft such as regional jets or business jets. The user charge systems currently in use reflect a continuum of how much of the air traffic control costs should be born by each type of user.

A user charge system also has the ability to reflect the special circumstances of some segments of aviation. For example, for small general aviation aircraft who make relatively little use of the air traffic control system it may be more efficient not to bill them on a per use basis but rather to make some other arrangement. NAV CANADA does not apply the weight and distance charges to very small, general aviation aircraft. A small, single-engine aircraft such as a Cessna 172, pays only an annual fee equivalent to about $62 (US). In the United States, the same plane would pay that much in fuel tax if it consumed 323 gallons of avgas per year. At a typical fuel consumption for this aircraft, this represents less than 35 hours of flight time per year.[7] A similar approach is available in Australia with the "light aircraft option" which would charge a plane such a Cessna 172 as little as $123 per year if the plane made no more than 7 flights.[8] If the plane was used more frequently, the fee would be higher. EUROCONTROL exempts aircraft weighing less than 2 metric tonnes, which would include most small single-engine aircraft such as the Cessna 172, from

---

7   http://www.voyageraviation.com/cessna172.html.

8   Airservices Australia, Charges for Facilities and Services, ABN 59 698 720 886, Standard Contract Terms, July 1, 2006.

en route charges.[9] Here again, the user fee systems used in other developed countries are not nearly as monolithic as some opponents of user fees characterize them.

The example in Table 16.2 shows that systems of user charges such as those found in NAV CANADA, Airservices Australia, and EUROCONTROL would be less sensitive to changes in industry structure than the system of taxes used in the United States. In the user charge systems, flights by different aircraft types that impose about the same costs on the air traffic control system pay closer to the same amounts than under the system of taxes used in the United States. Changing the mix aircraft types won't change revenue nearly as much under user charges as under the US tax system. Even these user charge systems, however, don't have charges that precisely mirror the costs various aircraft impose on the air traffic control system. Thus, even a system of user charges might have to be readjusted from time to time in the face of large changes to the aviation industry, although the needed adjustments would likely be smaller and less frequently needed than under a system of indirect taxes.

Equitable charges

Agreeing on a fair way of allocating the costs a service across different users is most easily achieved when the costs of the services are largely variable in nature, and where capacity constraints are not severe. The air navigation services, however, are characterized by high fixed costs, and sharply rising marginal costs when capacity is reached. This cost structure has a high proportion of joint and common costs, which then need to be allocated across users.

The general aviation and business aviation communities argue that, "The size, complexity, and cost of the National Airspace System are dictated by the commercial airlines and their hub-and-spoke models."[10] They go on to claim that, "if general aviation were grounded immediately, the cost of operating the system would not change appreciably."[11] Neither of these statements stands up to close scrutiny. The second statement illustrates the difficulties in allocating common costs in a high fixed cost, low variable cost environment. It may well be true that, in the very short run, grounding general aviation would not change the operating costs of the air traffic control system appreciably. However, the same claim would be equally valid for any segment of aviation, including the scheduled passenger airlines. With high fixed costs and low marginal costs, having any segment of aviation exit the system in the very short run is unlikely to have much of an immediate impact on total costs.

On the other hand, if general aviation left the system permanently, then the system would not need to be as large or extensive. Recall from Table 15.6 that general aviation accounts for 52 percent of terminal operations at all airports with FAA towers. Even at Large Hubs and Middle Terminals, general aviation accounts for 27 percent of terminal operations. With general aviation accounting for this

---

9   http://www.eurocontrol.int/crco/gallery/content/public/docs/circulars/cond_appl_ 2006_en.pdf.

10 http://web.nbaa.org/public/govt/issues/funding.php.

11 http://web.nbaa.org/public/govt/issues/funding.php.

large of a share of operations handled by the air traffic control system, it's clear that that system was designed for and has evolved to accommodate the needs of both commercial passenger service and general aviation. Thus, it is appropriate for general aviation to pay for a portion of both the capital and the operating costs of the air traffic control system. General aviation is not a marginal user of the air traffic control system.

Revenue adequacy and stability

The question of revenue adequacy has two parts: (1) will the revenue be adequate initially when the rates are set, and (2) will the charging scheme adjust to both to growth and to changes in the mix of operations to maintain adequate revenue over time. With respect to the first question, just about any funding mechanism could be set at a level that would be adequate initially. The more difficult question is whether the scheme will adjust to changing needs of the air traffic control system.

Revenue stability presents a different challenge. The Airport and Airway Trust Fund has not provided a particularly stable source of funding for FAA. Figure 16.1 shows the trust fund revenues as a share of FAA appropriations. As can be seen, there has been wide variation in the trust fund's contribution from year to year. Some of this variation has been due to the budget process discussed in the previous chapter. Some variation is because activity in the aviation industry has historically been sensitive to changes in economic conditions and fuel prices as well as events such as the 9/11 terrorist attacks and the SARS outbreaks. Whether the air traffic control system is funded by user charges or by indirect taxes, these changes in aviation activity

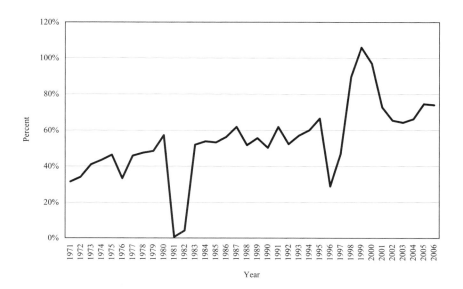

Figure 16.1   Trust fund revenues as a percent of FAA appropriations

will result in changes in the flow of revenues to support the system. In a system whose cost structure is characterized by high fixed costs and low variable costs, the fluctuations in total costs caused by these external factors are likely to be smaller than the fluctuations in revenues. In such a world, it is critical to have some sort of a reserve fund from which funds can be drawn in times of low revenue compared to costs and to which funds can be contributed during times of high revenue compared to costs. The need for such a fund is independent of whether the source of revenue is a system of user fees or a system of indirect taxes as the recent experiences of the United States, NAV CANADA, and NATS have shown.

Safety incentives

One concern expressed about some user fee proposals is that they might compromise safety, particularly among general aviation users. For example, it is feared that if there were separate charges for weather briefings, some general aviation pilots might choose to forgo those briefings rather than pay the charges to obtain them. Should this happen, the result might well be more accidents from pilots encountering unanticipated adverse weather conditions. The concern here is whether there is an added marginal cost for these safety items. One possible solution would be to include the cost of these briefings as part of some other charge such as a fuel tax as in the United States or a ATC access fee as used in NAV CANADA or Airservices Australia. Another option would be to pay for these safety related items out of the general fund. So long as the marginal cost of taking actions that improve safety, such as obtaining weather briefings, was zero there should be no concern about decreased safety from a charging mechanism. Still another option would be to require that pilots use these briefings as a condition of flying, in much the same way that the federal government requires that automobiles must be equipped with seat belts as a condition of being sold and some states require drivers and passengers of automobiles use those seat belts as a condition of using an automobile.

Administrative costs

Some argue that the fuel tax should be preferred to user charges because "there are no administrative costs associated with compliance," whereas user fees "require a large bureaucracy to administer."[12] Neither of these statements is accurate. In the case of fuel taxes, it's true that there are no FAA administrative costs associated with compliance, but that's because the Internal Revenue Service is charged with collecting the fuel taxes. In collecting these taxes the Internal Revenue Service must account for the fact that gasoline is taxed at a different rate than aviation gasoline and that kerosene is taxed at one rate in general use, but a different rate if used as an aviation fuel. In general, the Internal Revenue Service is governed by extensive rules and regulations in the collection of these taxes.[13] Similarly, a user fee system need not require a large bureaucracy to administer. The aircraft movements

---

12 http://web.nbaa.org/public/govt/issues/funding.php.
13 http://www.irs.gov/pub/irs-irbs/irb98-30.pdf.

are already monitored via the air traffic control computer system, so assessing the charges to the appropriate aircraft is straightforward and easily automated. Similarly, aircraft ownership information is also readily available through aircraft registration information and is easily automated and linked to usage information. As an example, EUROCONTROL's Central Route Charges Office (CRCO) combines a high recovery rate (average 99.48% for 1996–1999) with administrative costs which usually amount to little more than 0.5% of the charges collected.[14]

Addressing the first challenge

The first challenge – the disconnect between the factors that drive the costs of providing services and the factors that drive the revenue used to provide financial support – could be addressed while leaving the ATO as a part of FAA. In principle, there is nothing that would make funding the ATO with user fees while it was still part of FAA impossible. Indeed, as discussed later in this chapter, FAA proposed a new funding system that included user fees in 2007. GAO has investigated this question and found no evidence that moving to a direct charge or user fee system would require any change in FAA's governance structure.[15] One question is how the user fees would be set. The ATO's cost allocation system has improved substantially in recent years, but no matter how good the cost allocation system is, there will almost certainly still be controversy about the structure of user fees. Simply put, any change to a system of user fees will almost certainly change what various users of the system pay. Those asked to pay more will object, while those asked to pay less will applaud the change. Implementing any change where there are winners and losers is difficult, but when the losers are clearly defined and well-organized groups, the change is even more difficult. Nevertheless, financing air traffic control with a system of user fees would address the first challenge and could be done with the ATO remaining within FAA.

Diffused Accountability

A second challenge ATO faces is diffused accountability which has lead to continuing poor performance and high costs of its capital investment programs. As the Mineta Commission reported, "There are 'too many cooks' making authority and accountability too diffused."[16] The influence that Congress and the administration periodically exert on the FAA, and thus on the ATO, can be viewed as part of their legitimate oversight roles. But the result of this oversight is that FAA is much less accountable for its actions, because the accountability is shared with both Congress and the administration. One aspect is that budgetary decisions about how much

---

14 EUROCONTROL History: 1963–2003, "40 Years of Service to European Aviation," http://www.eurocontrol.int/corporate/public/standard_page/history.html.

15 US Government Accountability Office, Aviation Finance: Observations on Potential FAA Funding Options, GAO–06–973, September 2006.

16 National Civil Aviation Review Commission, Executive Summary, December 11, 1997.

money is available to support the operations of the ATO and the investment in capital are determined through the standard federal budget process. As second aspect is that this diffused accountability can result in inadequate incentives for financial discipline. As seen in the previous chapter, differences in investments and financial management are among the most striking differences between FAA and both NAV CANADA and NATS. As the Mineta Commission also reported, "Because there is so much dispersed power and authority in making budget decisions, FAA managers, industry, and the Congress can always point fingers when something goes awry."[17]

The problems of diffused accountability are inherent in the structure of ATO's relationship with other agencies, notably FAA and DOT, and with Congress. There may be periods of time when the specific individuals involved are able to work well together to minimize these problems as has arguably been the case in the early years of the ATO, but the structure will allow problems to crop up again in the future, as they have cropped up periodically in the past. Also, because accountability is spread among other government agencies, the administration, and Congress, there is relatively little direct accountability to the users of the air traffic control system. Again, this is in sharp contrast with NAV CANADA and NATS as well as with most other commercialized ANSPs where the users have considerable input into both operating and investment decisions. So long as ATO's funding is determined as part of the federal budget process, the problem of diffused accountability will remain. To address this challenge, the ATO would have to have its funding determined independently from the federal budget process. Removing the ATO from the FAA and providing it with a dedicated stream of funding might well be necessary to address the problems caused by diffused accountability.

Lack of Organizational Independence

The ATO's lack of organizational independence creates two types of problems. One is the risk that the ATO will get caught up in some government-wide movements that affect their ability to operate but are unrelated to the needs of the air traffic control system. At various times in the past, FAA has had to reduce the number of employees irrespective of their particular needs and has been restricted in spending Trust Fund monies because of budget deficit concerns. At other times, FAA has repeatedly been thwarted by Congress when it's tried to consolidate or close facilities. The issue is not whether those particular problems may reappear, some may and some may not, but rather the ATO's continued vulnerability to this sort of government-wide program.

A second type of problem is that FAA both operates the air traffic control system and regulates itself in its operation of that system. Self-regulation of air traffic control creates long-recognized potential conflicts of interest when there are decisions to be made about trade-offs between safety and capacity. Following the formation of the ATO, FAA has attempted to place greater separation between the regulation of air traffic control and its operation. Starting in 2005, FAA's Office of the Associate

---

17 National Civil Aviation Review Commission, Section III, December 11, 1997.

Administrator for Regulation and Certification established a separate Air Traffic Safety Oversight Service, which has the responsibility to establish, approve, and/or accept safety standards for the ATO. This restructuring has added more separation between operations and regulation. However, all of these units are still within FAA, so there remains a degree of self-regulation. Specific problems that emerge from self-regulation can always be corrected once they are identified, but they are only identified once self regulation has failed. Such problems are endemic to self-regulation.

Removing the ATO from FAA would provide the organizational independence necessary to eliminate the potential problems from self-regulation and, depending on the organizational structure that was used, it might also help insulate the ATO from government wide movements that could impede its ability to provide air traffic control services. It's important to understand that removing the ATO from the FAA is not the same thing as privatizing air traffic control nor does it mean removing the ATO from government oversight. While some have advocated privatization, that's not the only organizational option. An alternative would be some form of government corporation, along the lines of the approach used in both Australia and New Zealand. Indeed, Congress has created about 20 government corporations already including the Tennessee Valley Authority, the Corporation for Public Broadcasting, Amtrak, and the United States Postal Service. A government corporation was proposed for air traffic control by the Clinton Administration in the mid-1990s.

FAA's 2007 Reform Proposal

In February 2007, FAA presented a proposal to reform the way air traffic control services are funded in the United States. One central feature of the proposal was the elimination of the taxes levied on passengers and cargo (Table 15.1) and the replacement of these taxes by user fees. Little detail was provided in the proposal about what the level of user fees would be. The fees for the en route portion of flight would be based on distance and the fees for the terminal portion of flight would be based on weight. The terminal fee might also vary based on time of day and day of the week and might also be different for more congested airports. Because the fees weren't specified, it's not possible to tell the extent to which substituting fees for taxes would impact the various segments of commercial aviation.

A second central feature of the proposal was changing the fuel tax, both in structure and in magnitude. The structure of the tax changed in that a specific fuel tax of $.136 per gallon was proposed for both aviation gasoline and jet fuel used both by commercial and general aviation as a dedicated source of funding for the Airport Improvement Program. This tax represented an increase in the fuel tax for commercial users from the current tax of $.043 per gallon. Then, for general aviation and additional tax of $.564 per gallon was proposed for both aviation gasoline and for jet fuel. Thus, for general aviation the combined fuel tax was $.70 per gallon, which is a substantial increase over the current tax leveled on general aviation of $.193 for aviation gasoline and $.218 for jet fuel. General aviation flights would not be subject to the user fees unless they operated in the terminal airspace of one of the largest 30 or so airports (the Large Hubs).

The user fees and fuel taxes would continue to be subject to the normal budget appropriations process except that the user fees would be credited as off-setting collections which, under federal budgeting rules, could provide some limited protection for the FAA from some kinds of government-wide spending caps. There would also be a 13-member Air Transportation System Advisory Board, the majority of whose members would represent aviation stakeholders including various categories of commercial carriers, general aviation, business aviation, airports, and aviation manufacturing.

Confronting the challenges

How well would this proposal address the three challenges confronting the FAA? In terms of the disconnect between the cost drivers and the revenue drivers, this proposal appears to be an important step in the right direction. For the commercial users of the air traffic control system, a user fee system based on the miles flown in en route airspace and the number of terminal operations is a substantial improvement in matching the cost drivers to the revenue drivers to a tax on passenger tickets or on the charges paid by shippers for cargo. The number of flights in terminal airspace and the number of miles in en route airspace are important cost drivers for air traffic control. Without knowing the exact level of user fees, it's not possible to assess whether or not the commercial carriers will be paying and amount that covers the costs they impose on the system, but the FAA proposal appears to put a better structure of fees in place than the current taxes. In particular, this set of user fees should be better positioned to accommodate the anticipated growth in commercial aviation and the added demands that will be placed on the air traffic control system.

The revisions to the fuel taxes also appear to be a step in the right direction, although again without knowing the full set of user fees, it's not possible to determine the relative contributions of general aviation versus commercial aviation. However, given the demonstrated disparity between general aviation's contribution to the trust fund and the costs they impose on the air traffic control system, these tax imposed to fund the air traffic control system appear to be a reasonable step toward closing that gap. It's also encouraging to see a separate source of funding directed at the Airport Improvement Program (AIP) instead of having it intermingled with air traffic control. By making funding for the AIP transparent it will make it easier for all stakeholders to determine whether the level of funding is appropriate. Not charging general aviation user fees is consistent with the practices of other major ANSPs, but the exception of charging user fees when general aviation aircraft enter the terminal airspace of large hubs is reasonable since these are the most congested facilities and since general aviation activity at large hubs is almost exclusively high performance turbine aircraft (business jets).

With regard to the second challenge of diffused accountability, the FAA proposal opens the door for a small step in the right direction. The proposed Air Transportation System Advisory Board has the potential to provide a single voice for how the users of the air traffic control system view such things as user fee rates, major capital infrastructure decisions, and the development and operation of ATO's performance metrics. The Board is only advisory with the authority for final decisions resting with the FAA Administrator and the Secretary of Transportation so accountability is still diffused within the Administration and ATO funding is still subject to the appropriation process so accountability is still diffused with Congress. But the FAA Administrator is a member of the Board, as is a representative of the Department of Defense, so the Board has the potential to reduce the diffusion of accountability within the Administration. The problem of diffused accountability is not solved, but the proposal makes what could become a small step in the right direction.

Finally, the challenge of a lack of organizational independence is not addressed by the FAA proposal. The operator of the air traffic control system remains a part of FAA, as does the regulator of the air traffic control system, so the proposal doesn't address the potential problem of self-regulation.

Summary

While, the formation of the Air Traffic Organization (ATO) within the Federal Aviation Administration (FAA) has been an important step in improving the management of the air traffic control system in the United States, three fundamental challenges still remain. Until these challenges are addressed, ATO will be severely limited in how much progress it can make.

The first challenge, the disconnect between the cost drivers and the revenue drivers, could be most easily addressed by changing the manner in which the ATO is financed from a system of taxes unrelated to the cost of providing air traffic control services to a system of user fees that more closely matched the cost drivers. The choice between the current system of taxes or a system of user fees is not a binary one. There is significant variation in the relationship among charges to various aircraft within these three user charge systems examined earlier in the chapter. None of the user fee systems used by the major ANSPs charges every user of the system the same. All retain some degree of cross-subsidy in the form of reduced charges for smaller aircraft such as regional jets or business jets. Similarly, as seen in the experiences of NAV CANADA, EUROCONTROL, and Airservices Australia, a user fee system need not impose high costs on small general aviation aircraft. The user charge systems currently in use in other countries reflect a continuum of how much of the air traffic control costs should be born by each type of user. The choice for the United States is not taxes versus user fees so much as where along this continuum its air traffic control financing system should the financing system be located.

The second challenge – diffused accountability – are inherent in the structure of ATO's relationship with other agencies, notably FAA and DOT, and with Congress. So long as ATO's funding is determined as part of the federal budget process, the problem of diffused accountability will remain. To address this challenge, the ATO would have to have its funding determined independently from the federal budget process which would probably require having the ATO removed from FAA.

The third challenge – the lack of organizational independence – can best be addressed by removing the ATO from the FAA. To avoid potential problems of self regulation, most other countries have established their ANSP as organizationally independent from their civil aviation regulator and the United States needs to do the same thing.

Addressing these three challenges does not mean that the ATO needs to be privatized. Instead, the experience in other countries shows that there are a variety of organizational form that allow these challenges to be addressed. Airservices Australia is a state-owned authority and Airways New Zealand is a state-owned enterprise. Both are the equivalent of government corporations in the United States. Putting air traffic control into a government corporation with dedicated funding was proposed during the Clinton Administration. NAV CANADA is organized as a private non-share capital corporation which functions much as a stakeholders cooperative. NATS was formed as a public-private partnership and functions as a regulated private entity. Other countries have used variants of these approaches to avoid the challenges facing the ATO.

SECTION FIVE
Cross-Cutting Issues
and Lessons Learned

The final section of the book, Chapters 17 and 18, examines the cross-cutting issue of labor relations and the lessons learned from examining ANSPs from around the world. Chapter 17 looks at the challenges posed by labor issues and why labor relations are more contentious with some organizational structures and funding mechanisms than others. Most ANSPs have periodic labor relations issues, but some ANSPs seem to have more contentious labor relations than others. Bilateral monopoly situations have the potential to produce contentious labor relations as each side seeks to increase its bargaining position to seek more favorable contract terms. The contentiousness is compounded in the United States by the tax-based funding system for FAA, where labor has no responsibility for where the revenue comes from to pay for the contract. In contrast, for NAV CANADA, responsibility is more spread across the interest groups with the unions having two of the fifteen seats on the Board of Directors, while airlines have four and business aviation has one. A challenge for all ANSPs is to be sure that controllers are closely involved in the design of the new technology that they will be using in the future. Another labor issue that all ANSPs face is labor's attitude toward commercialization, which raises the question in many minds of facility consolidation. A final labor problem faced throughout the world is the ability of the regulators of the air traffic control system to recruit and retain the technical expertise needed to regulate effectively.

Chapter 18 compares the strengths and weaknesses of the different organizational structures that are used in different countries throughout the world. Five different types of organizational forms are considered covering the continuum from a fully private corporation to a traditional government agency. There is no one single form that is an automatic solution for all of the challenges facing ANSPs. Each form has some dimensions at which it excels and each has other dimensions at which it is not the strongest. The changes in how air navigation services have been provided present a spectrum of organizational, financial, and operational initiatives. Each experience was shaped at least in part by the legacy of the organization which preceded and the political process through which the change was made. In almost every case, these legacies and processes created problems in transition. The variety of experiences not only allow an examination of the lessons learned, but also provide insight into the mix of approaches that might be best able to improve a country's (or region's) air navigation services.

Chapter 17

Labor Issues

Introduction

Almost all Air Navigation Service Providers (ANSPs) seem to have labor issues from time to time and in some cases they can be quite contentious. The best known and most highly publicized example was the strike by the Professional Air Traffic Controllers Organization (PATCO) in the United States in 1981, which led to President Reagan firing the striking controllers. As discussed in Chapter 14, this strike and subsequent firing were simply the culmination of several years of increasingly contentious labor relations.

Strikes threats of strikes, or other job actions by air traffic controllers continue to be seen in many countries. For example, in June 2006, Aeroports de Paris, the French airport operator, reported around 30 flight cancellations or diversions owing to a strike by air traffic controllers at Paris Le Bourget airport. The strike followed a demand that the airport be reclassified from category 3 to category 2, which would result in an increase in pay for air traffic controllers.[1] In November 2006, a so-called "work-by-the-book" slowdown by air traffic controllers in Brazil caused the delay or cancellation of hundreds of domestic and international flights. The controllers claimed they were understaffed, overworked, and underpaid.[2] In March 2007, Italian air traffic controllers struck in Rome causing Alitalia to cancel 150 flights and delay 50 more. Other airlines were similarly affected. Again, working conditions and compensation seemed to be the cause of the strike.[3] Strikes have also recently been threatened in Spain and Germany, but were avoided in last minute negotiations.

This chapter examines the labor issues facing ANSPs throughout the world. It begins by discussion the economic characteristics of a bilateral monopoly that describes relations between ANSPs and air traffic controllers. The chapter then turns to two specific issues of concern in the United States: 1) the task of replacing a wave of retiring controllers and 2) the problems faced in the most recent contract negotiations. The chapter next examines three important themes found throughout the world: 1) labor's role as a stakeholder in air traffic control modernization, 2) labor's concerns regarding the movement toward commercialization, and 3) the challenge of attracting and retaining technical expertise in the regulatory agencies that oversee the ANSPs.

---

1   "Strike Disrupts Air Traffic at Paris Le Bourget," *Europe Intelligence Wire*, June 28, 2006.

2   "Passengers Put Out By Controllers' Slowdown In Brazil," *Aviation Daily*, Vol. 366, Number 25, page 5, November 6, 2006.

3   "175 Flights Cancelled as Rome Air Traffic Controllers Strike," *Europe Intelligence Wire*, March 14, 2007.

Bilateral Monopoly – One Buyer and One Seller

In a competitive market for labor, a prospective employee has several potential employers to choose from, each of whom would like to hire someone with his or her skills and training. Similarly, a prospective employer seeking to hire an employee will have multiple potential employees to choose from, all with similar skills and training. A situation where there was only one buyer of labor, one employer, and many sellers of labor, potential employees, would be characterized as a monopsony and the wage rate would tend to be lower than in a competitive market. On the other hand, if there were only one seller of labor, a trade union for example, and there were many potential employers, then the situation would be characterized as a monopoly and the wage rate would tend to be higher than in a competitive market.

In the case of air traffic controllers, there is both a single buyer of their services, the ANSP for that country, and since air traffic controllers are almost always represented by a union, there is also a single seller of air traffic controllers, the union.[4] The supply of air traffic controllers can't be expanded quickly because of the training requirements and because there is relatively little mobility of controllers from the ANSP of one country to the ANSP of another. Similarly, the skills of an air traffic controller don't readily transfer to other occupations. This situation is called a bilateral monopoly and the resulting wage rate is likely to be somewhere between that of the monopoly situation and that of the monopsony situation. Where, exactly, the wage rate will fall depends on the relative bargaining power of both sides. Thus, bilateral monopoly situations have the potential to produce contentious labor relations as each side seeks to increase its bargaining position to seek a more favorable wage rate.

However, labor relations in all ANSPs don't seem to be equally contentious. Depending on the governance structure, some commercialized ANSPs seem to have better labor relations than is found at FAA, a traditional government agency. For example, in August 2005, NAV CANADA and its controllers union reached agreement on a four-year contract after less than five months of negotiation.[5] In NAV CANADA's case, responsibility is more spread across the interest groups with the unions having two of the fifteen seats on the Board of Directors, while airlines have four and business aviation has one. Thus, the lines between labor and management are not nearly as sharply drawn for NAV CANADA as is the case with the FAA where user groups and other stakeholders, including unions, are not represented in FAA's governance structure. With NAV CANADA, the union is represented on both sides of the table during the contract negotiation, although its interests clearly lie more on one side than on the other. In the case of FAA, as a government agency, there is a much sharper line between management as the buyer of controllers' services and the union as the seller of controllers' services. Also, because FAA is funded by a

---

4   The widespread unionization of air traffic controllers is easily understood as a way of having a bilateral monopoly rather than a monopsony where wages would be expected to be lower.

5   "Nav Canada Controllers Ratify New Four-Year Contract," *Aviation Daily*, Volume 361, Number 41, August 29, 2005.

system of excise taxes set by Congress supplemented by contributions from general tax revenues rather than user fees set by the ANSP, the union does not have to take any responsibility for addressing the financial implications of its contract settlement. With representation on the Board of Directors, the unions in the NAV CANADA case share responsibility of setting the user fees or taking other actions to cover the costs of the contract settlement.

In the United States with both a government agency ANSP without labor represented in the governance structure and with a tax-based funding system where labor has no responsibility in setting the tax rate, the contentiousness is probably inherently worse than with some other organizational and funding forms. Here, the negotiation process is much more dependent on relative bargaining powers. Much of the effort of the National Air Traffic Controllers Association (NATCA) to cultivate support among members of Congress can be viewed as an attempt to increase their bargaining power with respect to the Federal Aviation Administration. As will be discussed later in this chapter, in the discussions about possible moves to a more commercialized approach, NATCA has consistently opposed more commercialization and argued to keep Congress closely involved in FAA oversight and decision-making. In the most recent round of contract negotiations, NATCA repeatedly appealed to Congress to intervene and secure contract terms more favorable to controllers. All of this behavior is consistent with seeking to increase union bargaining power in a contentious bilateral monopoly.

The Challenge of Controller Retirements in the United States

The origins of the problem

The 1981 PATCO strike resulted in the firing of approximately 11,000 controllers out of a total union membership of 15,000. This created a massive need to hire a new generation of controllers at an unprecedented level. On October 2, 1981, FAA entered into a $10 million contract with the University of Oklahoma to help train new air traffic controllers to replace those fired for participating in the illegal strike. The agreement proved to be the first in a series of controller training contracts with the University of Oklahoma and others. Through these training programs, FAA was eventually able to rebuild the number of controllers to the point where the last of the special flight restrictions that had been imposed when the strike began were lifted in 1984. One important legacy of the strike which was recognized at the time was that the large number of controllers hired during this rebuilding period would all become eligible for retirement within a short period of time, creating another potential shortage of controllers in the future.

The nature and magnitude of the problem

FAA estimates it will lose about 72 percent of its air traffic controller workforce over the ten-year period between 2006 and 2016.[6] As far back as 2002, Congress and the Department of Transportation's Inspector General raised concern about the FAA's level of preparation for the retirement wave. To address these losses, FAA plans to hire about 15,000 controllers between 2007 and 2016.[7] Figure 17.1 shows the actual controller losses and hires from 2002 through 2006 and the forecast losses and hires in the 2007–2016 period. The hiring targets shown in the figure are higher than those that had been projected in June 2006 to reflect that controllers were found to be retiring at a more rapid rate than FAA had originally forecast. For example, FAA projected 341 retirements for fiscal year 2005 but 465 controllers actually retired – 36 percent more than FAA's estimate. Similarly, in fiscal year 2006, 25 percent more controllers retired than FAA projected. According to FAA and NATCA officials, the large jump in actual retirements was a result of the breakdown in contract talks (discussed below).[8] Controllers are eligible to retire at age 50 if they have at least 20 years of service and can retire at any age after 25 years of service. Moreover under a law in effect since 1971, most controllers are required to stop handling traffic when they reach age 56. Thus for many controllers, there is considerable flexibility about when they can retire.

In looking at Figure 17.1, it's apparent that FAA's hiring plan is clearly ambitious compared to what they were able to accomplish in 2002 to 2005. Indeed, the low number of new hires in 2004 and 2005 caused considerable concern in many aviation circles, although some of that concern abated with the large number of hires in 2006. It's also apparent that the planned sustained increase in the number of new hires will stretch FAA's training capabilities. In June 2005, FAA began considering whether prospective controllers who graduate from aviation-related programs in certain colleges could bypass the currently required academy training and instead proceed directly to an ATC facility to begin on-the-job training. Such a change in the training program holds potential for cost savings and has been endorsed both by union officials and by one of the colleges that prepares graduates for careers in aviation.[9]

---

6   United States Government Accountability Office, *Federal Aviation Administration: Key Issues in Ensuring the Efficient Development and Safe Operation of the Next Generation Air Transportation System*, Statement of Gerald L. Dillingham, Ph.D., Director Physical Infrastructure Issues, Testimony Before the Subcommittee on Aviation, Committee on Transportation and Infrastructure, House of Representatives, March 22, 2007. GAO–07–636T.

7   Federal Aviation Administration, *A Plan for the Future – 2007–2016*, The Federal Aviation Administration's 10-Year Strategy for the Air Traffic Control Workforce, March 2007.

8   US DOT Office of the Inspector General, *FAA Continues to Make Progress in Implementing Its Controller Workforce Plan, But Further Efforts are Needed in Several Key Areas*, Federal Aviation Administration, Report Number: AV–2007–032, Date Issued: February 9, 2007.

9   United States Government Accountability Office, National Airspace System: *Transformation will Require Cultural Change, Balanced Funding Priorities, and Use of all*

There are currently 14 colleges and universities approved to participate in the Air Traffic Collegiate Training Initiative, a program established by FAA in 1991.[10] Under this initiative, participating schools produce candidates with college degrees and a broad knowledge of the aviation industry. These candidates have at least a basic level of training in air traffic control and have demonstrated their interest in the field by the investment they have made in their own training. The hope is that through this and other initiatives, FAA can achieve greater success than it did in the 1980s, when it last hired large numbers of controllers, but had problems with retention. At that time most of the candidates were recruited with no prior background in aviation or air traffic control with the result was that over 40 percent of the candidates failed before completing their training.

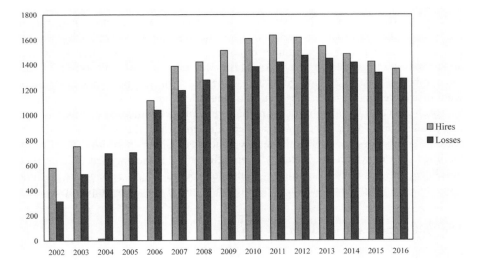

Figure 17.1   Historic and planned controller hires and loses

The hiring challenge is more complex than might be inferred from simply looking at Figure 17.1. The controllers who are retiring are fully certified controllers while the bulk of the new hires must first attend the FAA Academy for 12 weeks of training. Some of the hires may come from the Department of Defense with prior training in

---

Available Management Tools, October 2005, GAO–06–154.

10 The institutions are: University of Alaska Anchorage, Mt. San Antonio College in California, Embry-Riddle Aeronautical University and Miami-Dade College in Florida, Purdue University, Minneapolis Community & Technical College, Daniel Webster College in New Hampshire, Vaughn College and Dowling College in New York, University of North Dakota, Community College of Beaver County in Pennsylvania, Inter American University of Puerto Rico, Middle Tennessee State University and Hampton University in Virginia.

air traffic control, but the military has recently increased incentives for controllers to remain in the service so that former military controllers may be less of a source in the future than they've been in the recent past. After receiving the initial training, the controllers will work as "developmental controllers" until they complete the requirements to be certified for all the air traffic control positions within a defined area of the facility.[11] It typically takes 2 to 4 years for a developmental controller to become fully certified, so that with the planned hiring program, a large portion of the controller workforce may be trainees or developmental controllers and not fully certified. Based on FAA's hiring and retirement projections, even by 2010, about 40 percent of the air traffic controller workforce will still have 5 or fewer years of experience.

In addition to the challenge of hiring and training new air traffic controllers, it will be important to deploy controllers to individual facilities to match changing air traffic demands. FAA's recent controller workforce plan is based on facility-by-facility staffing standards. The staffing standards are intended to take into consideration facility-specific information, such as air traffic operations, productivity trends, expected retirements, and the number of controllers in training. The new standards appear to be an improvement over FAA's historical approach, which was to compute the number of controllers needed system-wide and then negotiate how controllers were distributed among facilities with the controllers union. The previous staffing approach did not fully take into account the significant differences in complexity and workload among FAA's 300 terminal and en route control facilities. However, FAA's current staffing does not align with the new standards at about one-third of FAA's 314 facilities – 93 of which are currently overstaffed and 11 understaffed. The current misallocation adds further complexity to the controller hiring, training, and staffing issues as does the potential effect of new technologies that may be implemented.

The 2006 Contract Negotiation

In 1996, the Clinton administration allowed NATCA to bargain with FAA over wages and benefits, a right enjoyed by few federal-employee unions. NATCA negotiated a new contract in 1998 and between then and 2006, NATCA controllers' compensation increased by 74 percent to an average of $166,000 a year. As a point of comparison, this compensation is slightly above the 2006 pay for rank and file members of the House of Representatives and the Senate. The FAA began contract negotiations with NATCA in July 2005. In April 2006, after reaching an impasse in negotiations with NATCA, FAA used its authority under the law to settle the impasse by imposing a contract on its air traffic controllers. Rules governing the negotiations between the two parties allowed FAA to deliver its final contract to Congress, and if legislators didn't act on it for 60 days, it could be ratified. In the contract, FAA attempted to control costs by offering a proposal that would protect the total compensation of all current controllers, but would reduce the compensation of new hires by offering $127,000

---

11 US Department of Labor, Bureau of Labor Statistics, *Occupational Outlook Handbook* (www.bls.gov/oco/ocos108.htm).

in salary and benefits in the first five years. Congress chose not to intervene and the contract was imposed on NATCA. Congressional sympathy for the controllers may have been dampened by the fact that the 100 top NATCA union members make $197,000 a year, a salary substantially above even that paid to Majority and Minority Leaders of Congress and to cabinet secretaries. Subsequent attempts by NATCA to get Congress to force FAA to reopen contract negotiations were not successful. In August 2006, the President of NATCA during the contract negotiations, John Carr, was defeated in his re-election bid.

From FAA's perspective, the new contract was not entirely about compensation, but also provided increased management flexibility to match staffing to workload. FAA had limited flexibility to alter staffing to changing needs under the previous contract. For example, following TWA's bankruptcy in 2001 and subsequent acquisition with American Airlines, traffic at the St. Louis airport dropped off dramatically, reducing total controller workload in the area. The FAA, however, was contractually bound to a negotiated number of controllers at the facility and hence had too many controllers and not enough work. Similarly, when a new carrier, Independence Air, saw its traffic dramatically increase at Dulles Airport, FAA was limited in its ability to realign staffing to handle that increase.

The impasse in contract negotiations followed by the imposition of a contract on controllers certainly has not helped the already contentious labor relations between FAA and NATCA. In NATCA's view controllers are working under imposed work and pay rules rather than a contract agreed to by both sides. Pat Forrey, NATCA's new president continues to ask Congress to force FAA to return to the bargaining table with NATCA to resume the contract negotiations.[12] Ill will resulting from the imposition of a contract may already have aggravated the controller retirement issue and has the potential to increase early retirements in the future. Moreover, the lingering resentment is not likely to make the next round of contract negotiations go any more smoothly.

Labor's Role in Air Traffic Control Modernization

The contentious labor relations situation in the United States is also reflected in the planning process for modernization of the air traffic control system. In 2003, the enactment of P.L.108–176 (Vision 100 – Century of Aviation Reauthorization Act) laid out the mandate for Next Generation Air Transportation System (NGATS) initiative and proposed a public/private partnership managed by the Joint Planning and Development Office (JPDO) to carry it out. The JPDO involves representatives from the Departments of Transportation, Defense, Homeland Security and Commerce and the FAA, NASA and White House Office of Science and Technology Policy.

The JPDO is at the heart of a large and complex effort to design the air navigation and air traffic control systems of the future. It seems beyond dispute that any such effort should involve those who operate the current system and who will be operating the future system. Originally, NATCA assigned a controller to JPDO as

---

12 "Problem solving through dialogue," *Air Traffic Management*, Spring 2007.

part of its liaison program with the FAA. However, On June 28, 2005, shortly before the start of the air traffic controller contract negotiations, FAA notified NATCA that it was terminating the liaison assignments effective July 29, 2005, citing budget constraints and the implementation of the ATO. The controller who had been acting as the liaison within JPDO's Agile Air Traffic System Integrated Product Team was among the controllers who returned to his facility. Through the end of March 2007, no active controller participated in the NGATS planning effort of JPDO.[13] The lack of involvement of such a key party as air traffic controllers in the early stages of system planning is disturbing. As GAO reports:

> Our work on FAA's current air traffic control modernization program has shown that without early and continuing stakeholder input, costly rework and delays can occur late in system development. Similarly, the input of active controllers on JPDO's planned research – especially on how controllers interact with pilots and air traffic systems in a highly automated environment – can help to identify potential safety issues early, before costly changes become necessary. Controllers' input could also inform JPDO's analyses of issues such as timeliness, cost-effectiveness, and the safe transformation of the nation's air traffic control system.[14]

The situation in the United States with a lack of controller input on modernization to JPDO is in marked contrast to the situations in both Canada and the United Kingdom. With both NAV CANADA and NATS, controllers are heavily involved in virtually all aspects of hardware and software design and system modernization. Indeed, many of the improvements at NATS have originated with ideas from the controllers. Controllers at NATS and NAV CANADA are thoroughly involved in the design, testing, and implementation of new equipment and procedures.

As one looks to the future of labor's role in the air traffic control system, concerns have been raised that unions have little or no incentive to adopt some of the new technologies because they are designed to handle more aircraft with fewer people, thus threatening controller employment.[15] Some have argued that for nearly 20 years, NATCA has worked to slow down almost all technology deployment that might decrease controller workload and increase controller productivity.[16] A related concern is that improvements in technology will change the future role of air traffic controllers to one of monitoring air traffic rather than controlling or directing it.

---

13 United States Government Accountability Office, *JOINT PLANNING AND DEVELOPMENT OFFICE Progress and Key Issues in Planning the Transition to the Next Generation Air Transportation System*, Testimony Before the Subcommittee on Space and Aeronautics, Committee on Science and Technology, House of Representatives, GAO–07–693T, March 29, 2007.

14 United States Government Accountability Office, *Responses to Post-Hearing Questions for the Record, The Future of Air Traffic Control: The R&D Agenda*, Subcommittee on Space and Aeronautics. Committee on Science, House of Representatives, GAO–06–778R, Submitted May 17, 2006.

15 United States Government Accountability Office, *NATIONAL AIRSPACE SYSTEM: Experts' Views on Improving the US Air Traffic Control Modernization Program*, GAO–05–333SP, April 2005.

16 George Donahue, "US Air Transportation: An Approaching Perfect Storm," *Aerospace America*, August 2006, page 26.

While in principle, there may be some basis for these concerns, it's easy to overstate them because the future of air traffic control is unlikely to involve a dramatic increase in controller productivity or a sudden change in the role of the controller.

It's certainly true that some of the new technology is designed to ease controller workload. As discussed in Chapter 2, ADS-B has the potential to shift some of the responsibility for maintaining separation between aircraft from the controller to the pilots. But ADS-B is not the first example of using technology to enhance the controller's ability to maintain separation. Already, there are computer programs to alert controllers of potential conflicts before separation is lost. Even TCAS (Traffic Collision Avoidance System) can be viewed as technology that aids in maintaining separation.

These sorts of technologies are likely to have the biggest impact in the en route environment. Even here, the likely change will be to allow aircraft to fly more efficient routes and altitude profiles. As technology allows more of the responsibility for route selection and maintaining separation to be transferred to the pilots, the en route controllers' role will shift more toward monitoring flights and away from directing each flight's every direction and altitude change. But these changes are already starting to occur and the changes in the future will be gradual and evolutionary rather than a dramatic shift of controller responsibilities. There is much more of a continuum between directing traffic and monitoring traffic than a sharp distinction and even the en route controller's job will continue to have some of both kinds of duties in the foreseeable future.

In terminal airspace surrounding congested airports, controllers are likely to retain a primary role of directing both departing and arriving traffic with less of the responsibilities for route selection and maintaining separation transferred to pilots. With aviation traffic forecast to grow much more rapidly than airport runway capacity, there is little doubt that more and more airports will become more and more congested. With runway capacity increasingly scarce, there will be even more pressure to use runways efficiently with both arrival and departure streams maintained to minimize any moments where runways are underutilized. In the foreseeable future, controllers will continue to play a key role in making sure these facilities are efficiently utilized. As more and more airports become congested, it's almost inconceivable that there would be any technologies with sufficient productivity gains that would be enough to reduce the overall need for terminal airspace controllers.

Labor and Commercialization

While labor unions have been largely opposed to commercialization in the United States and Europe, that hasn't been the case everywhere. Indeed, the unions supported the creation of NAV CANADA, in part because they had endured a six-year long wage freeze under Transport Canada. But since the formation of NAV CANADA, labor relations have been far less contentious than previously. Similarly, neither NATS nor Airservices Australia have had labor problems following their commercialization, although in the United Kingdom, some senior trade union leaders have called for the renationalization of air traffic control, along with the railways and other public services.[17]

In the United States, NATCA is strongly opposed to commercialization in any form. They oppose user fees primarily because they see user fees as a first step toward commercialization, which they consistently refer to in its most extreme form as privatization. NATCA continues with its long-standing argument air traffic control is an "inherently governmental" function and opposes any participation by a "contracted service provider."[18] In NATCA's view, the February 2007 reform proposal is a first step toward privatizing air traffic control in the United States.

NATCA's opposition to commercialization is most easily understood in the context of seeking bargaining power in a bilateral monopoly. In the current organizational arrangement, NATCA relies heavily on direct appeals to Congress as a means of attempting to improve its bargaining position. Even after Congress refused to intervene in the 2006 contract negotiation, NATCA continued to lobby Congress to overturn the contract.[19] While the effort was ultimately not successful, they did find a sympathetic ear among some in Congress.

NATCA has also found a sympathetic ear among some members of Congress with regard to facility consolidation. While NATCA does not publically oppose the consolidation of air traffic control facilities, it supports consolidation only when the process involves "all of the FAA stakeholders, including controllers and Members of Congress."[20] Members of Congress, of course, have generally opposed consolidation when it involves job loss in their districts or relocation to other districts, as consolidation inevitably does. The Department of Defense faced a similar problem in trying to consolidate military bases and close unneeded facilities. A Base Realignment and Closure (BRAC) process was developed in 1988 that greatly reduced the political challenges of closing facilities by having multiple facility closures considered as a group rather than on a one facility at a time basis. The BRAC process has been very successful in de-politicizing military facility closings and allowing the needed consolidations. In FAA's February 2007 proposal, it included a BRAC-like process to consider air traffic control facility consolidations. NATCA opposed this feature of the proposal by arguing that it would leave inadequate redundancy to maintain safety.

The experience with commercialization in Europe has also raised controller concerns about facility consolidation. The dominant characteristic of the air traffic control system in Europe is that it is highly fragmented. Recall that Europe's airspace covers 6,120 square kilometers but has 57 separate ANSPs with 75 area

---

17 Robert Watts, "Brothers tell Labour what they want in return for their millions," *The Sunday Telegraph*, January 28, 2007.

18 Patrick Forrey, "A Review of FAA Operational and Safety Programs," Testimony before the House Committee on Transportation and Infrastructure, Subcommittee on Aviation, March 22, 2007.

19 "NATCA Turns to Congress to Overturn FAA Contract," *Aviation Daily*, Volume 367, Number 46, March 9, 2007.

20 Patrick Forrey, "A Review of FAA Operational and Safety Programs," Testimony before the House Committee on Transportation and Infrastructure, Subcommittee on Aviation, March 22, 2007.

control centers employing 42,000 people. The air traffic control systems of the US and Canada, in contrast, together cover an area over three times as large with two and one half times the number of aircraft movements, but control that space with slightly more than one third the number of area control centers and employ fewer people. The need to reduce fragmentation in Europe has been evident since the 1960s. The failure to establish a unified air traffic control system in Europe's upper airspace is the result of a long-standing basic tension between national sovereignty and operationally efficient airspace design.

As European ANSPs become increasingly commercialized, considerations of national sovereignty may begin to take on less prominence relative to considerations of efficient airspace design and pressures to consolidate facilities are likely to increase. Air Traffic Controllers European Unions Coordination (ATCEUC) was created in 1991 and is composed of 20 professional and autonomous trade unions representing more than 11500 air traffic controllers throughout Europe.[21] In the view of ATCEUC, the Single European Skies initiative (discussed in Chapter 7) has the goal of getting rid of any notion of frontier or border in the air and providing the tools to rationalize and reorganize the airspace.[22] ATCEUC foresees two potential paths: cooperation among existing ANSPs or competition between them. Not surprisingly, ATCEUC argues for cooperation among existing ANSPs and rejects any notion of competition. It further argues that cost reductions should not be achieved through savings on ATM personnel.

A variation on the theme of cooperation as opposed to competition has been put forth in Project Mosaic, a regional initiative, launched by ATCEUC members from France, Maastricht UAC, Belgium, the Netherlands, Luxembourg, Switzerland, Italy, and Germany. This group opposes any attempt at introducing competition between ANSPs and argues instead for a the eventual step-by-step creation of a single entity to provide air traffic control services in the airspace of these countries based on extensive cooperation among the ANSPs.[23] This organization would rely either on user charges or state subsidies or some combination of both. Of most significance, the entity would be under the direct supervision of the Ministers of Transport of the participating countries and the staff would be employed under the European civil servant general conditions of employment. The members of Mosaic explicitly reject the proposed privatization of DFS, the German ANSP and are clearly proposing a movement away from commercialization.

In sum, NATCA opposes commercialization in part because it could diminish Congressional influence over ANSP management and thus potentially weaken the

---

21 Membership includes: AATCU (Serbia), ATC Branch of IMPACT (Ireland), ATCOR (Romania), ATM PP (Italy), BATCU (Bulgaria), EEEKE (Greece), GdF (Germany), GLCCA (Luxembourg), HSKL (Croatia), ITUATC (Serbia), LIFSZ (Hungary), MATCA (Malta), MATCU (FYROM), Skycontrol (Switzerland), SINCTA (Portugal), SNCTA (France), SSKL (Slovenia), TUEM (Eurocontrol), USCA (Spain), ZZKRL (Poland).

22 Air Traffic Controllers European Unions Coordination, Roadmap for Future ATM, Position Paper, July 2006, (http://www.atceuc.org/atceuc_documents.php).

23 "Air traffic controllers and trade unions: working to create a single Air Navigation Service Provider over their own countries," Press Release, Common Statement, (http://www.project-mosaic.eu/home.htm).

union's position in bilateral monopoly negotiations. Where this might be most clearly seen would be in an easier path to facility consolidation. The experience in Canada lends credence to that concern because facility consolidation and closure was politically much more difficult before the formation of NAV CANADA than it has been since. Fear of facility consolidation would also seem to be the major concern of labor unions in Europe where commercialization can be expected to lead to growing pressure to address fragmentation.

Retaining Technical Expertise

While the advantages of separating the operation of the air traffic control system from its regulation are clear and well understood, one potential downside of this separation is that it can be more difficult for the government regulatory agency to retain the technical expertise it needs. When the separation involved a commercialized ANSP, the problem was often aggravated. When NAV CANADA was established, much of the staff who had been involved with overseeing safety moved to the new organization, leaving Transport Canada with inadequate staff to conduct timely safety inspections in the early months following the transition. In the United Kingdom, the CAA has expressed similar concern about its ability to oversee the safety of NATS's operations and Germany has similar concerns regarding it move toward privatization of DFS. Regulators also need the expertise of experienced air traffic controllers, but the high salaries of controllers working for ANSPs makes recruiting qualified staff for regulatory positions difficult.

The problem of retaining technical expertise isn't confined to controllers. As long ago as 1988, the Aviation Safety Commission raised concerns about the FAA's ability to retain safety inspectors with sufficient technical expertise. The same skills that made these inspectors valuable to the FAA also made them valuable to the private sector, particularly airlines, airframe manufacturers, and component manufacturers. Compounding the problem in the United States is the fact that the FAA also faces a wave of retirement of safety inspectors. By 2010, 44 percent of FAA's inspector workforce of about 3,865 will be eligible to retire.[24] To begin addressing this situation, FAA has requested funding to hire an additional 87 inspectors in fiscal year 2008, but that number will have to be increased sharply in the near future to keep pace with the expected retirements. FAA also employs over 6,000 technicians who maintain the air traffic control equipment. As with the safety inspectors, these technicians have skills and expertise that is in demand elsewhere in the aviation industry, often at higher wages.

---

24 United States Government Accountability Office, *Federal Aviation Administration: Key Issues in Ensuring the Efficient Development and Safe Operation of the Next Generation Air Transportation System*, Statement of Gerald L. Dillingham, Ph.D., Director Physical Infrastructure Issues, Testimony Before the Subcommittee on Aviation, Committee on Transportation and Infrastructure, House of Representatives, March 22, 2007, GAO–07–636T.

Summary

Most ANSPs have periodic labor relations issues, but some ANSPs seem to have more contentious labor relations than others. At the United States' FAA, labor relations can be described as a bilateral monopoly, where there is a single purchaser of air traffic controller's services, the FAA, and a single seller of those services, the controllers' union, NATCA. In a bilateral monopoly, the wage rate and working conditions that emerge from negotiations depends on the relative bargaining power of both sides. Bilateral monopoly situations have the potential to produce contentious labor relations as each side seeks to increase its bargaining position to seek more favorable contract terms. The continuing effort of the National Air Traffic Controllers Association (NATCA) to cultivate support among members of Congress can be viewed as an attempt to increase their bargaining power with respect to the Federal Aviation Administration. The contentiousness is compounded in the United States by the tax-based funding system for FAA, where labor has no responsibility for where the revenue comes from to pay for the contract. In contrast, for NAV CANADA, responsibility is more spread across the interest groups with the unions having two of the fifteen seats on the Board of Directors, while airlines have four and business aviation has one. With this kind of representation on the board, the lines between labor and management are not nearly as sharply drawn. NAV CANADA's unions share responsibility of setting the user fees or taking other actions to cover the costs of the contract settlement.

Against the backdrop of an inherently more contentious labor relations environment, FAA faces two critical labor problems. The first is replacing the large number of air traffic controller retirements expected by 2016. This coming wave of retirements stems from the large number of controllers hired in the wake of the PATCO strike in 1981 beginning to reach retirement age. To address these losses, FAA plans to hire about 15,000 controllers between 2007 and 2016, but hiring and training such a large number of controllers in such a short time period will be a challenge. The task will not be made any easier by the second problem, the failure of the FAA and NATCA to agree on a contract in 2006. When the contract talks failed to reach agreement, FAA, under the law and with Congressional approval, imposed contract terms on the union. Understandably, this action provoked lingering resentment among the controller workforce.

A challenge for all ANSPs is to be sure that controllers are closely involved in the design of the new technology that they will be using in the future. The degree of involvement varies across ANSPs. For commercialized ANSPs such as NAV CANADA and NATS, controllers are closely involved in all phases of the conceptualization, design, and testing. By contrast, at FAA, controllers were once involved, but that involvement was sharply reduced at about the time that the latest round of contract negotiations began.

Another labor issue that all ANSPs face is labor's attitude toward commercialization. The unions supported the creation of NAV CANADA, in part because they had endured a six-year long wage freeze under Transport Canada. In the United States and Europe, labor unions have been largely opposed to commercialization. In the United States, the opposition would seem to stem from a concern that commercialization could reduce Congressional influence on how the ANSP was operated and thus reduce labor's bargaining power. The experience with commercialization in Europe has raised controller concerns about facility consolidation as Europe seeks to reduce the problem of fragmentation.

A final labor problem faced throughout the world is the ability of the regulators of the air traffic control system to recruit and retain the technical expertise needed to regulate effectively. Regulators need the expertise of experienced air traffic controllers to oversee the system, but the high salaries of controllers working for ANSPs makes recruiting qualified staff for regulatory positions difficult. The problem of retaining technical expertise isn't confined to controllers but is also a concern for safety inspectors and maintenance technicians, whose skills and expertise are also valued by ANSPs, airlines, and elsewhere in the private sector.

Chapter 18

Lessons Learned and Challenges for the Future

Approaches to Commercialization

The preceding chapters have examined the evolution of Air Navigation Service Providers (ANSPs) around the world and the challenges they face as they look to the future. All ANSPs face the same basic tasks of providing separation between aircraft, both on the ground and in the air, so as to avoid collisions and providing efficient routing between the origin and destination of each flight. Prior to the 1987, almost all ANSPs were government agencies, including some that were part of the military, but since then there has been a widespread move toward commercialization under a range of organizational options.

This chapter begins with a summary of how each of the principal organizational options compares according to the ten criteria introduced in Chapter 3. Five different types of organizational forms are considered covering the continuum from a fully private corporation to a traditional government agency. Examples of each of the organizational forms have been examined in detail in the preceding chapters and are cited in the discussion that follows. There can be considerable variation within each of these organizational forms in how the organization actually functions. The details of the charter of each organization and the initial conditions under which the organization is established can make an enormous difference in how well a specific organization functions. As will become clear in the discussion that follows, there is no one single form that is an automatic solution for all of the challenges facing ANSPs. Each form has some dimensions at which it excels and each has other dimensions at which it is not the strongest. The chapter next turns to some lessons regarding labor relations and then examines the sources of resistance to commercializing ANSPs. The chapter concludes with the challenges that the future will bring.

The organizational forms

The first form is a fully private corporation. While there is often talk about privatizing air traffic control, typically by those opposed to moves toward commercialization, there are not currently any examples of a fully private ANSP. Perhaps the closest to a fully private ANSP would be Deutsche Flugsicherung (DFS) in Germany which was converted from a state-run organization to a corporate form in 1993 and became a commercial, self-supporting government company. The German parliament has passed legislation to permit the sale of 74.9 percent of the company to private investors, which, depending on the terms of the sale, could have made DFS a private company. Those plans were delayed in 2006 because of the objection of the German president, Horst Kohler, who called for the legal and constitutional status of the planned privatization to be examined more closely.

The next form is a public-private partnership and the example is the United Kingdom's National Air Traffic Services (NATS). NATS operates with the government owning 49 percent of the shares, a group of British airlines owning 42 percent, the employees of NATS owning five percent and BAA, plc, the operator of most British airports owning four percent. With this distribution of shares, the government's has effective control over NATS, but that could conceivably change were the government to sell some or all of its shares.

The third form is a private, non-share capital corporation and the example is NAV CANADA. Because of the corporation's non-share capital status, there are no shareholders to receive profits. This structure means that any surpluses of revenue over costs could be used for capital investment, to pay down debt, or to go towards reducing future air navigation charges. The associated financial reporting structure required that any surpluses in a given period would be directed into a reserve fund account. Since there would be no shareholders, the Canadian Corporations Act provided for member organizations that could nominate Board directors. This board structure is designed to provide major stakeholders a significant role in governance. The Board is supported in these efforts by an Advisory Committee comprised of representatives from various aviation groups across Canada.

The fourth organizational form is a government corporation and the examples are Airways New Zealand and Airservices Australia. Airways New Zealand was the first ANSP to become a commercial government corporation in 1987 and Airservices Australia was converted to a government corporation in 1995. Government corporations vary in their details both from country to country and even from organization to organization within a country. The most important attributes is that they typically have the independence to operate along commercial lines but remain entirely within the government.

The final organizational form is a government agency with the Federal Aviation Administration (FAA) as the example. As with government corporations, government agencies can operate under a variety of conditions. For example, while the FAA is funded by a combination of excise taxes and contributions from the general fund, a government agency could also be funded through user fees. In the case of FAA, the air traffic control system is operated by a separate branch, the Air Traffic Organization (ATO).

The dimensions of performance

Safety   The most critical element of air traffic control is the ability of the system to maintain separation between aircraft both in the air and on the ground. All ANSPs maintain that safety is their highest priority and it is embedded in the culture of air traffic controllers. However, not all ANSPs are equally effective in providing safe service and the expected growth in air traffic will place additional burdens on maintaining a safe system.

Separation of operation from regulation The value of arms-length regulation, where the organization that regulates how a system should be operated is not the same organization that operates the system is well recognized in virtually all sectors of the economy and in most segments of the aviation industry. For many years in many countries, however, the same government agency that operated the air traffic control system also regulated it. As more and more countries have moved to a more commercial approach to providing air traffic control services, they have also moved to separate regulation from operation. Some countries have put more separation between regulation and operation than others but some have yet to separate the functions in any meaningful way.

Matching cost drivers to revenue drivers A critical issue for every ANSP is how it is funded, and whether the funding mechanism is linked to the costs of operating the system. If the factors that drive the costs of an air traffic control system aren't closely matched to the factors that drive the revenues, one problem that can emerge is that that the share of the revenue contributed by each segment of the industry may not reflect the share of the costs that segment imposes on the air traffic control system. A second potential problem is that changes in how the industry operated, for example the mix of aircraft or the pattern of flights, could have much different impacts on revenue than it did on costs.

Effective capital investment A modern air traffic control system is a capital intensive operation. It's critical that the capital investments that are made deliver the expected performance, are completed on time, and are completed within budget.

Financial structure and capacity Aviation activity, both commercial and private, has historically varied with the business cycle. An important element of ANSP financial structure is the ability to weather the financial implications of variations in traffic brought about by the normal business cycle or other external events.

Need for economic regulation While there are many ANSPs around the world, the provision of air traffic control services in a given geographic area is not suitable for competition and is more safely provided as a monopoly. However, granting a monopoly to a service provider immediately raises the question of whether the service provider will exploit that monopoly power and either charge user fees or taxes that are above that necessary to cover costs or not provide all the services that are needed. One way to guard against this possibility is to make sure that the incentives or the governance structure is designed to prevent monopoly abuses. Another approach is to regulate the prices charged and the services rendered.

Organizational independence One recurrent problem that ANSPs have encountered when they were government agencies is other parts of the government imposing decisions or actions on them for reasons unrelated to the efficient operation of the air traffic control system. In some cases, the decisions might prevent consolidation so as to preserve jobs in a particular location and in other cases the decision might be budget cuts or personnel cuts in response to overall government deficit concerns.

Clear lines of accountability   For an organization to operate effectively, it must have a clear set of objectives and a well defined system of accountability to judge its performance in achieving those objectives. Diffused accountability to multiple other organizations can result in little or no effective accountability.

Ease of interoperability   With the past and anticipated growth in international traffic, the ability of an air traffic control system to interact smoothly with adjacent air traffic control systems – interoperability – is increasingly important. To the extent that ANSPs are restricted in their choice of equipment suppliers, perhaps to ones from the same country, or operate with different incentives, then interoperability will be more difficult to achieve.

Pursuit of social and political goals   In most countries, there are aviation activities that are deemed to be valuable to society but may not be able to pay for the costs they impose on the air traffic control system without undue financial hardship. Maintaining airport services in small or remote communities or supporting small private aircraft in the air traffic control and air navigation system are two examples frequently cited as being in this category. One possibility would be to support these activities out of a country's general fund. A more common approach is to cross subsidize losses in providing these services with surpluses generated by charging more than the cost for other services. Such cross subsidies are easier to do under organizational structures than under others.

Comparing the organizational forms

In Table 18.1, each dimension has two rows of information. The top row in each category contains a summary assessment of how effective that particular organizational form might be along this dimension. Below that, is a list of the issues associated with that particular dimension that each organizational form would have to confront.

Safety   Examples of each of the four organizational forms have amassed very good safety records. For both the government corporation and the government agency forms, the biggest challenge is responding quickly to a changing safety environment. Government agencies in particular often find it difficult to respond in a timely manner to changing external environments often because they face greater restrictions in redeploying employees to different assignments or different geographic locations. Government corporations may face slightly fewer restrictions in this regard, but would usually still be more constrained than organizations with non-government employees. For both the non-share capital corporation and the public-private partnership the principle issue is getting and maintaining the right mix of public and private objectives. In the short run, at least, safety usually involves tradeoffs with economic objectives, so that steps to improve safety may come at the expense of steps to reduce costs or increase capacity. In the public-private partnership, the public's role is clear from the outset, but in a non-share capital corporation, there is the additional challenge of defining the public's role. For the private corporation there has to be clear regulatory safety oversight, so a main issue is making sure that the regulator has sufficient access to information about the operations of the corporation to regulate effectively. As in any regulatory situation, it's also important to structure the corporation's operating and investment incentives to maintain safe operations properly.

Separation of operation from regulation   The biggest issue in this area for a government agency is the extent to which the separation is enough to be meaningful. If the regulatory body is simply a different branch of the same umbrella organization, then regulatory disputes are more likely to be settled behind closed doors and self-regulation can remain a problem. In situations like this, the fear is that the much larger operating agency will be dominant. With a government corporation, the issue of sufficient independence remains, but it's more likely that there will be a fully independent regulator than with a government agency. With the other three organizational forms, it's virtually certain that there will be sufficient separation of regulation from operations. Here the issue is whether the regulator will be able to hire and retain people with sufficient technical expertise to regulate effectively. Many of the technical skills that the regulator needs are the same skills that the operator needs, but the operator will typically be able to offer more compensation for these people. A second issue for the private corporation and for the non-share capital corporation is whether or not the regulator can get sufficient access to the information needed to regulate. The public role in the public-private partnership means that this is less likely to be a problem with this form.

Match cost drivers to revenue drivers   It's possible to match cost drivers and revenue drivers in a government agency, but it's least likely to happen there of all the organizational forms, as the experience with FAA has shown. Since government agencies are often perceived as having the general fund to fall back on, the main issue is often making sure that the revenues cover both operating and capital costs and that costs are controlled so that the funds are used efficiently. With a government corporation, matching cost drivers and revenue drivers is easier and more likely. A final potential problem with private corporations or public-private partnerships is the degree of monopoly power and the associated need for economic and safety regulation and oversight. In the case of the government corporation, an additional issue is the extent to which the financial returns are shared with the government. A second issue, which is also common to non-share capital corporations, public-private partnerships, and private corporations is what sort of financial reserve policy is adopted. Since aviation activity is sensitive to the business cycle, some accommodation needs to be made to short run swings in revenue that are not easily matched by corresponding swings in costs. One approach is to maintain a reserve fund to carry through downturns in the economy. A final issue with public-private partnerships and particularly with a private corporations is the monopoly power they would have and the incentive to take advantage of that monopoly power.

Table 18.1   Summary of organizational forms

	Private Corporation	Public-Private Partnership	Non-Share Capital Corporation	Government Corporation	Government Agency
Examples	None to date	NATS	NAV CANADA	Airservices Australia and Airways NZ	FAA
Safety	Good	Very Good	Very Good	Very Good	Very Good
Issues	Acces to information; regulatory oversight; incentives	Relative mix of public and private objectives	Relative mix of public and private objectives; defining the public role	Ability to respond to changing safety environment	Ability to respond to changing safety environment
Separation of Operation from Regulation	Virtually Certain	Virtually Certain	Virtually Certain	Likely	Possible but least likely
Issues	Technical ability of the regulator; access to information	Technical ability of the regulator	Technical ability of the regulator; access to information	Independence of the regulator from the operator	Independence of the regulator from the operator
Match Cost Drivers to Revenue Drivers	Excellent	Very Good	Very Good	Good	Possible but least likely
Issues	Profit maximization and monopoly power	Profit maximization and monopoly power	Degree of profit maximization and reserve policies	Degree of profit maximization and reserve policies and financial returns to government	Insuring that revenue covers both operating and capital costs; cost efficiency
Effective Capital Investment	Very Good	Very Good	Very Good	Good/Very Good	Poor/Fair
Issues	Relative role of ANS provider and suppliers in technology; better project management	Relative role of ANS provider and suppliers in technology; better project management	Relative role of ANS provider and suppliers in technology; better project management	Relative role of ANS provider and suppliers in technology; better project management	Relative role of ANS provider and suppliers in technology; annual budget cycles
Financial Structure and Capacity	Good	Good/Very Good	Good/Very Good	Good/Very Good	Fair

Continued – Table 18.1   Summary of organizational forms

	Private Corporation	Public-Private Partnership	Non-Share Capital Corporation	Government Corporation	Government Agency
Examples	None to date	NATS	NAV CANADA	Airservices Australia and Airways NZ	FAA
Issues	Degree of leverage and type of equity	Degree of leverage and type of equity	Degree of leverage and reserves policy	Degree of leverage and reserves policy	Access to public resources and long term capital; annual budget cycle
Need for Economic Regulation	High	Moderate/High	Low/Moderate	Low/Moderate	None
Issues	Access to information and incentives	Access to information and incentives	Degree of stakeholder representation	Access to information and incentives	
Organizational Independence	High	Moderate	Moderate	Moderate	Low
Issues	Stakeholder representation	Nature of the charter and incentives for public involvement	Nature of the charter and incentives for public involvement	Nature of the charter and incentives for public involvement	Incentives for micromanagement
Clear Lines of Accountability	Very Good	Very Good	Good/Very Good	Fair/Good	Poor
Issues	Public interest issues	Clarity of objectives	Clarity of objectives	Clarity of objectives; government oversight	Accountability to multiple government entities
Ease of Interoperability	Very Good	Very Good	Very Good	Very Good	Limited
Issues	Incentives	Degree of commerical orientation	Degree of commerical orientation	Degree of commerical orientation; national suppliers	Diversity of organizational goals; national suppliers
Pursuit of Social and Political Goals	Very Low	Moderate	Moderate	Moderate/High	High/Very High
Issues	Public interest input	Incentives for cross subsidy	Incentives for cross subsidy	Incentives for cross subsidy	Degree of cross subsidy

Effective capital investment   Government agencies have the greatest difficulties making effective capital investments of any of the organizational forms. Part of the problem is the financial uncertainties and the difficulty in making long term commitments due to the annual government budget cycle. A second problem is that there is often pressure to use national suppliers for capital equipment. With a government corporation, there may be similar pressures to use national suppliers, but the annual government budget cycle does not pose a problem and it's much easier to make long-term commitments. As a result, it's more likely to have better project management with a government corporation. Better project management is also a characteristic of a non-share capital corporation, a public-private partnership, and could be expected for a private corporation. For these forms, there is also an issue of the relative roles of the ANSPs and suppliers in developing new technology, but here the issue is where the research and development should originate. Traditionally, much of the research and development has been funded by the government because traditionally, the only customers were government agencies and because these government agencies had a tendency to try to buy only from suppliers based in the same country. More commercially oriented and independent ANSPs will not feel obligated to buy only from national vendors, so vendors developing new technology will have a broader array of potential customers. Thus, from an research and development perspective, air traffic management becomes like many other industries where the vendors have an incentive to conduct research and development in order to gain more market by developing better products.

Financial structure and capacity   An issue with a government agency is whether it will have the ability to undertake long term financing to match the long term capital investment programs needed to modernize the system. With a government agency, the annual budget cycle makes this difficult if not impossible. For a government corporations or a non-share capital corporation, the issue is the degree of leverage and the policy on establishing and maintaining financial reserves. Too much leverage, particularly in the early years before financial reserves are established or if inadequate reserves are established can leave an ANSP vulnerable to economic downturns and the accompanying effect on aviation traffic and thus revenues from fees. With a public-private partnership and a private corporation, equity has the potential to be a partial substitute for financial reserves, but the issue is the nature of the equity. One potential problem is that to the extent that equity is held by elements of the aviation industry, such as airlines, they would be affected by the business cycle in the same way as the ANSP so that they might not be in a position to put in more equity at the point it would be most needed.

Need for economic regulation   In any given geographic area, a single ANSP will have a monopoly since it's not possible to have competing ANSPs in the same airspace. With a single ANSP, the issue is preventing the abuse of monopoly power. When the ANSP is a government agency, there is no need for any economic regulation. With a government corporation, there is still direct government involvement, so there is only a low to moderate chance that economic regulation will be needed. The same is true for a non-share capital corporation if there is sufficient stakeholder representation in the governance structure. There may be a greater need for economic regulation with a public-private partnership, depending on the role of the public interests in decisions about rates and fees. Even with significant public involvement, there may still be the need for some economic regulatory oversight. If so, then the issue is making sure that the regulatory body has access to the information it needs to regulate rates. With a private corporation, there is clearly a high need for economic regulation so that the issue is, as with a public-private partnership, the ability of the regulatory body to get the needed information from the ANSP.

Organizational independence One of the biggest drawbacks of a government agency is the lack of organizational independence. One issue is that legislators may micromanage to preserve jobs in particular locations or favor particular suppliers. As a government agency, the ANSP may get caught up in government-wide programs to reduce employment or cut budgets because of overall deficit concerns unrelated to the needs of air traffic management. With a government corporation, a non-share capital corporation, or a public-private partnership, there will likely be much greater organizational independence. With these forms however, the issue is making sure that they all have sufficient incentives or mechanisms for some public involvement. Typically, this issue is addressed in the charters of these organizations. The greatest degree of organizational independence would be with a private corporation. Here the issue is making sure there is adequate stakeholder representation in reaching major decisions.

Clear lines of accountability Organizations perform best when they have unambiguous objectives and clear lines of accountability holding them to achieve those objectives. With a government agency, it's likely to be accountable to both the administrative and legislative branches of government and to multiple entities within each branch. Such diffused accountability can also result in multiple and often conflicting objectives and can approach having no accountability at all. A government corporation will still have government oversight, but will likely have much greater clarity of objectives. A non-share capital corporation and a public-private partnership will also likely have still greater clarity of objectives and less government oversight of day-to-day operating decisions. With a private corporation, there is less of an issue of clarity of objectives, but a greater issue of accountability to public interest objectives.

Ease of interoperability Interoperability is the ability of ANSPs to easily hand off traffic to and from one another. With government agencies, a barrier to interoperability is the diversity of goals these agencies may have. For example, if maintaining higher levels of employment than efficient operations would dictate is an implicit goal, then the system may have more facilities than needed which can complicate smooth handoffs. Similarly, if supporting national equipment vendors is a goal, then adjacent ANSPs may have equipment built to different standards and conventions, again making interoperability more difficult. To the extent that ANSPs have a commercial orientation and are not constrained to use national vendors, then they are likely to achieve very good interoperability. To the extent that there is still some pressure to use national vendors, government corporations may have slightly more difficulty achieving interoperability than non-share capital corporations, public-private partnerships, or private corporations.

Pursuit of social and political goals   There can be social and political goals beyond simply the efficient operation of an air traffic management system. Examples of such goals might be maintaining service to small or remote airports without charging the full cost for such service or providing service to business or general aviation at less than the costs they impose on the system. Such goals are commonly provided through a system of cross subsidies where some users of the system are charged more than the cost they impose on the system so that other users can be charged less. Virtually all the ANSPs in the world have some cross-subsidy build into their user fee systems through the ICAO endorsed weight and distance formula, but the degree of cross subsidy varies from ANSP to ANSP as they use different coefficients in the formula. Government agencies have the highest tendency (and ability) to use cross subsidies. Government corporations probably have somewhat less tendency to use extensive cross subsidies, while non-share capital corporations and public-private partnership would have still less tendency. Private corporations would have the lowest tendency. With this form, the issue is the extent to which there would be any public interest input.

How do the forms compare?

Government agency   The government agency form of ANSP has strengths in that it doesn't require economic regulation and it can most easily implement cross subsidies to pursue social and political goals. It can do a very good job with safety, but may have some difficulty adapting quickly to a changing industry environment. In every other dimension represented in Table 18.1, however, it is a less attractive organizational form than the others. Of greatest importance, it is inherently more difficult in a government agency to manage an effective capital investment program, to achieve organizational independence, to have clear lines of accountability, and to achieve interoperability with other ANSPs.

Private corporation   At the other end of the spectrum, a private corporation is likely to be particularly good at matching cost drivers to revenue drivers and at achieving organizational independence. However, this organizational form also poses some difficult challenges were it to be used for an ANSP. Because of the incentives to maximize profits and take advantage of monopoly status, it would require the highest degree of economic regulation. It is also the worst suited organizational form to pursue social and political goals through cross subsidy. It may also be the most difficult to regulate for safety since it could easily pose the greatest challenge to the regulator to gain access to the information needed to regulate effectively.

Two of the organizational forms, government agency and private corporation, seem to be clearly less promising for application to an ANSP than the other three. For much different reasons, these two forms are just not inherently as well suited to providing air traffic control and air navigation services. The other three forms, government corporation, non-share capital corporation, and public-private partnership, have similar strengths and weaknesses and can each be effective if carefully designed and implemented.

Government corporation   A government corporation is the smallest step away from a government agency, but has the potential to have similar strengths to a non-share capital corporation and a public-private partnership. With a government corporation, it may be slightly less likely to achieve complete separation of regulation from operation than with the other two forms, but it clearly can be done. Similarly, achieving effective capital investment and closely matching revenue drivers to cost drivers may be a little more difficult. However, pursuing social and political goals may be somewhat easier.

Non-share capital corporation and public-private partnership   Both of these forms can be very effective, as the experiences of NAV CANADA and NATS have shown. If there is sufficient stakeholder representation with a non-share capital corporation, it might have less need for economic regulation than a public-private partnership. On the other hand, it may have slightly less clear lines of accountability.

Lessons from Restructuring

The level and patterns of growth and changes in the operating environment have raised both the visibility of air traffic management and the urgency of addressing its problems. Growth in domestic and international traffic, in both the developed world and the developing countries, has highlighted the current strains and possible future shortcomings of today's air navigation systems and organizations. The potential for significant general/business aviation growth through the adoption of Very Light Jets (VLJs) have heightened the concerns about managing both capacity and the associated costs of managing this growth.

Additionally, historically low profit margins for airlines have increased their attention to all costs – especially ones that are rising. Air navigation charges now represent between three and seven percent of airline costs, and have been trending upward. Environmental concerns about energy use, noise, and aircraft emissions place greater pressure on more direct and fuel efficient aircraft routings, and thus more pressure for improved performance from the world's air navigation service providers.

The restructurings that have characterized air navigation over the past twenty years have resulted in more effective, efficient and more commercially-oriented organizations. Safety does not appear to be systematically affected by the organizational structure; in fact, the more commercially oriented structures may be better able and quicker to introduce and implement improved or upgraded technology that makes the skies safer. The evidence indicates that user fees tend to lead to greater stakeholder input and involvement which leads to better and more effective capital investment.

The challenges that some of the major ANSPs have faced have largely been transitional challenges stemming from the legacies of their creation and aren't signs of long-term weaknesses of the organizational structures. Moreover, the variety of different structures have each weathered serious challenges in recent years, including the consequences of the September 11 air terror attacks, airline bankruptcies, SARS, and various country economic and fiscal crises.

Cross-Cutting Issues

There are two kinds of cross-cutting issues that are found in both developed and developing countries: labor relations and resistance to commercialization.

Labor relations

Most ANSPs have periodic labor relations issues, but some ANSPs seem to have more contentious labor relations than others. Unionized labor forces are almost universal in ANSPs and the skills and training are quite specialized and take considerable training to acquire. As a result labor relations often take on the characteristics of a bilateral monopoly, where the ANSP is the only employer and the labor union is the only source of trained employees. In such situations, labor relations can become quite contentious as both sides work to increase their bargaining power and tend to view the negotiations as a zero-sum game where one side's gain is automatically the other side's loss.

NAV CANADA's experience suggests that labor relations may be less contentious where labor also has a voice in decisions regarding charging and financial issues. With broader involvement in these charging and financial decisions, labor negotiations seem to take on less of a zero-sum game character. With less contentious labor relations, there is a better chance that controllers will be closely involved in the design of the new technology they will be using in the future. For commercialized ANSPs such as NAV CANADA and NATS, controllers are closely involved in all phases of the conceptualization, design, and testing.

Resistance to commercialization

While there has been widespread movement toward commercialized ANSPs, there has also been resistance to commercialization in many countries. Part of that resistance comes from organized labor, whose concerns seem to fall primarily into three categories. First, there is a concern that commercialization will lead to consolidation of facilities and that consolidation may lead to fewer jobs and will certainly lead to employee relocations. Second, there is a concern that a move to commercialization will increase pressures to reduce ANSP costs with corresponding downward pressure on wages and benefits. Third, there is a concern that commercialization will lead to contracting out of some functions with a resulting loss of union jobs.

Politicians and military leaders have also raised concerns about commercialization and also about cross-border regional approaches to air navigation. The concerns come in two areas. The first is a security concern regarding the ability to move military aircraft as needed in times of emergency or conflict when the air traffic control system is run by an outside organization or by a multinational group. The second concern is one of giving up sovereignty of airspace to an outside organization or a multinational group.

Implications

One implication of these cross-cutting issues is that new technology alone is not enough to solve air navigation and air traffic control problems. To be effective, the technology needs to be developed, from the beginning, in cooperation with those who will use it – the controllers and the maintenance technicians. NATS has been particularly effective at involving controllers in new technology whereas the FAA has largely excluded controllers in recent years. Even with controller involvement, the technological challenges are substantial. Air navigation is faced with changing its fundamental approach from ground to satellite systems, and from air traffic control to air traffic management. There is a much greater coordination and decentralization of individual decision-making in cockpits, in towers, and in operations. At the same time, the globalization of travel demands and the underlying features of satellite-based technologies make integrating national systems a challenge and put more pressure on interoperability.

A second implication is that cross-border cooperation is easier when the ANSPs are commercialized rather than when they are government agencies or military operations because issues of airspace sovereignty are likely to be less of a stumbling block and because commercialized ANSPs are more likely to have common goals and common concerns than are government agencies. Cross-border cooperation is also likely to be easier when the countries involved are politically stable and have good diplomatic relations.

Summing Up: Challenges for the Future

What might the future hold? The process of globalization of air traffic control has meant that much of the world has gone from national, government ANSPs to a variety of organizational structures. However, while there are differences in structure, successful air navigation reforms have tended to share many underlying features, as described in the beginning of this chapter. As the British proverb states, "There are many ways to skin a cat."

Technology and scale have accelerated the globalization of air navigation. Commercialized ANSPs tend to operate on very similar principles, which make cooperation between them easier than is likely to be the case for the national government ANSPs. The United States, although still the largest aviation market in the world, may increasingly become out of step with the rest of the world and may thus be unable to share as easily in some of the progress lead by other countries. Greater cooperation among commercialized ANSPs could well lead to consolidation or contracting out for certain services from other ANSPs. Whether the result is a more interconnected system or an ongoing consolidation of air navigation organizations across borders remains to be seen.

Air traffic management has advanced markedly over the past decade, with greatly improved communications, navigation, technologies, and organizational capacity. At the same time, air navigation has faced more challenges and change in the past decade than in the fifty years following the Chicago Convention. Looking ahead, air navigation is likely to require even more from those whose job it is to manage the skies.

Glossary

ADS-B – Automatic Dependent Surveillance System.

AIMS – Aircraft Autonomous Integrity Monitoring Systems.

Airline Group – a consortium of airlines comprised of British Airways, bmi British Midland, Virgin Atlantic, Britannia, Monarch, easyJet, and Airtours that is a part owner in NATS.

Airservices Australia – a wholly government-owned corporation created in 1995 that provides air navigation services in Australia.

Airways Corporation of New Zealand – the state-owned enterprise that took over the provisions of air navigation services in New Zealand in 1987.

ANSP – Air Navigation Service Provider is the term most typically used to describe the organizations that provide air traffic control services and also air navigation services. These two activities together are also often referred to as air traffic management.

ARTCC – Air Route Traffic Control Center.

ATC – air traffic control.

ATO – Air Traffic Organization, a performance-based organization within the Federal Aviation Administration formed in 2004 that manages the air traffic control system in the United States.

Austro Control GmbH – an independent limited liability company which undertakes all state duties related to civil aviation in Austria.

Avinor AS – a state owned limited company that owns and operates 46 airports and is responsible for air traffic control services in Norway.

CAA (US) – Civil Aeronautics Authority an agency formed by the United States government in 1938 whose duties included the encouragement of civil aeronautics and commerce, establishment of civil airways, provision and technical improvement of air navigation facilities, and the protection and regulation of air traffic along the airways.

CAA (UK) – Civil Aviation Authority is the government aviation safety and economic regulatory agency in the United Kingdom.

CAATS – Canadian Automated Air Traffic System.

CANSO – Civil Air Navigation Services Organization.

CATCA – Canadian Air Traffic Controllers Association, the labor union representing air traffic controllers in Canada.

Category I – a precision instrument approach and landing with a decision height not lower than 60 m above touchdown zone elevation and with either a visibility not less than 800 m or a runway visual range not less than 550 m.

Category II – a precision instrument approach and landing with a decision height lower than 60 m above touchdown zone elevation but not lower than 30 m, and a runway visual range not less than 350 m.

Category III – a precision instrument approach and landing with:

1. a decision height lower than 30 m above touchdown zone elevation, or no decision height; and a runway visual range not less than 200 m. (Category IIIA) or,
2. a decision height lower than 15 m above touchdown zone elevation, or no decision height; and a runway visual range less than 200 m but not less than 50 m. (Category IIIB) or,
3. no decision height and no runway visual range limitations.(Category IIIC).

Central Flow Management Unit – an operational unit of EUROCONTROL, enhancing safety through coordinated flow and capacity management services of the air traffic in Europe.

Controlled Airspace – in controlled airspace, air traffic control separation is provided to all aircraft operating under instrument flight rules. If flights operating under visual flight rules are present, the IFR flights have the responsibility of separating themselves from VFR flights and VFR flights have the responsibility of separating themselves from both IFR flights and from other VFR flights. In the United States, airspace above 18,000 feet is essentially reserved for IFR flights only. Most of the rest of the airspace in the US is also controlled, but allows both IFR and VFR flights.

CRCO – Central Route Charges Office is the organization that operates a centralized system for collecting a single charge per flight on behalf of the EUROCONTROL.

DFS – Deutsche Flugsicherung, Germany's air navigation service provider.

DGAC – France's civil aviation authority.

DSNA – France's air navigation service provider.

EATCHIP – European Air Traffic Control Harmonisation and Integration Programme was a program launched by EUROCONTROL in the 1990s that emphasized cooperation among ANSPs rather than a more efficient consolidated airspace.

ECAC – European Civil Aviation Conference whose members include: Albania, Armenia, Austria, Azerbaijan, Belgium, Bosnia and Herzegovina, Bulgaria, Croatia, Cyprus, Czech Republic, Denmark, Estonia, Finland, France, Georgia, Germany, Greece, Hungary, Iceland, Ireland, Italy, Latvia, Lithuania, Luxembourg, Malta, Moldova, Monaco, Netherlands, Norway, Poland, Portugal, Romania, Serbia, Slovakia, Slovenia, Spain, Sweden, Switzerland, the former Yugoslav Republic of Macedonia, Turkey, Ukraine, and the United Kingdom.

En Route Centers – facilities established to provide air traffic control service to aircraft operating on IFR flight plans within controlled airspace, principally during the en route phase of flight.

ENAV, S.p.A – a publically controlled joint stock company, formed in 2001, that is Italy's air navigation service provider.

EUROCONTROL – European Organisation for the Safety of Air Navigation is an international organisation whose primary objective is the development of a seamless, pan-European Air Traffic Management (ATM) system.

EGNOS – European Geostationary Navigation System.

FAA – Federal Aviation Administration.

FAB – Functional Airspace Block.

FANS – Future Air Navigation System.

FIR – Flight Information Region.

Free Flight – a navigation and air traffic control approach that would allow aircraft to proceed directly from origin to destination using the most direct and efficient flight path. It would put the responsibility for maintaining separation on the pilots of the aircraft, aided by systems that detected potential conflicts, rather than on air traffic controllers.

Galileo – a global navigation satellite system under development by the European Commission.

GAO – United States Government Accountability Office.

GLONASS – a global navigation satellite system under development by Russia.

GNSS – Global Navigation Satellite System.

GPS – Global Positioning System is a global navigation satellite system developed and operated by the United States.

IATA – International Air Transport Association.

ICAO – International Civil Aviation Organization.

IFF – Identification Friend or Foe is a system developed by the military as a means of positively identifying friendly aircraft from enemy.

IFR – Instrument Flight Rules are a set of regulations and procedures for flying aircraft whereby separation to other aircraft and terrain is maintained with reference to aircraft instruments only.

ILS – Instrument Landing System.

LAAS – Local Area Augmentation System.

LFV Group – a Swedish state enterprise which operates and develops State-owned civil aviation airports and also provides peace time air navigation services for civilian and military aircraft.

LVNL – Luchtverkeersleiding Nederland, the civilian air navigation service provider in the Netherlands.

MSAS – Japanese Multi-Function Satellite Augmentation System.

NATCA – National Air Traffic Controllers Association, the union representing air traffic controllers in the United States that was formed in 1987.

NATS – National Air Traffic Services, the public private partnership that provides air navigation services in the United Kingdom.

NAV CANADA – a private, non-share capital corporation that owns and operates Canada's civil air navigation system. NAV CANADA began operations in 1996.

NERL – NATS En Route Ltd is the portion of NATS that is responsible for en route and oceanic air traffic services.

NSL – NATS Services Ltd is the portion of NATS which competes for contracts to provide air traffic control at airports in the UK and overseas, as well as providing other services.

PATCO – Professional Air Traffic Controllers Organization, the union representing air traffic controllers in the United States that was formed in 1968.

PPP – Public-Private Partnership.

PSR – Primary Surveillance Radar.

RAIMS – Receiver Autonomous Integrity Monitoring Systems.

RNP – Required Navigation Performance.

RPI-X – an approach to rate setting that sets prices at the level of the inflation less a factor to account for productivity.

RSA – Rate Stabilization Account, the reserve fund established by NAV CANADA to allow them to absorb fluctuations in revenue without having to change rates frequently.

RVSM – Reduced Vertical Separation Minima.

SARPS – Standards and Recommended Practices.

SARS – Sudden Acute Respiratory Syndrome.

SES – Single European Sky.

SESAR – Single European Sky ATM Research program.

Skyguide – Switzerland's air navigation service provider.

SSR – Secondary Surveillance Radar.

TAAATS – The Australian Advanced Air Traffic System.

TCAS – Traffic Collision Avoidance System.

TRACON – Terminal Radar Approach Control.

Uncontrolled Airspace – in uncontrolled airspace, both VFR and IFR flights have responsibility for separating themselves from all other aircraft. In the United States, typically uncontrolled airspace is below 1,200 feet and away from busy airports.

VDB – Very High Frequency Data Broadcast.

VFR – Visual Flight Rules is a flight regime where it is the responsibility of the pilot of the aircraft to maintain separation from other aircraft so as to avoid collisions. The basic method of maintaining separation under these conditions is through the concept of "see and avoid" where pilots look out the cockpit window and make sure they don't get too close to other aircraft.

WAAS – Wide Area Augmentation System.

Bibliography

Aviation Journals

"175 Flights Cancelled as Rome Air Traffic Controllers Strike," *Europe Intelligence Wire*, March 14, 2007.

"Air traffic controllers and trade unions: working to create a single Air Navigation Service Provider over their own countries," Press Release, Common Statement, (http://www.project-mosaic.eu/home.htm).

"Air Travel in Crisis," *Aviation Week and Space Technology*, Vol. 151, No. 17, 95, October 25, 1999.

"Airline Groups Criticize Slow Pace Of Single Sky Initiative," *Aviation Daily*, Vol. 363 No. 30, February 15, 2006.

"Airline News – Latin America," *AirGuide Magazine & AirGuide Online*, March 19, 2007.

"Airport Privatization in Australia," Case HKU150, Centre for Asian Business Cases, School of Business, University of Hong Kong, August 2001.

"Argentina Raises Air Traffic Controller Pay Amid Safety Fears," *Dow Jones Newswires*, May 23, 2007.

"ATNS: The Next Step Forward," *Air Traffic Management*, Spring 2006.

"Brazil's President Admits Govt. Role in ATC Woes," *Aviation Daily*, March 30, 2007.

"Caribbean and South America Regional Air Navigation Plan," IBAC Technical Report Summary, www.ibac.org/Library/ElectF/iran/CAR_SAM_3.pdf.

"Congested Airports, Delays Will Hamper Brazil Holiday," *Aviation Daily*, December 22, 2006.

"FAA Reorganizing Agency Flight Operations in Wake of Crash," *The Weekly of Business Aviation*, April 18, 1994, Vol. 58, No. 16.

"Getting Airport Ready for the Games," *Financial Times Information Limited – Asia Intelligence Wire* (www.Chinadaily.com.cn), January 23, 2007.

"Grounded: Aviation in Brazil," *The Economist*, US Edition, December 16, 2006.

"NATCA Turns to Congress to Overturn FAA Contract," *Aviation Daily*, Vol. 367, No. 46, March 9, 2007.

"Nav Canada Controllers Ratify New Four-Year Contract," *Aviation Daily*, Vol. 361, No. 41, August 29, 2005.

"Near Misses on Runways Spark Debate at Hearings," *Pittsburgh Post-Gazette*, July 1, 2002, Page A-12.

"NTSB Issues Scathing Report on Deficiencies in FAA Flight Operations," *The Weekly of Business Aviation*, November 29, 1993, Vol. 57, No. 22.

"Out of Control," *Flight International*, June 25, 2002.

"Passengers Put Out By Controllers' Slowdown In Brazil," *Aviation Daily*, Vol. 366, No. 25, 5, November 6, 2006.

"Problem solving through dialogue," *Air Traffic Management*, Spring 2007.

"Single minded: The dawn of the Single European Sky will be a long time coming, and the route toward it remains a political minefield," *Flight International*, July 13, 2004.

"Southern Star," *Air Traffic Management*, Spring 2005.

"Strike Disrupts Air Traffic at Paris Le Bourget," *Europe Intelligence Wire*, June 28, 2006.

"Surveillance on a Grand Scale," *Air Traffic Management*, January/February 2001.

"When No One Watches the Watchers," *Business and Commercial Aviation*, January 1994, Vol. 74, No. 1.

"Who's To Blame?; Finger-pointing continues in Brazilian midair collision probe," *Aviation Week & Space Technology*, January 29, 2007.

Primary Resources

Air Traffic Controllers European Unions Coordination, Roadmap for Future ATM, Position Paper, July 2006, (http://www.atceuc.org/atceuc_documents.php).

Airservices Australia, *Annual Report 2005–2006*.

Airservices Australia, Charges for Facilities and Services, ABN 59 698 720 886, Standard Contract Terms, 1 July 2006.

Airservices Australia, *Corporate Plan July 2005–June 2010*.

Airways New Zealand *Annual Report, 2005*.

Australian Civil Aviation Safety Authority, "Airspace Management Reform in Australia," September 2006.

Aviation Safety Commission: *Final Report and Recommendations* (Washington, DC: Government Printing Office, 1988).

Bradley, Perry and Gordon A. Gilbert, "Assessing International ATC," *Business and Commercial Aviation*, Vol. 80, Issue 3, March 1997.

Business and Management Practices, Air Traffic Management, December 2006, SECTION: Pg. 21 Vol. 15 No. 4 ISSN: 0969–6725.

Civil Air Navigation Services Organisation, *Corporatisation of Air Navigation Services*, August 1999.

Convention on International Civil Aviation done at Chicago on the 7th Day of December 1944, http://www.icao.int/icaonet/arch/doc/7300/7300_orig.pdf.

Donahue, George, "US Air Transportation: An Approaching Perfect Storm," *Aerospace America*, August 2006, page 26.

Doyle, Tim and Andrew T. Gillies, "Smart Skies," *Forbes*, February 26, 2007.

EUROCONTROL History: 1963–2003, "40 Years of Service to European Aviation," http://www.eurocontrol.int/corporate/public/standard_page/history.html.

Federal Aviation Administration, *A Plan for the Future – 2007–2016*, The Federal Aviation Administration's 10-Year Strategy for the Air Traffic Control Workforce, March 2007.

Federal Aviation Administration, Airports Data Package for Stakeholders, September 2, 2005, http://www.faa.gov/about/office_org/headquarters_offices/aep/aatf/media/Airports%20Data%20Package.pdf.

Federal Aviation Administration, Status of FAA's Major Acquisitions: Cost Growth and Schedule Delays Continue to Stall Air Traffic Modernization, Federal Aviation Administration, Report Number AV–2005–061, date issued: May 26, 2005.

Forrey, Patrick, "A Review of FAA Operational and Safety Programs," Testimony before the House Committee on Transportation and Infrastructure, Subcommittee on Aviation, March 22, 2007.

Halls, Mike "Official: Single European Sky off course," *Air Traffic Management*, Spring 2007.

Hughes, David "Russian ATC Reform," *Aviation Week and Space Technology*, Vol. 166 No. 9, February 26, 2007.

International Air Transport Association, Fact Sheet: Economic and Social Benefits of Air Transport, www.iata.org/pressroom/facts_figures/fact_sheets/economic_social_benefits.htm.

International Air Transport Association, Fact Sheet: IATA www.iata.org/pressroom/facts_figures/fact_sheets/iata.htm.

International Civil Aviation Organization, "International Standards & Recommended Practices – Air Traffic Services," Annex 11 to the Chicago Convention, 12th edition, July 1998.

International Civil Aviation Organization, *Icao's Policies on Charges for Airports and Air Navigation Services*, Doc 9082/7, 2004, Appendix 3.

International Civil Aviation Organization, *Tariffs for Airports and Air Navigation Services*, ICAO, Doc 7100 (2002).

MBS Ottawa, Inc., *Air Traffic Control Commercialization Policy: Has It Been Effective?*, January 2006, page 16.

McDougall, G., "The Privatisation of the Canadian Air Navigation System," in *Defining Aerospace Policy*, edited by K. Button, J. Lammersen-Baum, and R. Stough, (Aldershot, England: Ashgate, 2004).

Mhatre, Kamlakar "Millennium Facelift for Indian ATC," *Air Transport World*, March 2000.

Morrocco, John D. and Pushpindar Singh, "Tragedy Hits Just Prior to Indian ATC Upgrade," *Aviation Week and Space Technology*, Vol. 145, Issue 21, November 18, 1996.

Moxon, J "Testing Times," *Flight International*, December 15–21, 1993.

National Business Aviation Association, "Costs Incurred and User Fees Recovered by the Federal Government for Services to Business General Aviation," October 2004.

National Civil Aviation Review Commission, Final Report, December 11, 1997.

Official Journal of the European Union, L96, Volume 47, 31 March 2004.

Performance Review Commission, *A comparison of performance in selected US and European En-route Centres*, Eurocontrol, May 2003.

Poole, Robert W. and Cordle, Vaughn, *Resolving the Crisis in Air Traffic Control Funding*, Policy Study 332, Reason Foundation, May 2005.

Schlumberger, C. "Financing of Essential Air Transport Infrastructure," mimeo, (Washington: The World Bank, 2006).

Shubert, Francis, "The Single European Sky Controversial Aspects of Cross-Border Service Provision," *Air and Space Law*, Vol. 28, Issue 1, 2003, pages 32–49.

Stander, W., "Lessons from the Commercialization of Air Navigation Services in South Africa," in *Essays on Air Navigation: Flying through Congested Skies*, (Montreal: McGill University Institute of Air and Space Law and the International Civil Aviation Organization, 2007), pp. 21–24.

Strong, J. et al., *Moving to Market: Restructuring Transport in the Former Soviet Union*, (Cambridge, MA: Harvard University Press for the Harvard Institute for International Development, 1996).

"Suspect Parts Found in FAA Aircraft," *Aviation Week and Space Technology*, March 15, 1993, Volume 138, Number 11.

United States Department of Labor, Bureau of Labor Statistics, Occupational Outlook Handbook (www.bls.gov/oco/ocos108.htm).

United States Department of Transportation, Office of the Inspector General, *FAA Continues to Make Progress in Implementing Its Controller Workforce Plan, But Further Efforts are Needed in Several Key Areas*, Federal Aviation Administration, Report Number: AV–2007–032, Date Issued: February 9, 2007.

United States Department of Transportation, *Perspectives on the Aviation Trust Fund and Financing the Federal Aviation Administration*, Statement of the Honorable Kenneth M. Mead, Inspector General, US Department of Transportation, Before the Committee on Transportation and Infrastructure, Subcommittee on Aviation, United States House of Representatives, May 4, 2005.

United States Government Accountability Office, *Air Traffic Control, FAA's Modernization Efforts – Past, Present, and Future*, Statement of Gerald L. Dillingham, Director, Physical Infrastructure Issues, GAO–04–227T.

United States Government Accountability Office, *Aviation Finance: Observations on Potential FAA Funding Options*, GAO–06–973, September 2006.

United States Government Accountability Office, *High-Risk Series: An Update*, GAO–05–207.

United States Government Accountability Office, *Federal Aviation Administration: Key Issues in Ensuring the Efficient Development and Safe Operation of the Next Generation Air Transportation System*, Statement of Gerald L. Dillingham, Ph.D., Director Physical Infrastructure Issues, Testimony Before the Subcommittee on Aviation, Committee on Transportation and Infrastructure, House of Representatives, March 22, 2007. GAO–07–636T.

United States Government Accountability Office, *JOINT PLANNING AND DEVELOPMENT OFFICE, Progress and Key Issues in Planning the Transition to the Next Generation Air Transportation System*, Statement of Gerald L. Dillingham, Ph.D., Director, Physical Infrastructure Issues, Testimony Before the Subcommittee on Space and Aeronautics, Committee on Science and Technology, House of Representatives, GAO–07–693T, March 29, 2007.

United States Government Accountability Office, *National Airspace System, Experts' View on Improving the US Air Traffic Control Modernization Program*, GAO–05–333SP.

United States Government Accountability Office, *National Airspace System, Transformation Will Require Cultural Change, Balanced Funding Priorities, and Use of All Available Management Tools*, GAO–06–154.

United States Government Accountability Office, *Next Generation Air Transportation System: Preliminary Analysis of Progress and Challenges Associated with the Transformation of the National Airspace System*, Statement of Gerald L. Dillingham, Ph.D., Director, Physical Infrastructure Issues, Testimony Before the Subcommittee on Aviation, Committee on Commerce, Science, and Transportation, US Senate, GAO–06–915T, July 25, 2006.

United States Government Accountability Office, *Responses to Post-Hearing Questions for the Record, The Future of Air Traffic Control: The R&D Agenda*, Subcommittee on Space and Aeronautics. Committee on Science, House of Representatives, GAO–06–778R, Submitted May 17, 2006.

van Marle, Alexandra "Indian Search for Safety," *Air Traffic Management*, Vol. 13 Issue 4, Winter 2004.

Warfield, Murray "Technology and Flight Safety – Benefits to be Realized," in *Essays on Air Navigation: Flying through Congested Skies*, (Montreal: McGill University Center for Research of Air and Space Law and the International Civil Aviation Organization, 2007).

Watts, Robert "Brothers tell Labour what they want in return for their millions," *The Sunday Telegraph*, January 28, 2007.

Index